CW01017614

INTRUDERS OVER
BRITAIN

INTRUDERS OVER BRITAIN

The story of the Luftwaffe's
night intruder force
– the Fernnachtjager

SIMON W. PARRY

AIR RESEARCH PUBLICATIONS
in association with
KRISTALL PRODUCTIONS

First published 1987 by
Air Research Publications
in association with Kristall
Productions Ltd, 71b Maple
Road, Surbiton, Surrey.
KT6 4AG. England.

ISBN O 904811 07 7

Typeset by Qualitext, Salisbury,
Wilts. SP2 7BE
Printed and bound in Great Britain
by LR Printing Services Ltd,
Crawley, West Sussex RH10 2QN

'When I want to kill wasps, I smoke out their nest. I don't swat the insects in the air one at a time, I go to the nest when they are in!'

General Josef Kammhuber
1940

Contents

Introduction

By Emil Nonnenmacher
former Luftwaffe night fighter pilot with III/NJG2 and IV/NJG3.

In any war, fate decrees that some events live on in the memory of those who witnessed them whilst other, no-less meritorious episodes fade into obscurity and are seldom referred to. One such chapter of the Second World War, and one in which I became personally involved, was the story of the long-range, night intruders (*Fernnachtjäger*) which operated over Britain.

To understand the importance of these sorties, one has to consider the progressively worsening situation that Germany's leaders faced. The Allied bomber offensive, and in particular the RAF's night bombing, caused ever increasing destruction and hardship to industry and the population throughout the country. Efforts to protect the Reich from these attacks diverted vital resources from other theatres and weakened Germany's overall war effort. How best to counter the mounting bombardment was therefore a matter of great concern at the highest level.

To intercept an aircraft at night was a difficult task. No matter how effective the defences were, the majority of the bombers got through to the target. At their peak, the German defences could only account for some 10% of the raiding force. As horrific in terms of life as this may seem, it still meant that 90% of the force returned to make another attack. Whether the RAF's resources could have sustained this loss rate for a prolonged period is now a matter of doubt, but the fact remains that the Luftwaffe was forced to make every effort to protect their home-land.

During the early stages of the war, the RAF bombers attempted to fly individually to their far distant targets with only minimal navigational aids. Such were the tactics employed in early 1941 when the first of the Luftwaffe's intruders attacked the bombers over Britain. Even though the RAF's bomber force was small, by comparison with that of later in the war, the then primitive home defence night fighters had great difficulty locating and destroying them. At this time the Luftwaffe's night fighters were not equipped with airborne Radar and the night fighter arm as a whole was given a low priority compared to other branches. The prospect of attacking the bombers at their most vulnerable moments and when they were easiest

9

to locate was therefore attractive. Both of these factors occurred when the bombers were over their own bases in Britain. When aircraft were either taking off or landing they were at their most vulnerable and many lights had to be illuminated for safety both on the airfields and in the air. All these lights made airfields and aircraft comparatively easy to locate in the black-out. Crews were also inclined to relax their guard when not over enemy territory and many fell to the guns of the I/NJG2 intruders who began to claim more aircraft destroyed than the home based defences.

When the order to stop the intruder sorties came in October 1941, the *Fernnachtjäger* crews were shocked. What nonsense was this! Rumours said that Hitler himself had given this stupid order because he wanted his night fighters to shoot the bombers down over the Reich, not over far away Britain. The German people should see the 'Terrorflieger' burning in front of their homes.

For two years no *Fernnachtjäger* were sent to Britain. Instead of attacking the bombers at there most vulnerable they must be hunted down and destroyed one-by-one in the skies over the Reich, with all the difficulties this presented. And all the time the attacks became heavier.

In late 1943, some Me 410s, which were strictly speaking attached to the bomber forces, began to be used on intruder sorties. These attacks continued on a very small scale until the Allied invasion in Normandy, when other more urgent targets presented themselves.

Some die-hards had not forgotten the idea of intruder sorties, which were being flown almost continuously by the RAF. Even so, it was not until late 1944 that the ideas were allowed to proceed beyond the planning stage and by the time that they materialised, in the form of *Operation Gisela,* it was too late to have any telling effect.

What difference it would have made to the course of the air war over Europe had intruders been employed on a large enough scale early in the war, is difficult to estimate. What can be said for certain is that the Allied bomber offensive would have been severly hampered and the losses greater had they not been given total freedom over Britain.

The story of the intruders over Britain illustrates another of those chapters in the Second World War which have hitherto been largely ignored. I would therefore like to thank my young British friend, Simon Parry, for his research into the *Fernnachtjäger*. The public have known little of this story until now. May this book help make the whole episode more transparent.

Sincerely

E. Nonnenmacher

Emil Nonnenmacher.

Acknowledgements

The story of the Luftwaffe intruders over Britain is, first and foremost, that of the young men who flew and often died in the name of their respective countries. Having been born thirteen years after the war's end I cannot have, and do not profess to have, first hand knowledge of life in those times. But I have been struck by the eagerness of those fine gentlemen who played a part in the events described in this book, to help me in any way they could.

Therefore, I firstly extend my sincere gratitude to those aircrew, both German and British, who took the trouble to respond to my appeals for information and recollections. Without their words this book would mean little, for they and their fellow comrades are what this book is about. There seems little reason to impassionately list them here for within these pages you will read of them all.

There is a second group of people who, although they have no direct connection with the events detailed in this book, have been a major factor in its completion. These are the aviation historians who devote much of their spare time to recording and collating information regarding the Second World War. Notable amongst these has been John Foreman, who has used his vast wealth of information to weed out the most obscure of facts. Philippa Hodgkiss has also been ready to search her detailed files and has often answered seemingly impossible questions. Frank Marshall has provided much indispensable advice on Luftwaffe matters over the years, as has Stephen Burns. Brian Bines has often had this book at the back of his mind when researching and has come up with several nearly forgotten incidents which I might otherwise have missed. Others who have provided information relating to their specialist areas are: Bob Collis, Peter Foote, Andy Saunders, Ian McLachlan, Stewart Evens, Brian Cull, Ab Jansen, Winfried Bock and Nick Pointer from the Public Record Office.

A man who has a place in both the aforementioned groups is Emil Nonnenmacher. He has given me much help, both from the point of view of a fighter pilot and historian, and was instrumental in obtaining much of information relating to the Luftwaffe's part in Operation Gisela.

Two organisations which have helped are the *Gemeinschaft der Jagdflieger* and the Royal Air Force Association. Both were kind enough to insert appeals for information of their respective magazines: *Jägerblatt* and *Air Mail*.

Finally, this book would probably never have been started if it had not been for the encouragement of Jan Harman. She has provided guidance for, and worked on, the manuscript from its earliest days to the last full stop. Should you find any spelling or grammatical errors, they are mine   not hers!

Part I

CHAPTER ONE

Germ of an idea – the creation of the night intruder force

During 1939 and for the greater part of 1940, Germany had no cohesive night defence policy or structure to protect her vital industrial areas, such as the Ruhr Valley, from air attack. So great was the feeling of invincibility held by the Oberkommando der Wehrmacht (the German High Command), that little thought had been given to the possibility of any such attack. It had been realised however, that should a strategic bomber offensive be launched against Germany, these industrial targets would bear the brunt of it. To counter this threat a line of defence had been established by the end of 1939. This was the L.V.Z. or Western Air Defence Zone which extended in a line stretching from Münster in the north, to Stuttgart in the south. This defensive line consisted almost entirely of searchlights and flak batteries, with only a token number of night fighters available to intercept raiders.

By December 1939, RAF Bomber Command's strictly limited attacks had caused little consternation within the German High Command. Raids were few in number and hopelessly inaccurate. Even when the propaganda leaflets, which had at first been dropped, were exchanged for bombs there was little reaction. This total lack of effectiveness, coupled with the singular lack of success of the meagre number of night fighters, led to the abandonment of any expansionist schemes that may have been entertained at the Reichluftfaht-ministerium (RLM), the aviation ministry. The official view was that it would be a waste of precious resources. Eventually only a single

Gruppe remained charged with Germany's night defence. This was IV(Nacht)/JG2 under the command of Hauptmann Blumensaat and it was equipped with the Messerschmitt Bf 109D-1. This unit was the result of an amalgamation of 10 and 11 Staffeln JG2 and 10(Nacht)/JG26 which was based at Jever in the Heligoland Bight. It is believed that three British bombers were shot down in the space of four months but the task of the night fighters was made almost impossible by their wholly unsuitable equipment and the tactics employed.

The Bf 109 may have been a superb fighter in daylight but it was totally unsuited, if not positively dangerous, when used for operations at night. It could not be flown on instruments alone and the pilot had to take off and land on a fragile narrow track undercarriage making accidents all too common. To compound the discomfort of the pilots, the canopies of many aircraft were removed to prevent its pilot being dazzled by searchlight beams reflecting in the perspex. As if these problems were not restricting enough, the fighters could only operate on nights when heavy cloud cover was present, for on clear nights the flak and searchlights had priority. This left the pilots of IV(N)/JG2 operating on nights when they could fly above cloud, and meant that they could be given no assistance from the ground. Bombers had to be located by moonlight alone. When these factors are considered, it is hardly surprising that little success was achieved.

Following the German invasion of Denmark in April 1940, the Danish airfield of Aalborg became a Luftwaffe base and as such soon received the attentions of British bombers. A Staffel of IV(N)/JG2 was based at Aalborg and shared the airfield with I/ZG1. This was a Zerstörer Gruppe under the command of Hauptmann Wolfgang Falck equipped with Me 110Cs. Falck, together with some of the Gruppe's more experienced crews, began to experiment in the defence of their own airfield and at length an effective technique was devised. The basic theory was that aircraft, co-operating with ground radar stations, would orbit specific areas until they could be directed on to a target by the ground control station. This system would become common place in years to come but in 1940 it was an innovation ahead of its time. Falck was convinced of the soundness of his ideas, even if no aircraft had actually been brought down. Success would have come in time but the invasion of France in May 1940 halted the experiment. I/ZG1 moved to Gütersloh where Falck set about producing a report on his findings on night fighting for the RLM.

In Germany there was still little interest in defence. The Blitzkreig

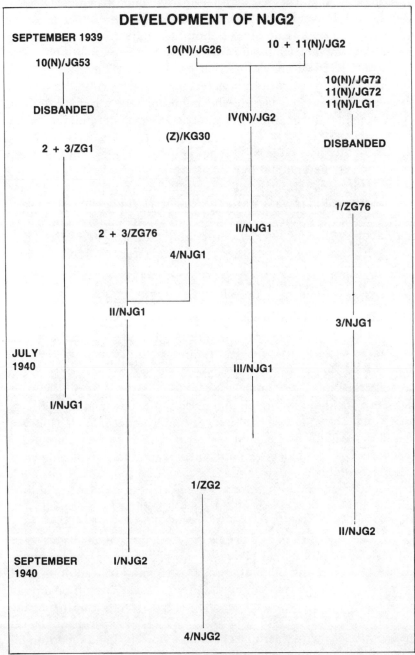

DEVELOPMENT OF NJG2

SEPTEMBER 1939

10(N)/JG53

10(N)/JG26   10 + 11(N)/JG2

DISBANDED

2 + 3/ZG1

(Z)/KG30

IV(N)/JG2

10(N)/JG72
11(N)/JG72
11(N)/LG1

DISBANDED

1/ZG76

2 + 3/ZG76

II/NJG1

4/NJG1

II/NJG1

3/NJG1

**JULY
1940**

III/NJG1

I/NJG1

1/ZG2

II/NJG2

**SEPTEMBER
1940**   I/NJG2

4/NJG2

*The Gruppen of NJG2 remained subordinate to NJG1 until the Stab of NJG2 was established
in November 1940*

A Ju 88C outside one of the camouflaged hangars at Gilze-Rijen. This is believed to be the usual mount of Hauptmann Karl Hülshoff. (Ab Jansen).

A fitter works on a Ju 88C's guns. (M. Merker).

Testing the guns of a Ju 88C. (M. Merker).

was preparing to roll across Europe and the Luftwaffe was riding on a wave of victory. On May 10th, 1940, Holland, Belgium and Luxemburg were invaded in Operation Gelb. The war machine had changed up a gear. That night the RAF bombed Münchengladbach and in the coming weeks many more towns in Germany itself would become targets. Although the scale and accuracy of these attacks could scarcely be regarded as a serious threat, aircraft had flown over and bombs had fallen on the Reich. Göring's famous claim had lost its credibility.

The embarrassment caused by these raids made itself felt in both the political and military hierarchy. Heads turned to Göring for an answer and he, in turn, looked to Falck.

Wolfgang Falck had already met with the Chief of Luftwaffe Supply General Ernst Udet, State Secretary Erhard Milch and the Chief of General Staff Albert Kesselring, with whom he had discussed this report on night fighting. The reaction to his report took Falck by surprise for within a week of submitting it he was summoned to an hotel at Wassenaar, near the Hague, where the higher echelon of the Luftwaffe had assembled. At this meeting Göring declared night defence to be the 'Achilles heel' of the Luftwaffe and promptly appointed Falck, Geschwaderkommodore of the new Nachtjagdgeschwader 1, in July 1940. He was the first Hauptmann to be given such a position. Once more, in a time of reorganisation, units began to change their identities rapidly, as was often the case within the Luftwaffe. From Falck's old unit, 2 and 3 Staffeln ZG1 became I/NJG1. IV(N)/JG2, after a short period as II/NJG1, changed again to III/NJG1. The new II/NJG1 was formed from the Zerstörer Staffel (Z)/KG30 together with 2 and 3 Staffeln ZG76.

As the Gruppenkommandeur of I/ZG1, Wolfgang Falck was of the opinion that each unit should adopt an emblem of its own. Previously he had been Staffelkapitän of the 'Ladybird Staffel', so called because of the design of its emblem which was a ladybird. He firmly believed that such a device added to the identity of the unit and to the esprit de corps of the men within it. Thus, as Gruppenkommandeur, Falck invited suggestions for an emblem to suit I/ZG1. Various designs were submitted by members of the Gruppe but Falck's favourite sketch came from Oberleutnant Victor Mölders, brother of the famous Werner Mölders who became General der Jagdflieger. The emblem consisted of a coat of arms on a shield with a segment of the globe at its base. This showed the unit's theatre of operations: Norway, Denmark, Germany, France, the Atlantic coast and England. Above

20

The Ju 88 V7, prototype of the Ju 88C.

A Do 17Z-10 of 2/NJG2.

21

this was a white falcon, the Falck family crest, diving and carrying a red lightning flash aimed at Southern England. This design was adopted in June 1940, just before Falck was appointed Geschwader-kommodore of NJG1. In view of the change in the unit's role to night fighting, the colours of the emblem were changed to give a black background instead of the previous light blue. Very shortly the new badge began to appear on the noses of the unit's aircraft, then on vehicles, buildings and personal badges. When I/NJG2 was formed, a red border to the shield was adopted to differentiate it from NJG1 who used a white border.

Unlike the other night fighter units who were now equipped with Me 110s, (Z)/KG30 flew Ju 88s. This Staffel had been stationed at Trondheim in Norway and, under the command of its Staffelkapitän Oberleutnant Bönsch, claimed to have destroyed four Blenhiems on April 30th, 1940. The unit's principal task during this time had been coastal and anti-shipping strikes. It would take some time for the crews to adjust to the idea of using the Ju 88s as night fighters.

The RLM had given their consent for the conversion of the seventh Ju 88 prototype, the V-7, to a Zerstörer in the summer of 1939. The conversion involved the fitting of three MG 17 machine guns and a single 20mm cannon to the standard glazed nose. Despite its size and weight, the Ju 88C proved to be fast and stable as a gun platform. This impressed the Luftwaffenführungsstab, but there seemed to be little need for a second Zerstörer type as the existing Me 110 performed the role perfectly adequately. A project to fit BMW 801 radial engines to produce a Ju 88C-1 variant was shelved as the engines would be needed for the new Focke-Wulf Fw 190, when it went into production. Permission was however, granted to convert a few Ju 88A-1s already on the production line to Ju 88C-2 specification. The Ju 88C-2 retained its V-12 Junkers Jumo 211B-1 engines and was in most respects a standard Ju 88A-1. The most fundamental change was made to the nose. A 'solid' nose fairing replaced the perspex nose of the bomber version and an armoured bulkhead served both to protect the crew and to provide support for the heavy armament. So similar was the fighter to the production Ju 88 that even the bomb-bay was retained, allowing it to carry a bomb load of ten 50kg bombs. The crew was reduced from four, as normal for the bomber, to three. These were a pilot, a Bordmechaniker who also reloaded the 20mm MG FF cannon, and a Bordfunker who looked after the rearward firing MG 15 machine gun. On some of I/NJG2s Ju 88s the 20mm cannon was later replaced by a belt fed MG 151, 15mm cannon, but in all cases the three MG 17s were belt fed from three containers. Two of these were placed between the rudder pedals and the third was positioned on the starboard side of the cockpit.

Fully loaded the aircraft tipped the scales at well over ten tons. This would be the aircraft that was to fly over England, but this was still a long way off when the Zerstörer Staffel of KG30 took delivery of the first twenty machines.

In July 1940, (Z)/KG30 moved to Düsseldorf where they were redesignated 4/NJG1 and began their training in night fighting. Soon a fifth Staffel was formed under the command of Oberleutnant Schultze which was equipped with the one and only Dornier Do 17Z-6 'Kauz I' and a few Do 17Z-10s 'Kauz II'. Like the Ju 88C-2, the Do 17 based night fighters were conversions of the standard bomber variants. Initially a nose from a Ju 88C-2 was literally grafted on to a Do 17Z-3 but only one such aircraft was completed which was the Do 17Z-6. A custom built nose of a similar design to that of the Ju 88C-2 but holding four MG 17s and two 20mm cannon, was fitted to create the Do 17Z-10 'Kauz II'. The Screech Owl, as this aircraft was named, was fitted with a device unique to this type known as the spanner-anlage. This was a detector, fitted in the nose of the aircraft, which was capable of picking up the infra-red emissions from the hot exhaust gases of other aircraft. The image was displayed on a small screen fitted into the cockpit, the so called 'Q tube'. It was hoped that the pilot would be able to home in on his otherwise unseen enemy as with more sophisticated AI equipment. Similar infra-red devices had been experimented with by the RAF but had been abandoned in favour of radio based AI equipment.

Thus armed, II/NJG1 continued to train at Düsseldorf and expand as crews from other units, who had experience in night flying, joined. Amongst the airmen reporting to Düsseldorf that July was twenty-two year old Herbert Thomas from the town of Bochum. More than forty-five years later he can still recall the events which brought him to NJG2.

'At the age of fourteen I was already a glider pilot—this was in 1932. Then I began my flying training at the A/B school Berlin Schönwalde and after this I flew with Jagdgeschwader Richthofen in Berlin Döberitz from 1936 to 1939. When the Polish campaign began I was attached to with KG4 'General Wever'.

In the summer of 1940, I went to Düsseldorf–Lohausen for a 'special duty'. Crews from many Geschwadern had been gathered together to sort out which of them would become night fighter crews. My crew were all experienced in night flying and we were posted to II/NJG1.

All our aircraft at the school were modified Do 17Zs and with these we practiced night flying and landing. We also began co-operating with the searchlight and flak batteries in preparation for defensive sorties. The Do 17s had been improvised for night flying and were slow and unmanoeuverable. We had no fighter control, Lichtenstein or Freya, and flew by what we called the 'wooden eye'. That is, without any aids to help us.'

Düsseldorf was however unsuitable for their night flying activities and soon the units were on the move, to Schiphol near Amsterdam. Herbert flew in one of the first aircraft.

'We arrived at Schiphol in the early evening and went immediately to the Hotel Krasnapolsk in Amsterdam in the taxis of KLM, the Dutch airline. A group of Dutch people sat around the tables enjoying their meals when we marched in, wearing full German uniform. We stayed there until midnight, then we left with the music still playing in the bar. The driver of the KLM taxi opened the door for us and drove us back to the airfield.'

The organisation was rapidly expanding to beyond the point where Falck, a lowly Hauptmann acting as Geschwaderkommodore, could effectively control and influence those around him. Thus on July 17th 1940, the First Night Fighter Division was created with Oberst Josef Kammhuber at its head. Kammhuber had been captured during the invasion of France and had recently returned from a prisoner of war camp. The new night fighter division came under the over-all control of Kesselring's Luftflotte 2 and soon established its Headquarters in Brussels.

A few days later on July 24th, Feldwebel Wiesse and Feldwebel Schramm both claimed to have brought down Wellington bombers and opened NJG1's account. Göring sent his congratulations, but little else. The unit still had no Gruppenkommandeur, few administrative staff, no transport, no equipment, very few ground staff or for that matter, aircraft. However, the situation improved over the following weeks.

A 6th Staffel, equipped with Ju 88s, was next established under Hauptmann Hülshoff. This was followed, in September 1940, by the arrival of Major Karl Heyse, a veteran of the Spanish Civil War, who became the Gruppenkommandeur. Then followed two workers companies, more administrative staff and air crew.

The air crew were still being posted from other operational units, but some, like Heinrich Beul, came straight from their training schools.

Above: Hauptmann Wolfgang Falck with I/ZG1 in Aalborg during the winter of 1939–1940. (Falck).

Above right: Wolfgang Falck, Geschwaderkommodore NJG1.

Right: Generalmajor Josef Kammhuber.

'I joined the military in 1936 and became an army radio, telephone and telex operator before I went into the Luftwaffe at the end of 1938 to train as air crew. A year later I was selected to become a Bordfunker (radio operator) and continued my training. Eventually I went to the school of army reconnaissance at Grossenhain and then to Weimar where they flew Do 17Ms. The crews were mixed from army and Luftwaffe personnel and it was here that I had an experience which I shall remember for the rest of my life. Near Weimar was the infamous 'K2'—Buchenwald, a concentration camp. The whole area was secret and marked as a prohibited area on our maps. We were not allowed to fly over it but sometimes our course took us near. When this happened our reconnaissance camera was removed before the flight. We saw little—a long, straight street of closely packed huts with pointed roofs. On a wide road, a column of forty or fifty people were marching. They marched three abreast with two or three guards to the front and rear. I take it that this column was being taken to 'K2'. I did not see the crematoriums. The first I saw of these was on film after the war. One Sunday I was invited to visit new settlement between Weimar and Buchenwald. There a group of soldiers had been ordered to build a road. They had a road roller but were pulling it along themselves, not driving it. They were from the SS. The sight shocked me. This was in 1940 and I still remember it to this day.

Our training at Weimar was complete. We had learned about equipment, weather, cameras, navigation, assisting the pilot and gunnery. We shot rifles on the range and fired at targets from the air. We were well trained in things that we would need to know at the front. In the summer of 1940 ten Bordfunker were posted to night fighter units, seven went to home defence units and three to the unit which flew to England. I was in the latter group.'

At this time the unit was still known as II/NJG1 and operated from Schipol. Kammhuber firmly believed that the converted bombers would be best employed in the role of long range night fighters, a form of operation which they had already begun to fly. Kammhuber had already been given permission by Göring to form two further complete Geschwadern of long range night fighters and directed Heyse to develop his unit to full Geschwader strength.

Training was coming to an end and soon operations would begin in earnest. Herbert Thomas reflected;

'Up until now we had been playing. We were young men and had forgotten the worries and dangers of flying at night. We were supposed to be ready for war but we were not. We were like boys setting out on an adventure. This way of fighting the war could not last for long.'

26

CHAPTER TWO

First tentative steps. August – December 1940

Herbert Thomas had been right and things soon changed, but NJG2's first flights over England bore little relation to what would come.

'The aim of our first flights over England was simply to stir the defences into action. We wanted to test the RAF's reaction and to get used to the idea of flying over enemy territory. The British defences were not prepared for a lone German aircraft. When our crews returned after four or five hours over England all there was to report was the sighting of a few lights. They had seen nothing of the British defences.

To goad the RAF into the air we later took flares and incendiary bombs with us. I made one such flight sitting in the Bola, the under slung gondola, of a Do 17 with a cannister of incendiary bombs beside me. The Bola had a small trap door in it only a little larger than the fuel cap of a car. The hole was for dropping flares through but until then no one had discovered what it was for!

Eventually we saw some smoke rising from a chimney and I prepared myself for action. I armed the bombs and pushed them out through the door. This was crazy, just like the bombers of the First World War. If a Lancaster bomb aimer had to do this he would have thought that he was at a kindergarten. Our Bordfunker called out that he could see lights and we took evasive action to lose the British fighter but the lights he had seen were only our own flares igniting. It was lucky for us that the defences were still inexperienced.'

Inexperienced as the RAF may have been at the time, they could still catch the unwary. In the early hours of August 18th, 1940 Pilot Officer Rhodes was flying a Blenheim 1F of No. 29 Squadron on a patrol of the area to the south of Chester. With no airborne interception equipment available, the early night fighters could only wait upon instructions from the ground to guide them to a target. It was with considerable luck therefore, that Rhodes saw what he took to be dim cockpit lights in the distance. For two hours Rhodes chased his foe, which was believed to be a Heinkel He 111, across England. Finally, some 25 miles off Spurn Head, Rhodes opened fire with the Blenheim's four machine guns. The following excerpt from his combat report records:

'I opened fire with my front guns and expended all the ammunition in the fixed guns.

The E/A appeared to be slowed down and I followed and manoeuvred on to the starboard side to allow the rear gunner to fire. The E/A circled slowly losing height and after a short sighting burst the gunner, Sgt. W. J. Gregory emptied his drum into the aircraft.

The E/A continued to lose height and the rear gunner saw it land gently on the water.'

The time was 03.20 hours, and somewhere off Cromer Knoll the first aircraft to be lost on intruder operations sank into the sea. No trace was ever found of it or of its three crew.

Earlier, in the evening of August 17th, Feldwebel Peter Laufs claimed to have shot down a Hurricane near Lowestoft. Although this has gone down in history as the ninth aircraft shot down by German night fighters, and the third by NJG1, no loss of an RAF aircraft has been found that would confirm Lauf's claim. Oberfeldwebel Merback claimed the destruction of a Hurricane on August 27th, but once again this cannot be confirmed. It is certain, however, that by the end of the month NJG1 had lost four aircraft and their crews. In addition to Feldwebel Schramm's aircraft which had been brought down by Pilot Officer Rhodes, three had crashed in Europe. The first of these was an Me 110 of 2/NJG1 which had crashed on June 29th. On July 27th a Do 17Z of 5/NJG1 crashed on a non-operational flight near Krefeld and killed two of its crew. The third loss occured during air gunnery practice on August 29th, when a Ju 88C-2 crashed at Elsdorf. This time all three of the crew were killed.

September 1940 brought news of yet another move for the unit. Once more ground staff and administrative personnel packed their bags to move, this time to the airfield of Gilze-Rijen. Before the outbreak of war, the Dutch had used Gilze-Rijen as a military landing ground and had begun to expand its facilities shortly before Holland was overrun. The airfield's name stemmed from its location which was adjacent to the Gilze to Rijen road, about two miles north of Gilze village. At the time of the German invasion, much of the ground work has been completed and the Germans carried through the original plans which culminated in a first-class airfield for night operations. The three concrete runways, each 1,700 metres long, were laid out in an 'A' pattern and a blind landing facility was provided on the northeast to south-west runway. Other facilities included two large hangars, two compass swinging platforms, workshops, ammunition dumps and 112 dispersal shelters. The main accommodation consisted of fifty barrack huts in a wooded area just outside the main airfield but many personnel were billeted elsewhere, in places such as the Gilze Village

Hall. It would be the unit's home for the next year. Already operational from Gilze-Rijen was Kampfgeschwader 30, a bomber unit equipped with Ju 88A-1s. From the night fighter's point of view this meant that equipment, facilities and expertise in the operation and maintenance of the Ju 88 were readily available.

Another change, made in early September 1940, was that the unit altered its identity from II/NJG1 to I/NJG2. This meant little to the personnel but was a significant step in the expansion of the German defences. Even though a new Geschwader had been formed on paper, I/NJG2 remained subordinate to NJG1. This state of affairs continued until NJG2 formed their own Headquarters and became a separate Geschwader, which did not happen until November 1941.

I/NJG2's equipment was still very much a 'mixed bag' and consisted, in the main, of Ju 88C-2s with a handful of Do 17Z-10s. There were also one or two Me 110s, but these were soon transferred to home defence units as they did not possess the range to operate over Britain. Throughout 1940 and 1941 the unit never exceeded a strength of more than twenty, fully operational aircraft.

The crews that flew with I/NJG2 were mainly in their mid-twenties and rapidly a great camaraderie developed amongst them. In the coming months some would achieve success and become 'Experten', but more would perish at the hands of the RAF. Still more would succumb to the unforgiving waters of the North Sea after their aircraft, for reasons such as mechanical failure or pilot error, had crashed into it.

Now established as an operational unit, procedures and tactics for intruder operations could be finalised. A seemingly effective method had been devised. Each day the German wireless telegraphy interception service would monitor the transmissions of British bombers preparing for operations on the coming night. At the head of this service was Major Kuhlmann, who reported his findings to the operations room at Gilze-Rijen at 15.00 hours. These messages became known to the crews as 'Kuhlmann meldungen', Kuhlmann reports. Based upon the information gathered it was planned that aircraft would be despatched in three waves:

First Wave.   To attack bombers as they prepared and took off from their bases.

Second Wave. To fly along the known routes taken by Bomber Command over the North Sea.

Third Wave. To fly to the RAF bases and lie in wait for the returning bombers.

29

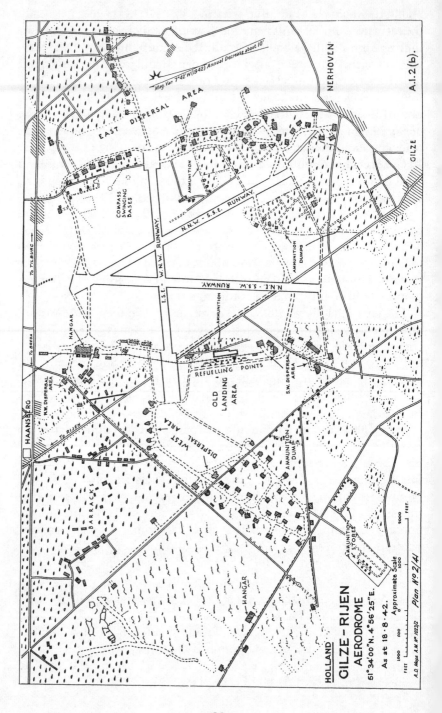

HOLLAND

GILZE - RIJEN AERODROME

51°34′00″N. 4°56′25″E.

As at 18·8·42.

A.D. Maps A.M. N° 1023/2   *Plan N° 2/41*

Approximate Scale

A.I.2(b).

Although sound in theory, applying this system in practice was a different matter. The information and navigation were seldom of a high enough standard to allow attacks to be made on take-off and there was no airborne interception equipment to locate bombers flying individually over the sea. It was, however, comparatively easy to follow a returning raid back to its illuminated airfields. When the bombers switched on their navigation and landing lights, with the crews being fatigued after their long flight, they were easy prey to any prowling night fighter.

For operational purposes, Eastern England was divided into three 'Raumen' or areas. To the north was 'Raum A', basically Yorkshire, bounded by Hull, Leeds, Lancaster and Newcastle. 'Raum B' covered the Midlands and Lincolnshire whilst 'Raum C' encompassed East Anglia bounded by the Wash, Peterborough, Luton and London.

Heinrich Beul's first task in NJG2 had been to prepare the recognition signal flares but on return from leave to visit his wife and daughter, he was posted to the First Staffel.

'I reported to my new Staffelkapitän who shook my hand and asked if I had made any operational flights. I said that I had not. I was told that in this Staffel I would have plenty of opportunity to fly and shortly after my arrival, I was ordered to make my first flight to England.

I was the Bordfunker and kept busy during the flight working the radio and taking fixes to locate our position. At one point, the pump which moved oil from the main tank to the engines, failed but there was a backup hand pump and for the return flight I had to work the oil pump all the time. My work was appreciated and I was rapidly accepted as a member of the Staffel.'

Not all crews were so lucky. On September 16th 1940, Feldwebel Palm's Ju 88 failed to return from a sortie and on October 14th, Unteroffizier Götz was returning to Gilze-Rijen in fog when his Do 17 hit the embankment of the Breda to Tilburg railway which ran to the north of the airfield. The Dornier bounced back into the air and crashed again. The machine was severely damaged but the three crew escaped with injuries.

By mid-October 1940, five claims had been made for aircraft shot down over England but as far as is known, no RAF aircraft were actually destroyed. There has always been, and probably always will be, dispute over the accuracy of the claims made by the crews of I/NJG2 in their sorties over Britain. There is no doubt that more claims were submitted and credited to crews than there were aircraft destroyed as a result of their attacks. This is understandable when one

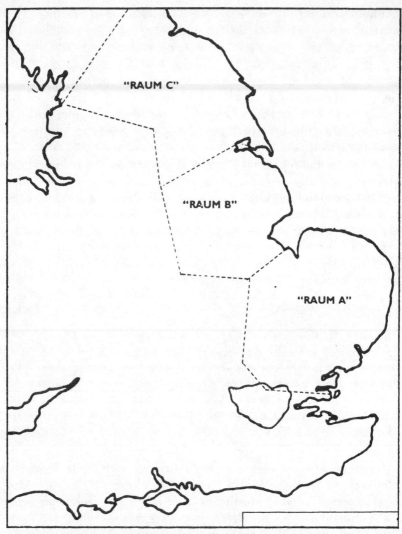

Patrol areas allocated to the intruders of Nachjagdgeschwader 2.

stops to think of the conditions under which these combats took place.

Night fighting was, in mid 1940, in its infancy and a crew who were inexperienced and tense can hardly be expected to have had the composure to examine what they had seen, objectively. In near total darkness, over a blacked out enemy country, any bright light or flash could appear dazzlingly brilliant to eyes accustomed to the darkness. An aircraft's engines misfiring upon sudden throttle changes could produce a brilliant flame, or a burst of return gun fire could well be misconstrued as evidence of damage or strikes from their own fire. In fact the aircraft could well have accelerated violently, returned fire indiscriminately and taken violent evasive action when its crew realised that they had come under attack. The night fighter crew, seeing the effect of their burst of fire, could well submit a claim, yet their target escape unscathed.

There were no means by which the Luftwaffe could confirm the accuracy of claims (as was possible in Europe where wrecks could be examined) and, for this reason, claims could only be taken at face value. In most instances there is some substance in the claims made and, in the heat of combat, mistakes in identification and navigation are understandable. There is little doubt however, that crews were convinced that they had brought their victims down. It is only through careful analysis of documents over forty years later and by taking an unbiased view of the recorded facts, that an accurate picture can now be compiled.

The first combat reported by I/NJG2 that can be confirmed, occurred on the night of October 24th, 1940. Oberleutnant Kurt Herrmann and Feldwebel Hans Hahn were among the night fighter pilots operating that night.

At 21.30 hours that evening, a Blenheim of No. 17 Operational Training Unit based at Upton, was engaged on a night cross country exercise over Norfolk when Kurt Herrmann made his attack. The Blenheim's hydraulic system was hit and the port fuel tank set on fire. The single .303 Browning machine gun, the aircraft's only armament, was unserviceable and only evasive action by the pilot prevented the destruction of his machine which he landed on Docking airfield. Both the aircraft and the crew survived to fly again. Five minutes later, whilst still near Docking, Herrmann attacked a Beaufort. This too was slightly damaged, a bullet having passed through a fuel tank, but no further damage was caused. At Linton-on-Ouse, home of No. 102 Squadron, nine Whitleys were preparing to take off for an operation to Berlin. Pilot Officer A. G. Davies had only just become airborne when Feldwebel Hahn's guns set the Whitley on fire. It crashed, killing two and injuring three of those on board. Four days later, on October 28th, Leutnant Heinz Völker attacked two Hampdens of No. 49 Squadron as they were returning from Hamburg to Lindholm. The first machine was damaged but was able to land safely. Völker then attacked a second which was not so lucky—his guns sent Pilot Officer Bufton and his crew to their deaths in the sea, half a mile off Skegness.

The cost of these victories was high. On November 1st,

Above: A Ju 88A-1 of KG30 ends up on its nose at Gilze-Rijen. (Böttner).

The nose of the Do 17Z-10, R4 + HK (WN 2817), of 2/NJG2 in which Oberfeldwebel Herbert Schmidt returned on 11th November, 1940. Schmidt and his Bordfunker, Paul Rosenberger, defected to Britain in May 1943.

Unteroffizier Lang's crew failed to return from a sortie and can be assumed to have fallen into the North Sea. On November 9th, Oberfeldwebel Schmidt brought his badly damaged Do. 17 back to Gilze-Rijen on one engine after surviving an attack by a Beaufighter. Then on November 23rd, came the first of a series of disasters for NJG2. A Ju 88 was being 'bombed up' in preparation for a sortie when one of the 50kg bombs exploded, killing two of the crew. The remaining aircraft took off for England as planned. Three claims were made but only one aircraft can be identified as lost. This was a No. 214 Squadron Wellington which failed to return from an attack on the Chancellory in Berlin.

Sergeant Oakley was outbound later that night in his No. 83 Squadron Hampden when he was attacked by three Ju 88s. Oakley threw his aircraft into evasive action, jettisoning his bombs to give greater manoeuvrability and dropped from 9,000 feet to 2,000 feet. His gunners blazed away at their attackers, one of which was seen to burst into flames and fall into the sea below. The others broke off the attack and turned away. Back at Gilze-Rijen they waited for the three aircraft to return. One landed safely but, as dawn broke, those on the ground realised that two aircraft and their crews would not come back. From the third Staffel, Feldwebel Schlicht was missing and from the Stab Staffel (Staff Flight), aircraft 'R4 + BB' had not returned. Its pilot was Major Karl-Heinrich Heyse, the Gruppenkommandeur. It was one of these aircraft (which one is unknown) that had been brought down by Sergeant Oakley's crew. It is certain however, that both Ju 88s fell into the freezing waters of the North Sea.

The loss of the figure-head of the unit shook its remaining crews. Immediately, Karl Hülshoff replaced Heyse as the Gruppen-kommandeur. Hülshoff's place as Staffelkapitän of 3/NJG2 was taken by Oberleutnant Ulrich Mayer, who was able to celebrate his twenty-sixth birthday as the new Staffelkapitän.

Operations were now limited by the inclement weather of the oncoming winter. Oberleutnant Paul Bohn and Oberfeldwebel Beier both made claims on December 17th and another operation was launched on the evening of December 21st. Once again aircraft of I/NJG2 ranged over the airfields of Eastern England. Leutnant Völker and Unteroffizier Blum both claimed aircraft destroyed but once more no evidence can be found to verify these claims. In search of targets the new Staffelkapitän brought his Ju 88 low over the airfield at Manby near Louth, Lincolnshire. As his incendiary bombs fell just short of their airfield's perimeter, the station's meager defences opened fire.

Hauptmann Karl Hülshoff.

The graves of Gefreiter Heinrich Dempewolf, Gefreiter Kurt Ludescher and Gefreiter Friedrich Rhode, who died when their Ju 88 crashed near Gilze-Rijen on 21st December, 1940. (Böttner)

Vickers and Lewis guns from the RAF and a Royal Artillery Anti-Aircraft Battery opened up. Even the Lewis gun on the station's Armadillo armoured car joined in with forty rounds. A light showed in the cockpit of the aircraft which was soon seen to be a fire, easily visible in the night sky. The aircraft flew on, losing height, until it hit the ground two miles further on. Instantly the plane exploded in a sheet of flame as the fuel tanks exploded and momentarily the surrounding countyside was lit up by the flames. When the blaze had died away the following morning, part of the Junkers's tail with the Swastika painted on it was borne away in triumph by the station personnel as their trophy. More seriously, the remains of three charred bodies were dragged out of the wreck. On one was found the name Oberleutnant Ulrich Mayer.

The other crews of NJG2 were not to know that they had already suffered the loss of one aircraft that night when Gefreiter Kurt Ludescher's Ju 88 came in to land at Gilze-Rijen. The Ju 88 crashed and burst into flames on the airfield killing all three aboard.

In the five months since the small unit had been formed, thirty-two aircrew had been killed and twelve aircraft lost. The pilots claimed to have destroyed eighteen RAF aircraft, of which two can be confirmed as destroyed and three damaged. NJG2 cannot be said, by any stretch of the imagination, to have got off to a good start but a new year was soon to begin. Things could only get better—or so the crews thought.

CHAPTER THREE

An eye for an eye. January–May 1941

The year 1941 began as 1940 had finished. The weather was foul, but some of the more experienced crews carried on. In the first three days of 1941, four claims were made for aircraft shot down over the North Sea. On January 9th, Unteroffizier Otto Kräher and his crew, flying in inclement weather, paid for their daring and disappeared themselves. Heinrich Beul, after his efforts to keep his aircraft's engines running, found a permanent place in the crew of Oberfeldwebel Otto Wiese and recalls:

'Otto came out of hospital and returned to the Staffel after being ill for some time with a stomach ulcer. During this time his Bordfunker had been posted missing when he failed to return from a sortie with another crew—I was his replacement. Hermann Mandel was our Bordmechanicker and we soon got to know each other and work well together, for upon co-operation everything depended. On one of our flights over England Otto saw a light flashing and attacked it with cannon and machine guns. It was a dangerous thing to do as the flak was firing at us. He asked me if the light was still flashing and when I replied that it was, he dived again but changed his mind and turned away. Otto apologised to us later and admitted that he had been careless. His actions had put us all in great danger.

My two comrades who had come from Fernaufklärungs training with me had, by now, both gone missing. At the end of January we flew back from England in very bad weather and had to make an emergency landing near Brussels. There was hardly any fuel left in the tanks and we only just made it. At our base in Holland we were overdue and my friends said that they were certain that the last of the 'three Fernaufklärung' had finally 'marched'. In our Staffel that meant that we had not returned. We were missing and would not come back to our loved ones who waited for us.

Life carried on as usual when we were not flying. The food was good and plentiful and our accommodation comfortable. We stayed in a room at the girls school in Wilhelmina Park, Breda. Here we found peace and quiet away from the airfield. We all had soft comfortable beds with fresh linen and our life style was relaxed. We did little in the way of exercise, only occasional rifle practice on the sand dunes of a small island south of Rotterdam.'

Operations continued throughout January, but only one more met with success. This was when Oberleutnant Schultz was credited with three Blenheims destroyed. In fact he had intercepted the night flying practice taking place at Church Fenton. Two Defiants and a Blenheim, none of which were carrying any gunners, crash landed but all the pilots were safe.

Early in February, the small number of Do 17Z-10s operated by 2/NJG2 was reduced still further when Oberleutnant Otto Heinrich Häuser's R4 + BK failed to return from a sortie. It seemed to many that I/NJG2 was losing aircraft on a one for one basis with the RAF, but the tide was turning.

On the night of February 10th, Bomber Command sent 105 bombers to Hannover, 102 to Hamburg and thirty-three to Rotterdam. Three aircraft did not return to England and for those that did, the intruders of NJG2 were waiting. For the first time the Do 17s and Ju 88s were lying in wait near the airfields in anticipation of the return of the bombers, just as had been intended. Among the first aircraft to take off had been Herbert Thomas's Do 17 flown by Hauptmann Jung, the Staffelkapitän of 2/NJG2. After attacking three airfields with incendiary bombs and chasing an unidentified aircraft without result, Jung saw a Wellington with its navigation lights on. Sergeant Rodgers, flying a No. 115 Squadron Wellington, had narrowly missed colliding with two other aircraft and was intent on avoiding a similar situation. Rodgers had attacked Rotterdam as strong winds had prevented him reaching his target of Hannover. He had also machine gunned two airfields in Holland on his way back. Near a flashing landmark beacon at Swaffham, Sergeant Rodgers switched on the Wellington's navigation lights. Almost immediately the machine's port engine was hit and Sergeant Hill, the rear gunner, wounded in his left arm. The aircraft began to lose height rapidly, but Rodgers was able to make a successful forced landing on a railway cutting. All the crew had time to escape before the wreck burst into flames and burnt out. Herbert Thomas recalls this flight:

'Just after this combat the English flak opened fire at us and hit us six times. We flew very low and just managed to get back home again.'

Nearly three hours later, Oberleutnant Semrau was flying over the blacked out countryside of Norfolk when he came upon two of No. 21 Squadron's Blenheims returning from their attack on Hannover. Squadron Leader Sabine's aircraft was hit in its starboard wing but he was able to make a landing which saved the lives of the crew but wrote off the machine. Sergeant Chattaway's Blenheim was hit on its final approach to Bodney and as the aircraft came to a halt, fire took hold.

Above: Unteroffizier Engelbert Böttner (Bordfunker 10/3/41) with other members of I/NJG2. (Böttner).

Left: Unteroffizier Herbert Thomas, 'Kampbeobachter', NJG2. (Thomas).

The gunner, Sergeant Birch scrambled out but the pilot was killed and the observer, Pilot Officer Sharvell, was grievously injured. He died that afternoon from his injuries.

One of the last crews over England that night was Oberleutnant Kurt Herrmann. His Bordfunker was Englebert Böttner, an Unteroffizier who had been with the Zerstörerstaffel KG30 in Norway. Herrmann already had four aircraft claimed as destroyed to

40

his credit when he opened his attack at 05.20 hours by releasing his ten, 50kg bombs which exploded in a field to the north-east of Lincoln. Twenty minutes later he chanced upon a No. 49 Squadron Hampden returning from Hannover to Scampton. A burst of fire set the Hampden alight. Two of the crew baled out safely whilst the other two perished as the aircraft crashed. A few minutes later another Hampden, this time from No. 144 Squadron and also returning from Hannover, was attacked as it circled Hemswell. Its pilot, Sergeant McVie, had been warned that intruders were operating in his vicinity and he had seen some tracers fired nearby. Despite these warnings he flew with the aircraft's navigation lights on. Herrmann's fire hit the Hampden's hydraulics, undercarriage and flaps. The lights went off and the Hampden dived away to land safely fifteen minutes later. Fellow No. 144 Squadron pilot, Sergeant Dainty, orbitted Hemswell but was refused permission to land on account of the intruders. Eventually, with fuel running out, the crew abandoned the aircraft which crashed near Newton.

This had been one of I/NJG2's most successful operations to date. Ten crews claimed five bombers without loss to themselves. Perhaps this augered well for the future?

Four days later, on February 15th, the RAF had some very close escapes when the aircraft of I/NJG2 returned. Bombs fell near the airfields of Bircham Newton, Feltwell and Sutton Bridge, which was also strafed. At Fulbeck two Oxfords were damaged but both were able to land. No. 44 Squadron at Waddington were also lucky. Flying Officer Penman dived his Hampden low to evade his attacker but Squadron Leader Smalies's Hampden was hit. With damage to his machine's port engine and its fuselage, Smalies landed on Waddington's blacked out runway. The crew had just walked away from their aircraft when another Wellington ploughed into it in the darkness.

Any jubilation at Gilze-Rijen was short lived however. Before the end of February 1941, two aircraft and six crew men had been lost in accidents only a few kilometres from the airfield. Both of the crews had been relatively inexperienced. As if to continue I/NJG2's 'eye for an eye' war with the RAF, Feldwebel Ziebarth attacked a Wellington of No. 218 Squadron as it came in to land at Marham on February 25th. Its pilot, Sergeant Hoos, tried to get his bomber to climb but the damage was such that it refused to gain sufficient height to enable the crew to bale out safely. Eventually the Wellington struck the ground near Swaffham. A fire broke out and began to spread as the crew scrambled out, one with a broken arm and another with his shoulder dislocated. Only Sergeant Stanley remained, trapped by his legs in his front turret. The other crew members returned to free him but despite their efforts he suffered serious burns. He was taken to King's Lynn Hospital where one of his shattered legs had to be amputated.

The next night Kurt Herrmann was once more over Lincolnshire when he sighted an Oxford making its final approach to Fulbeck. A burst of fire hit the Oxford but it flew on to crash land heavily near the airfield, catching fire as it did so. Acting Flying Officer Egan, an instructor with No. 2 Central Flying School, got out but his pupil, Flight Lieutenant Trench, was killed. Two personnel were killed by shrapnel from bombs which fell on the airfield. This Oxford was Herrmann's seventh victim and, to date, he was the highest scoring pilot. Engelbert Böttner was again his Bordfunker when he took off on March 10th.

'We took off from Gilze-Rijen at 23.00 hours and flew over Schouwen Island eastwards to England and the area of Lincoln. The night sky was clear and bright during our time over the mainland and we could see the flak firing at us. We were still trying to find a target when our right motor was hit by flak. Despite jettisoning the bombs, we lost height and had to make a crash landing near King's Lynn at about 00.15 hours. I was seriously injured in the landing and was taken to hospital for treatment.'

Following the landing, Herrmann and Wilhelm Rüppel set out to find help for their colleague and came upon four members of the Home Guard, headed by Corporal Buffham. As the injured Bordfunker was borne off on a gate, which served as a stretcher, other Home Guard members escorted their prisoners away at bayonet point. Engelbert Böttner, Kurt Herrmann and Wilhelm Rüppel were the first members of NJG2 to be taken prisoner.

Amongst the first to arrive at the scene of the crash the following morning was an officer from the RAF's Air Intelligence Section AI1(g). AI1(g)'s function was to gather as much material as possible relating to the equipment in use by enemy airforces. A key source of this information was the examination of downed aircraft. Since the outbreak of war Air Intelligence officers had toured crash sites reporting upon what they found. In many instances this was no more than a pathetic heap of fragments scattered over the countryside, but occasionally there was a greater prize providing much of value to the RAF. Herrmann's Ju 88 was the first German night fighter to be captured. The all black Ju 88C-2 lay in a field, its starboard wing and the centre section of the fuselage badly damaged. The markings, R4 + CH were painted in slate grey on the fuselage sides with the 'C' having a white outline. The cause of the crash was soon found. The number three conrod of the starboard engine had fractured and broken through the side of the crank case. The port engine showed signs of severe overheating, indicating a failure of the lubricating system. A new armament was found, the first time that anything of its type had been encountered on a Ju 88. This consisted of an MG 151 mounted below three MG 17s, all of which were fitted in the nose. After a brief examination, the wreck was dismantled for transportation to the Royal Aircraft Establishment at Farnborough where a thorough investigation took place.

Feldwebel Hans Hahn made attacks on two successive nights, March 12th and 13th, badly damaging a Blenheim and destroying a Manchester of No. 207 Squadron. Flying Officer Matthews, the pilot of the Manchester, had just taken off from Waddington when his machine was brought down. As the Manchester hit the ground, its bomb load exploded killing all but two of the crew. Of the two survivors, Sergeant Marsden died later in hospital.

A fourth Staffel had by this time been formed under the command of Oberleutnant Paul Bohn. Two aircraft and crews had been lost before the Staffel even became operational and, when it did, another loss was suffered almost immediately. Wing Commander Charles Widdows and his AI operator, Sergeant Ryall, were airborne in a No. 29 Squadron Beaufighter in the early hours of March 14th. They were operating under the control of the Orby Ground Control Interception Station who were attempting to vector the Beaufighter on to a 'bandit'. At first they had no success in intercepting the raid, but as Widdows reported:

> 'After a short time I was taken off this raid and put on to another proceeding directly towards me. I was brought round on curve of pursuit right astern of E/A. I sighted E/A before weapon was flashed. Closed to almost 100 yds and opened fire from dead astern with one short burst which could be seen entering the fuselage of the enemy. The pilot appeared to be killed as the aircraft went straight into a dive from which it never recovered.'

The 'enemy' had been a Ju 88C-4 of 4/NJG2. Gefreiter Hans Körner and his crew perished when their aircraft broke up in the air near Louth. Pieces of wreckage were subsequently found scattered over an area of two square miles, leaving little intact for AI1(g) to inspect, but the markings R4 + GM could be read.

A point that had been missed by the Air Intelligence officer who inspected the wreckage was that this aircraft had been one of the new C4 sub types. The Ju 88C-4 differed from the C-2 as it was based on the Ju 88A-5 airframe. This variant featured a longer wing span with pointed wing tips. It also had more powerful Jumo 211-G or Jumo 211-F engines replacing the earlier Jumo 211-Bs which were fitted to the Ju 88A-1 based machines. The armament remained similar to that of the Ju 88C-2 but a 20mm variant of the MG 151 was fitted in the nose replacing the MG FF 20mm cannon.

Another night fighter that had been operating that night was Sergeant Smith's No. 255 Squadron Defiant. Having patrolled the Humber to Grimsby area, Smith returned to Kirton-in-Lindsey.

'On returning to base I was informed that 'Rats' were active and that a diversion was suggested. I informed 'ops' that my 'gravy' was low and that a diversion was not on. It was agreed to allow me to return to Kirton and it was also agreed that precautions were to be exercised as it was a grass field and the flare-path consisted of four gallon petrol cans with one side cut away and with bulbs powered by a Chance Light generator. It was arranged that I should position myself down-wind and in line of the flare-path for my approach and landing. When I was on my final approach and touchdown, I would ask for the red 'obstruction light' on top of the Chance Light to be switched on to help me avoid it – that being the main hazard. It was clear half-moon night and as long as I missed the Chance Light I was confident I could get down O.K. The exercise was successful i.e. the red light on top of the Chance Light went on and not the flood light itself. I got a bearing on this for the landing run and I told 'ops' to switch off as I was O.K.

When approximately half way along the landing run, 'Jerry' opened fire on the starboard side – quite a distance away from my landing. Seeing this my gunner, a New Zealander named McKenzie attempted to operate the turret which was at rest in the forward landing position. In his anxiety to get the turret moving he pressed the 'high speed' button and fused the electrics so the turret refused to move. Whilst this was happening, 'Jerry's' cannon fire rained down just behind the tail of the Defiant and across the full width of the airfield. In the heat of the moment we had words regarding McKenzie not having a go at 'Jerry' as he had missed a unique chance of an aircraft on the deck shooting down an aircraft in flight and thus spoiling 'Jerry's' night out. McKenzie agreed that it was certainly a near miss for both of us saying, "it was a Junkers 88 – the bastard".'

In fact one aircraft was hit. A No. 65 Squadron Spitfire which was parked on the perimeter received several holes in one of its petrol tanks.

No. 149 Squadron sent eleven Wellingtons to Bremen on March 18th. As the returning bombers circled Mildenhall, Leutnant Rudolf Pfeiffer opened fire on Wellington 'M' Mother, flown by Sergeant Warren. On the ground at Beck Row, insurance agent Mr Titmarsh heard the gun fire and took shelter with his wife under their bed. No sooner had they done so than the Wellington, by now totally out of control, crashed near to their bungalow. The bungalow was destroyed but miraculously both Mr Titmarsh and his wife escaped with their lives. The six crew of 'M' Mother perished in the crash.

Towards the end of March the already badly hit 4/NJG2 suffered another loss when Gefreiter Otto Krüger and his crew disappeared into the North Sea.

The weather in April improved steadily allowing operations to be conducted on most nights. There was no lack of activity over Eastern England at this time as the 'Blockade of Brest', as it had become known, had begun. The German battle cruisers *Gneisenau* and *Scharnhorst,* in harbour at Brest, had been attacked by over one hundred bombers on the night of March 30th–31st. This was the first of sixty-three raids to be launched against this target during 1941. On April 3rd, Sergeant Thompson's Wellington was part of No. 115 Squadron's effort against the battle cruisers. Shortly after midnight 'H Harry' R4170, was returning to Marham, but when over the Wash the Wellington was hit by a burst of fire. Rapidly the aircraft lost height. Pilots, Thompson and Sergeant Chard, succeeded in holding the aircraft on an even keel until it eventually hit the mud flats off King's Lynn. The only man to get out alive was Sergeant Russell, the rear gunner, who was finally reached by rescuers several hours later. By this time he was suffering from exposure after being stranded on the bleak mud flats.

During the nights of April 7th–8th and 8th–9th four aircraft were damaged by intruders and one, a Hampden from No. 14 OTU, was destroyed by Feldwebel Hahn.

Berlin was the target for Bomber Command on April 9th. I/NJG2 came to England in search of the raiders, but the night's first casualty was once more a Ju 88 from 4/NJG2. Sergeants Bennett and Curtis were on patrol in Beaufighter R2122 of No. 25 Squadron when, shortly after 22.00 hours, a shower of incendiary bombs ignited below them. Sergeant Curtis, the operator, picked up an enemy aircraft on the airborne interception equipment and soon a vague shape was visible. It climbed and was lost to view but again Curtis guided the Beaufighter on to the tail of the enemy. Two bursts of fire from the cannon and machine guns hit the Ju 88 which dived away. Its Bordfunker and Bordmechaniker baled out but the pilot, Gefreiter Franz Brotz, was killed when the aircraft crashed near Oakham. As Unteroffizier Willi Lindler's parachute opened his boots fell off, leaving the Bordfunker to find his way into captivity bare-foot. Despite meeting a courteous soldier who wished him goodnight, it was not until he asked for the police station in Langham that anyone took any notice in him.

The first RAF loss of the night occurred two hours later, near the airfield of Bircham Newton. Wellington R1049 'B-Bertie' of No. 221 Squadron had just taken off when it was attacked by Feldwebel Peter Laufs. Sergeant Owens in the rear turret returned the fire but the Wellington was already on fire. Before anyone could escape the bomber crashed, killing its three crew. This was the first casualty that No. 221 Squadron had suffered since its formation.

At Bassingbourne, No. 11 Operational Training Unit suffered the first of many visits from I/NJG2 when Wellington L4253 was shot down. Fortunately its two crew were able to walk away from the blazing wreck.

Part of the RAF defence this night were the Hurricanes of No. 257 Squadron, based at Coltishall. Squadron Leader Tuck had already claimed that he had brought a Ju 88 down into the sea off Lowestoft and that he had attacked an He 111 before his wing man, Sergeant Truman, also met a Ju 88 over Norfolk. As Truman made his attack, return fire from the Ju 88 hit his Hurricane and Unteroffizier Alfons Köster made his claim for 'an unknown single engined machine'. Truman began to return to his home airfield, but when two-and-a-half miles short he was forced to bale out. Before Truman could extricate himself from his Hurricane, it crashed and he was killed. Another claim was submitted by Unteroffizier Hans Berschwinger who claimed to have destroyed a Wellington near Marham. No loss can be attributed to this claim but it has gone down in history as I/NJG2's twentieth victory. So far eight crews had been lost in accidents, seven had disappeared into the North Sea and five had been brought down by British defences.

When Herbert Thomas and Heinrich Beul had made their first flights over England in late 1940 there had been little real danger from British night fighters. Although the pilots of the slow and cumbersome Blenheims and Defiants put up a spirited defence, a German bomber would have to have been unlucky to have met one. No airborne interception equipment was carried and even if caught, the rifle calibre

Browning machine guns would need to score a considerable number of hits to bring a foe down. Some crews had been unlucky when something of importance was damaged by chance. But now there was a new and deadly opponent, the Beaufighter. Hans Körner's aircraft had been cut to pieces in the air by a No. 29 Squadron Beaufighter and now Franz Brotz had fallen to the guns of No. 25 Squadron.

In many ways the Bristol Beaufighter was similar to the Ju 88 night fighters for it too had come from bomber stock in the form of the Bristol Beaufort. It was however, far more refined, a thoroughbred night fighter. It was also the only aircraft of the time capable of carrying the AI. Mk.IV airborne interception equipment without reducing its performance. Once found, it could rip its target apart with a battery of four Hispano 20mm cannon and six .303 calibre machine guns. The Beaufighter, initially a private venture on the part of the Bristol Aeroplane Company, reached squadron service in late 1940. Fortunately, for the British, this was in time to play a major part in meeting the night Blitz and the intruders of NJG2. Nos. 25 and 29 Squadrons were the first to be equipped with Beaufighters which replaced their ineffective Blenheims in operations over Britain. No. 25 Squadron in particular would plague I/NJG2 from now on. When first formed in 1916, No. 25 Squadron's envisaged role was to intercept raiding Gotha bombers on their way to England. Twenty-five years later their descendants had a similar task. I/NJG2 had already dealt the squadron a blow when, on March 14th, six bombs fell on their base at Wittering. A hangar, the cinema, the Officers' Mess and some offices were hit, the squadron's records, a Magister, a Blenheim and three Beaufighters were destroyed. Casualties amounted to: five killed and fifteen injured. With the advent of effective night defences in addition to the more usual hazards, the odds were being stacked against NJG2. On April 17th, Feldwebel Hahn was successful in bringing down a Hampden of No. 144 Squadron and another of 4/NJG2's Ju 88s failed to return from England. The three crew of the Ju 88 were posted missing and the aircraft vanished, apparently without trace. This posed a mystery that would only be resolved when the wreckage of their aircraft was found some forty years later.

The next day, April 18th, an aircraft of 3/NJG2 crashed in Holland, killing all three on board. Casualties were high, but operations continued to gather momentum. Feldwebel Hahn brought down a Battle of No. 12 FTS on April 21st and Feldwebel Giessübel found a Wellington from No. 11 OTU in the early hours of April 24th. The aircraft was flying low over its base of Bassingbourne when it was shot down and it fell into a dispersal pen where another Wellington was parked. Both aircraft were destroyed and two men killed. That evening Heinz Völker was over Yorkshire where Flight Lieutenant R. W. Denison was flying solo in his Blenheim. He was attacked and the port engine of his Blenheim and its wing burst into flames as the petrol tank exploded. Denison managed to bale out and landed safely while Völker flew on to Church Fenton, by coincidence Denison's base. Here another No. 54 OTU Blenheim was hit by bullets but landed safely only to run into an obstruction on the runway. Later a third Blenheim landed and its undercarriage collapsed. Half an hour later, while the wrecks of the Blenheims were being cleared, another Ju 88 made a bombing attack on the airfield. Eight 50kg bombs exploded, destroying one aircraft and damaging five more, but no serious injuries were caused. Völker was credited with three Blenheims destroyed, which took his total to seven and brought congratulations from Generalfeldmarschall Kesselring. This, however, would prove to be the last time that Heinz Völker would celebrate destroying an aircraft.

No. 54 OTU and Church Fenton were the targets for Leutnant Pfeiffer two days later. This time a warning was given and visual signals were made instructing the pupils to put their navigation lights out and orbit a beacon until the danger had passed. For some reason Sergeant Crozier and Sergeant Bell, in a Defiant, failed to see or heed the warning. At 1,000 feet Pfeiffer attacked the illuminated aircraft. Gunner Bell in the turret returned the fire and Crozier threw his plane into violent evasive action. Perhaps the pilot performed his manoeuvres with too much vigor, for the Defiant hit a tree and exploded in a sheet of flame.

As has been mentioned, whilst justification can be found for many of the reports submitted, some incidents defy verification. An example is the report submitted by Oberfeldwebel Herrmann Sommer for a sortie made on the night of April 29th – 30th, 1941 when flying with Heinz Völker's crew.

> 'At about midnight on April 29th 1941, I flew to 'Raum B' near to the Wash. I saw an English aircraft fire recognition signals and flew towards it where I found an airfield, illuminated and very active. I joined the airfield's circuit at between 200 and 300 metres at 00.15 hours and after several circuits an aircraft came within range. I closed to between 100 and 150 metres and fired. After a short burst the aircraft exploded in the air and fell to the ground.
>
> At 00.20 hours I saw another aircraft landing with its lights on which

I attacked from behind and above at roughly 80 metres. The aircraft crashed after my burst of fire and caught fire on hitting the ground.

In the light of the flames from the two wrecks, I could see fifteen to twenty aircraft parked on the airfield. I dropped my bombs on these and flew to Hucknall where I saw an aircraft about to land. At about 00.50 hours I got behind the aircraft and opened fire from about 100 metres. The aircraft caught fire, hit the ground and burnt out.

After this I set course for home and was flying at 300 metres when my Bordfunker saw navigation lights to our right. I went to attack at 01.30 hours. As I could not approach from the rear, I attacked from the right hand quarter. The aircraft flew through my fire and crashed to the ground.

After shooting down the first two aircraft, I had attacked the airfield with bombs. I saw three aircraft on the runway with their landing and navigation lights on, a fourth taxiing and a fifth taking off. I dropped my bombs at 00.30 hours and scored direct hits, all five aircraft were blown into the air by the explosions which turned the sky blood red. The fires were still visible about an hour after the explosion.'

Sommer was credited with two Blenheims destroyed at Tollerton, another at Hucknall and finally one at Bircham Newton. Then there were the five aircraft destroyed on the ground at Tollerton by his bombs, surely there must be some evidence to support his claims?

Tollerton was an alternative name for Nottingham Airfield but there is no evidence recorded of an attack in this area. Bircham Newton found nothing worthy of note and Hucknall reported:

'Group Captain Garbinski attended a conference at Polish Inspectorate General, London. Oxford V3679 collided in air with Oxford V3588.'

Thirty miles away at Fulbeck (a relief landing ground for No. 2 Central Flying School, Cranwell) it was reported:

'One unidentified Enemy aircraft attacked Fulbeck RLG at 01.15 hours dropping incendiary bombs and 9 HEs some 75 yards from the flare path, but although 9 craters 20 feet in diameter and 10 feet deep were formed, nobody on the landing ground heard any explosions, no guns opened fire and there were no casualties.'

Fighter Command reported that a training aircraft was machine gunned over Driffield and bombs fell at RAF Sibson in Huntingdonshire but caused no damage. At Ipswich bombs destroyed a house near the airfield. The only damage caused seems to have been at Martlesham Heath where two enemy aircraft dropped bombs from 250 feet at 21.15 hours, which destroyed one Hurricane and damaged four more.'

49

Ground crew manhandle a Ju 88C at Gilze-Rijen. (Thomas).

Obergefreiter Wilhelm Beetz, pilot of the Ju 88C-4 which went missing on April 17th, 1941. Forty-five years later his body, along with those of his two fellow crew members, was found in the wreck of the aircraft when it was excavated near Peterborough. (Saunders).

An incident which has been associated with Sommer's claim is the attack on an Oxford flown by Leading Aircraftsman Patrick over Fulbeck. Records show, however, that the attack occured over 24 hours later, at 02.30 hours on May 1st and that the Oxford was landed safely, being only slightly damaged and continuing in service.

What, one wonders, had Herrmann Sommer been reporting? Is there any possibility that reports were falsified, for it is true that at this stage the intruders of I/NJG2 had more claims than all other German night fighter units put together? This is certainly not an isolated case and it has been suggested that intruder missions were eventually stopped partly because of the exaggerated reports. The answer lies in the interpretation put on reports by historians today.

A leading researcher into Luftwaffe night fighters, who was himself a pilot with II/NJG2, made the following comments on how the Luftwaffe term 'abschusse' has lead to confusion by todays' historians:

> 'Claims are not necessarily to be considered as victories. That is one of the reasons why the Luftwaffe seldom used the term 'victory' at all. Let us assume that I had definitely hit a bomber, the aircraft goes down aflame diving into solid cloud so that the actual crash cannot be observed. What are you to consider this to be? Are you to add it to your own personal score or add it to the score of the Staffel? How would the Gruppe count this in the Gruppen list? How would the OKW count it? Is it permitted to count it as an aircraft probably destroyed? If this is done then how does it show on the various lists?
>
> To get over these problems the Luftwaffe used the term 'abschusse'. The English equivalent would be 'claim'. Thus so long as abschusse, or claim, is used the statements are absolutely correct. Problems begin when you consider these claims to have been real victories.'

For the reasons described above, the term claim is used extensively, unless it can be shown through the use of contemporary records that particular parties were involved. Whatever doubts may be raised against the accuracy of the claims, some can be traced in surviving RAF records.

An example of a claim that can be verified occurred early in the morning of May 3rd 1941, when the crew of a No. 77 Squadron Whitley circled their airfield of Topcliffe. Leutnant Feuerbaum moved in behind the Whitley and opened fire. The Whitley's rear gunner returned the fire and the Ju 88 turned away but the Whitley's control surfaces had been damaged. The pilot, Sergeant Mills, landed his bomber but overshot the runway and ran through a hedge. Both aircraft and crew were safe.

Hans Hahn brought another two aircraft down on successive nights, 4th and 5th May, and Strunning made an attack on May 7th. His target was a Wellington from No. 11 Operational Training Unit. Flying Officer Warner was instructing Pilot Officer McAnally who was flying the down wind leg of the landing circuit at Bassingbourne when the attack occurred. At 900 feet a Ju 88 attacked the Wellington from astern and below, rear gunner Sergeant Stuart returned the fire but the port wing tank had already been hit and set on fire. Warner then took control, turned the aircraft into the wind and made a forced landing. Both Warner and McAnally were thrown out through the escape hatch and landed in a stream. Stuart was also thrown clear. Remarkably all escaped, shaken and bruised but otherwise unhurt. As was usual, several airfields were bombed. Notable amongst these were Methwold, where a Wellington was set on fire and destroyed, and Feltwell, where another aircraft was set ablaze.

CHAPTER FOUR

A game no more. May–June 1941

With thirty missions to his credit Herbert Thomas was regarded as one of his Staffel's old hands by the time he took off on the night of May 7th.

> 'On this night I had the job of introducing a new crew to making flights over England. The pilot was Willi Lettenmeier, Georg Herden was the Bordfunker whilst I was the Beobachter and Bordmechaniker.
>
> What feelings I had as we flew to England? Definitely not of being a big hero and not of being killed with the words of Adolf Hitler on my lips. I was twenty-two and proud to be fighting for 'the great Germany' and I would have liked to receive the Ritterkreuz. In some ways we were no different from the RAF boys. We understood the politics and what the future may have held but when we were flying we were 5,000 metres above the Nazis.
>
> That night we had already been over enemy territory for one-and-a-half hours but the airfields were blacked out and there were no aircraft to be seen. There was a deceptive silence, no searchlights in the sky. It seemed that no one in England was taking any notice of us.'

The principle target for the Lufwaffe's bombers that night was Liverpool. Although to Herbert Thomas all seemed quiet, three bombers had already fallen to the British defences and, before the night was over, a further eight would be destroyed over the West Country and the Midlands. As usual No. 25 Squadron's Beaufighters were on patrol. In one was Pilot Officer Thompson and his AI operator Pilot Officer Britain. At 4,000 feet, over the Wash, Britain got a 'blip' on his airborne interception equipment. Later Thompson reported:

> 'After a chase of about 3 minutes I saw an E/A about 400 yards away below and ahead at 13/14,000 and I definitely identified the E/A as a Do 215 against the bright cloud top 6,000 to 7,000 feet below, P/O Britain also identified the E/A as a Do 215 and we both were struck by the aid to identification afforded by the E/A being silhouetted against a brightly moonlit cloud layer below.'

Herbert Thomas climbed up from the Bola where he had been keeping a look-out and stood behind Willi Lettenmeier, looking for an airfield. Georg was looking behind for fighters while Willi turned and banked the Dornier from side to side to afford a better view. Pilot

Officer Thompson's report continues:

'Finding that I was approaching the E/A too fast, I throttled back which caused exhaust flames to appear from our A/C which was upmoon of the Do which apparently sighted the Beau and immediately made a steep turn to port in an attempt to evade and did evade the first burst of one second which I fired attacking on the starboard beam at a range of 100 yards. I followed the Dornier which continued on a straight course after making the steep turn to port giving me the impression that the pilot of the Dornier thought that he had succeeded in evading me. I followed him and fired two further one second bursts at about 100 yards range from below and to starboard and I saw hits from the first burst and after the second burst the port motor of the Do caught on fire.'

Herbert Thomas was caught unawares.

'Suddenly there was an awful crash and a grinding noise and the left motor began to burn brightly. The noise was terrific. My first reaction was to get the hood clear, close the fuel tap, cut the ignition, cut everything! I went to the control column to help Lettenmeier but our Dornier simply went down. The fire came nearer to the cockpit and together we gave the command to get out. Tracers went under me and the Bola. I could not find the switch for the bale out buzzer so with a great effort I forced open the hatch against the air stream. I climbed on to the Bordfunker's position and to my surprise found that Georg was still at his post. I screamed at him to jump and together we got out.'

Thompson had expended a total of 160 cannon shells on the Dornier, which he watched as it spiralled down near Boston. Willi Lettenmeier left it too late to get out and was found close to the gaping hole in a field that was all that was left of his aircraft. His parachute was unopened.

Herbert Thomas felt a sharp blow as his parachute opened.

'I struggled to get my breath and saw what seemed to be a house burning in the distance. It was in fact my Dornier. I hung firmly in my harness and suddenly found that it was completely quiet. I must have been unconscious. My parachute had opened and I was out of the crashing machine but an awful pain had come over me. I was down on English soil, but how long I lay in the field I do not know. I drifted in and out of consciousness. I could not believe my eyes – perhaps, I though, I was in Heaven. In the far distance I heard a tune. Then came a gift – I put a Woodbine between my lips. For a while I was with Georg. I was awake then on an operating table, having been taken to a small hospital. My overalls had been cut away leaving me naked and I was embarassed at being with a young nurse. I was put into plaster and taken to a ward, separated from an English patient by a partition. Next to me sat a soldier in full battle dress and armed with a rifle. An escape attempt was out of the question as the impact of the parachute harness had broken my left arm, strained two cervical vertibrae and I had sustained serious concussion when I hit the ground. The soldier said 'This fucking Nazi pilot won't get out.' Later we were to share the same cigarette.

An Intelligence Officer visited me and brought the sad news that Lettenmeier was dead. We sang a German song together in his honour.

Despite the pain I was in, I was made comfortable and the treatment in the hospital was excellent. Sunday was visiting day. The partition was moved aside as the visitors wanted to look at the evil German. One man was furious at a small boy who put a few sweets on my bed. My friend the soldier examined them, 'to see if they are poisoned', and then allowed me to eat them.'

Herbert Thomas stayed in Military Hospital No. 4 for four weeks before being moved to a camp in Oldham.

Other crews of NJG2 made claims for four aircraft destroyed on the night of May 7th–8th. Unteroffizier Köster claimed a Wellington and a Blenheim over the North Sea. Semrau and Beier each claimed Wellingtons over England, at Nottingham and Wells respectively. Bomber Command lost eleven aircraft on operations that night.

Shortly after Herbert Thomas's Dornier had been shot down an aircraft circled Wittering, the home of No. 25 Squadron. It descended from 10,000 feet to 800 feet and dropped ten 50kg bombs on the airfield. One bomb hit a barrack block and killed four people. Four hours later a Do 17 appeared over Barkston and shot an Oxford down in flames before dropping its ten 50kg bombs on the airfield and disappearing as quickly as it had come. The next night Wittering was attacked again. This time one man was killed and two Beaufighters damaged. Waddington was also bombed. Here the air raid warning had already sounded and the non-essential personnel, amongst whom were the women who staffed the NAAFI, had taken to the shelters. At 01.24 hours a bomb hit the empty NAAFI building but tragically another exploded in a trench shelter and killed seven of the staff. The airfield was attacked again on the following night but this time the bombs fell wide of their mark. Scampton also received bombs from I/NJG2 on May 9th, which exploded near No. 83 Squadron's dispersal but caused little damage. The next airfield to be attacked was Sutton Bridge. This occurred in the early hours of May 12th when sixteen bombs exploded in two attacks. Two aircraft were completely destroyed and seven more of No. 56 OTU's mixed bag of Hurricanes, Harvards, Masters and Battles were badly damaged. Two unexploded bombs were later found and defused. There was only a single casualty, a soldier injured by a bomb fragment.

Oberleutant Semrau rounded off this burst of activity by bringing down a Battle of No. 12 Flying Training School on May 18th near Grantham. The Battle's pilot, Flying Officer Thomas, was killed.

This claim by Oberleutant Semrau was the last made by I/NJG2 for more than two weeks as the unit was ordered to leave immediately for Brest with all available aircraft. I/NJG2's new task was to provide protection for the *Bismarck* as it attempted to reach Brest after its engagement in the North Atlantic. Protection was also to be given to the battle cruisers *Gneisenau* and *Scharnhorst* which were still trapped in Brest.

Before the *Bismarck* could reach Brest she was sunk in another naval engagement on May 27th and once again I/NJG2 returned to Gilze-Rijen to continue their intruder operations. Oberfeldwebel Sommer was the last member of I/NJG2 to take off on the ferry flight and flew alone. An Me 109 attacked the Ju 88 in error and damaged it so severely that it was forced to land at Lannion.

During the next two months intruder activity over England reached its peak. Only rarely did a night pass when the sky was free of I/NJG2's aircraft. RAF intelligence identified I/NJG2 operating on twenty-eight nights in July and twenty-six nights in August. In June it was estimated that 315 sorties had been flown, with 270 being flown in July and 257 in August. The usual strength amounted to only ten or eleven aircraft.

The month of June 1941 got off to a bad start for 2/NJG2 when, shortly after midnight on the 3rd, Leutnant Johannes Feuerbaum flew his Ju 88 headlong into a hillside at Skelder Moor, near Whitby. The aircraft, coded R4 + LK, disintegrated upon impact with the ground and scattered pieces far and wide among the heather. All three of the crew died instantly. Once more officers of AI1(g) made their examination and identified no less than three 20mm cannon. One of these had been mounted in the nose but the positions of the other three could not be ascertained (later the mounting would become clear during the investigation of another wreck). Three MG 17s, a single MG 15 and eight unexploded 50kg bombs were also found. Perhaps the most significant find was a small canvas case marked with British roundels. This contained pockets for eight two-coloured recognition flare cartridges. Their use was obvious to air intelligence for, with these flares, the correct 'colours of the day' could be fired to mislead or confuse defences if challenged. From now on there could be no certainty of identifying an aircraft from its flares alone.

Leutnant Feuerbaum's intended target had been the bombers returning from Düsseldorf. Two Hampdens of No. 144 Squadron, returning from this target, were attacked over the Wash. Aboard one of these aircraft Sergeant Tyler, the rear gunner, was injured. The other aircraft was slightly damaged before the Ju 88 broke off its attack. Both Hampdens returned safely to Hemswell. Only Oberfeldwebel Beier submitted a claim this night, for a Blenheim near Lowestoft.

At 02.00 hours on June 12th, the pupils of No. 16 OTU, Upper Heyford, were engaged on various night flying exercises when Unteroffizier Köster joined them. A Rhodesian pilot, Pilot Officer Buckley, was making his first night flight in Britain when a burst of machine-gun fire struck the starboard wing and engine nacelle of his Anson. The navigation lights had been on, making it an easy target, but Buckley dived away and switched off his lights. Later Pilot Officer Adams's Anson was also attacked and damaged. Infra-red bombing practice was taking place at nearby Northampton and as other aircraft were on similar exercises to himself, Pilot Officer Gunter switched on the navigation lights of his Hampden. Immediately he was attacked and the starboard wing of his aircraft hit. Gunter took evasive action and made his way back to Upper Heyford. Here the air raid alarm was still in progress and permission to land was refused, as it was for the pilots of other aircraft in the area. Among these was Pilot Officer Buckley who had the un-nerving experience of watching his attacker flying over the airfield. On board Pilot Officer Gunter's Hampden all seemed well and he continued on his bombing exercise once more. On the cross country flight however, the starboard engine failed and flames began to appear from around its airscrew which shortly fell off. The flames died away and Gunter decided to attempt an emergency landing on his remaining engine at Akeman Street landing ground. Misjudging his approach he overshot the landing ground. Two miles further on, the aircraft hit some high tension cables and ran through a hedge before it came to a halt with its undercarriage collapsed. All the crew walked away uninjured.

The next night, June 13th, Oberleutant Semrau was over Yorkshire and claimed the destruction of a four engined bomber. Another claim, for a Defiant near Thornaby, was submitted by Oberfeldwebel Beier. At Finningley a Wellington was brought down, and at Hemswell a

No. 61 Squadron Manchester was hit by bomb splinters whilst it was parked in its dispersal.

As dawn broke over Gilze-Rijen on the following morning, an air of gloom spread over the crews and ground staff of Paul Bohn's fourth Staffel. Since becoming Staffelkapitän three months previously, twelve men, four complete crews, had vanished. Now three more crews were long overdue – they too were missing.

At 22.15 hours the previous evening Richard Hoffmann, an Unteroffizier pilot, had left Gilze-Rijen with the other crews. Their destination was Norfolk 'Raum A'. At Wittering No. 25 Squadron's Beaufighters were ready for their nightly patrol. At 22.30 hours Squadron Leader Harold Pleasance left Wittering in Beaufighter T4634 with Sergeant Bent as his AI operator, their call sign being, 'Cockle 14.' The ground control interception station at Orby instructed them to patrol the coast at 11,000 feet. Twenty minutes after Pleasance had taken off, Pilot Officer Thompson left Wittering with Pilot Officer Britain as his AI operator. 'Cockle 33', as they were known, was put under the control of Digby GCI.

For nearly two hours 'Cockle 14' patrolled the coast before Orby gave the instruction to vector 260 degrees. At maximum range Sergeant Bent obtained a 'blip' on his AI set. The bandit flew at the same height (11,000 feet), away to starboard and heading west. Bent gave his orders which brought the Beaufighter to within 500 yards of his prey which Pleasance noted was flying at 200 mph. It had a single fin and showed no lights. His report continues:

'I attacked at once from dead astern and slightly below and fired a short burst at a range of 100 yards of which I saw no result.

I then closed to 75 yards and fired a second burst exhausting the contents of my four magazines which caused a vivid flash to come from the port engine of the E/A which went into a glide followed by a stream of white smoke.

After descending to 9,000 feet the E/A began to climb slowly doing 'S' turns at about 130 mph, I followed making wider turns but keeping the E/A in view and when the E/A had regained height to 10,000 feet fire began to spread over the E/A which then went down vertically in flames and exploded on the ground near Swaffham, when the E/A crashed I had descended to 5,000 feet.'

Richard Hoffmann and his crew had been taken completely by surprise. The whole aircraft appeared to be in flames as the three men jettisoned their canopy and baled out. Feldwebel Peter Meyer, the Bordmechaniker, landed safely but shaken. Richard Hoffmann broke one of his legs on landing but the Bordfunker, Gefreiter Johann Reisinger, was found dead after his parachute had failed to open.

As Harold Pleasance, his ammunition exhausted, returned to Wittering, 'Cockle 33' was called by Orby to replace him. Fifteen minutes later, Pilot Officer Thompson was vectored on to his target which was two miles ahead of him. After a chase which lasted twenty minutes he caught a glimpse of an aircraft. Twice he lost sight of it, but each time Britain guided him back until the Beaufighter sat just 100 feet away from Helmut Bähner's Ju 88. Thompson fired a short burst. The Junker's starboard engine burst into flames and the aircraft fell into a steep dive. Desperately Heinz Schulz, the twenty-five year old Bordfunker, tried to extricate himself from the bomber as it fell but to no avail as his body was found in the harness of his unopened parachute. Neither Helmut Bähner nor his Bordmechaniker, Jakob Ried, left the aircraft. They were blown to pieces as it exploded on the mudflats of Wingland Marsh.

This was the second aircraft of I/NJG2 that had fallen to Thompson's guns, the first having been Herbert Thomas's Dornier. A third member of the ill fated fourth Staffel, Unteroffizier Vitus Alt, survived the attentions of the east coast's defences and after an uneventful patrol set course across the North Sea for home. He and his crew were destined never to return.

The crew of an He 111 from 8/KG4 had been forced to ditch earlier on the night of June 13th, after their aircraft had been damaged during a raid on Chatham. They had been fortunate that the sea was calm and a safe landing allowed Feldwebel Neuenhöfer and all but one of his crew to scramble into their life raft before the bomber sank beneath them. Now it seemed that more good fortune lay in store as a Ju 88 flew over them. They must have wondered if they had been spotted. If they had, then their position would be radioed to the rescue service and they would soon be picked up by boat or a float plane from the Seenotdienst. If they had not, then they might never be found. Their question was answered when the sound of the Ju 88's engines returned to their ears and the bomber began to circle the dinghy. Bringing his aircraft lower, Vitus Alt tightened his turn around the men. A wing tip touched the water and in a flurry of spray the Ju 88 and its crew crashed into the sea. The following day the Heinkel crew were picked up by a Seenotstaffel aircraft. The SOS sent by Hans Suckow, Alt's Bordfunker, had been picked up. It was then that the tragedy unfolded and Paul Bohn learned of the fate of another of his crews. Heinrich Beul recalls this day well:

'A few days earlier we had seen an SOS flashed from the sea as we were returning from England. I sent a signal to our base from which they could get a fix on us and therefore on the SOS signal. Otto, my pilot, turned low over the sea and the signal flashed by beneath us. I told Otto that he should take more care, but he gave me a very unfriendly answer. 'You worry too much', he said.

The day after the Ju 88 had crashed into the sea we were on leave. Otto was very apologetic, bought me a beer and told me of the accident. I hoped that now he would take more care.'

CHAPTER FIVE

Sole Survivor. The story of Heinrich Beul

Heinrich Beul's leave was over all too soon and he returned to Gilze-Rijen to rejoin his crew. It was to begin a chapter of his life that he will never be able to forget.

'On June 22nd 1941, we left Gilze-Rijen at 00.15 hours, heading for England. Our route, as usual, took us over the North Sea to the Wash but the English flak did not appear as it usually did. From this we concluded that there must be night fighters in the area.

Our aircraft was coded R4 + JH, a Junkers Ju 88C-2, and carried eight 50kg bombs together with some incendiaries. The pilot was Oberfeldwebel Otto Weise and the Bordmechaniker Gefreiter Hermann Mandel. I was the Bordfunker, working the wireless, manning the rearward firing MG 15 machine gun and also keeping a look-out for British night fighters.

Over England other aircraft could often be made out in the darkness. It was possible that they could have been from our own Staffel or German bombers as well as English bombers.'

Just 100 yards away from Heinrich Beul was one of No. 25 Squadron's Beaufighters. 'Cockle 22' was flown by Flying Officer Michael Herrick, a New Zealander who had already destroyed four aircraft at night and had been awarded the DFC for shooting down two aircraft on September 5th the previous year. Herrick sat alongside the Ju 88 for some time as he contacted his ground control station at Orby to confirm that the aircraft was definitely 'hostile'. Satisfied with its identity, he dropped back behind and slightly below the four exhaust flames which were all that could be seen of his enemy. His first burst of fire missed by a narrow margin and Otto Weise threw the Ju 88 into a diving turn to starboard. Herrick went after it using his guns in the manner of a hosepipe as the pace of the combat was too great to make use of the reflector gun sight. Heinrich Beul recalled what followed:

'Our aircraft was hit from behind. Our right wing, with two 400 litre fuel tanks in it, caught fire. Otto went into a steep dive in an attempt to extinguish the flames but to no avail, in fact the flames grew bigger. Otto gave the order to bale out and Hermann tried to open the bottom gondola but couldn't, the handle having been damaged by a cannon shell. We had to jettison the cockpit hood. I stepped on to my seat and

61

rolled out. I was lucky to get out first and immediately tried to pull my parachute release. I was spinning over and over. I reached the handle on my chest and pulled. There was a tremendous jerk and I swung like a pendulum as I fell. I could see a streaking light like a question mark in the night sky. I thought that the fuel in the burning wing had exploded and that the aircraft had blown up but this was not the case. A little later I saw in front of me several explosions, both large and small. This was the aircraft crashing, the fuel tanks, bombs and ammunition exploding.

As I came nearer to the ground I could see a house and a stream. I thought I might land in the water so I inflated my life jacket. While I was still twenty to thirty metres from the ground I heard a whistle blow. The English soldiers were good – they had arrived whilst I was still in the air. The parachute fell in a small wheat field at the edge of the stream and I was dragged along. I hit my head hard. My arm hurt and I needed first aid. The army all carried their rifles and revolvers and took me to a house where the people were nice to me. They gave me some water as I was thirsty and I gave them my pocket knife in thanks.'

Heinrich Beul was the only one to escape alive from the aircraft which had crashed near to the church at Deeping St. James, Lincolnshire. When he was passed into the care of another of the RAF's Air Intelligence sections AI1(k), he finally discovered what had happened to his comrades.

Whilst AI1(g) dealt with the aircraft and the equipment, AI1(k) would gather information on Luftwaffe units and personnel. Due to the nature of the material gleaned from the interrogation of German personnel, most of AI1(k)'s records have either been destroyed or are still classified under the Official Secrets Act to protect those named. Once again Heinrich Beul provides a unique insight into the treatment that most Luftwaffe prisoners received.

'After a time the police came to the house. I was handcuffed and made prisoner. The police took me to a detention room at an airfield and the handcuffs were released. I hoped they would stay off. The room had no windows, just a door and above this a hatch. A wooden bunk was the only furniture. After about an hour the door opened and a soldier shouted, 'Kommandant!.' I got off the bunk.

'Boche', the Kommandant said, 'Deutscher Schweinehund.' And then I was introduced to the pilot who had shot us down. He was very friendly to me.

I was told what had become of my crew. Hermann had either jumped out over the burning wing or the fire had spread to the cockpit before he had time to bale out. His parachute had caught fire and he had fallen in flames. He had been the burning question mark I had seen in the sky. Otto Wiese went down with the aircraft and his body was found in its wreckage.

The following morning I was woken by a soldier and given breakfast. I could not eat. The happenings of the night had an effect on me. I did not feel hungry. The soldiers were friendly and sent me breakfast again later, but I refused it. About lunch time I was woken again by the soldiers and given several thin slices of meat with vegetables and potatoes. But the meat had hot English spice and was too salty for my taste. The soldiers gave me a dictionary and I was able to translate a few words.

Next I was put into a small military car and taken to London. The driver had to get out and ask the way as all the signposts had been taken down. In London I got out in a large park and was handed to someone else.

I was put into a room with a window. There was a large four sided tower nearby. The clockface on the tower had Roman numerals. The hour was chimed by a bell which could be heard well from my room. Soon the interrogation began.

The interrogator was an officer who called himself Hauptmann Humor (Flight Lieutenant Funny). He was anything but funny. He said malicious and inconceivable things:

I had changed my name. The radio frequencies and papers for the aircraft had been changed. When an aircraft was missing were the frequencies changed the same night? My military record was already known from other prisoners. Was I not a member of the NSDAP? And in the eye of Hauptmann Humor, a Nazi?

Then a 'spy' in Luftwaffe uniform came into my room. He spoke German with an Austrian accent. Again and again he talked of spying. I had a feeling we were being listened to, the room was bugged.

When the cross-examination began again there were two soldiers in the room with bayonets fixed to their rifles. During the examination Hauptmann Humor carried a revolver. I could see the barrel and that it was loaded with five cartridges. It was a large calibre revolver with a muzzle brake. I assume that the gun was to help extract the radio codes from me. I was in a dangerous situation. First I had been in a burning aircraft. The next second I jumped out. Of the men of my crew, I alone was still living. Now I could be killed. Why was I not already with my crew in the hereafter? I asked Hauptmann Humor, "Do the soldiers kill people in this business often?" I was frightened.

Hauptmann Humor was then a friend. Shortly after he asked me in a cynical way if I was married and if I had any children? I said that I was married and that I had a daughter. Did I also want a son? I replied that I did. Then Hauptmann Humor told me that in England the prison camps came under Polish command. If I went there, maybe I would not be able to have any more children. That was an unmanly threat. Then my sense of humour ran out.'

Heinrich Beul had been 'processed' by what had become an extemely efficient organisation which had begun its existence in the Tower of London just twenty-four hours after the outbreak of war. The basic idea of the intelligence gathering organisation had grown out of a meeting held in March 1939, attended by the War Office, Admiralty, Home Office and Air Ministry. As a result of this, a small group of RAFVR officers were chosen in August 1939, for their command of the German language and their previous business or professional connections. The first head of the 'Air Section' was Flying Officer Pollock and with Flying Officer Felkin, he moved into the Tower of London on September 2nd, 1939. The accommodation consisted of four rooms in the Welsh Guards' quarters and ten rooms for the prisoners. Fifteen of the selected officers were posted to RAF stations as field interrogators on the assumption that an airman would be at his most susceptible to interrogation immediately after his capture and whilst still under the influence of the initial shock.

In December 1939, the unit, now designated AI1(k), moved to Trent Park at Cockfosters in North London. Flight Lieutenant (later Group Captain) Felkin took charge and was to remain head of the organisation until its disbandment in February 1946.

One of the last reports issued by what was then the Assistant Directorate of Intelligence (k), was a summary of its methods. It is interesting in view of Heinrich Beul's experience to examine their procedure.

In the event of the enemy 'arriving by air' the nearest RAF authority would be informed and a field officer with his own car and driver would make his way to the scene of the aircraft crash to examine and remove all documents. Prisoners would be disarmed and searched by the police who would hand all documents to the field officer. From these documents the background of the prisoner would be established. Based upon an interview with the prisoner and knowledge gained from any documents, a preliminary report would be telephoned to the Headquarters in Trent Park. Whilst interrogation of prisoners of war was allowed under the Geneva Convention, a prisoner could not be expected to divulge more than his name, rank and number. AI1(k) had their ways of manoeuvring around this.

'A good interrogator', it was stated 'is a practical psychologist with a capacity for rapid appraisal of character. He should be a good linguist although understanding the language is more important than being able to speak it perfectly. Imperfect language can be beneficial as prisoners become suspicious of perfection in their language. Assumed imperfection on the part of the interrogator often produced good results.

Occasionally it might be necessary to deliberately lead a prisoner to untruth or impoliteness in order that the interrogator might take on a sterner tone. A little fierceness on the part of the interrogator, with the prospect of stricter camps and less comfortable surroundings, or the legitimate suggestion of handing over to another ally whose methods might give grounds for apprehension, would sometimes achieve a good result.'

AI1(k) also carefully collated all the information they could gather which would enable them to keep track of Luftwaffe activities. This included such diverse information as an index of names and signatures of parachute packers at airfields. From this, if all other means of identification had been destroyed, the base and therefore the unit of a wrecked aircraft could be established. A card index of names in the Luftwaffe was maintained which would include details of personnel as they became known. It was from this that the interrogator had been able to quote Heinrich Beul his career. Other details collected from previously captured comrades included the names and dates of birth of his wife and child, his dog's name and habits and tales relating to other members of his unit.

By the time Heinrich Beul was captured a fairly comprehensive picture of I/NJG2 would have been built up in its own loose leaf book. This file along with others was, it seems, destroyed at the war's end.

CHAPTER SIX

Attrition. June – September 1941

In June 1941, the basic tactics employed in intruder operations changed. No longer did they boldly patrol airfields over the English mainland. Instead, with occasional exceptions, the majority of interceptions took place over the North Sea, away from the RAF defences which had taken such a heavy toll. In June, twenty-two claims for aircraft destroyed were submitted, of which eighteen were over the sea. Of the other four, only one can be confirmed as resulting in the loss of an aircraft. This was a Wellington which was shot down by Oberleutnant Semrau on 13th June, near Finningley.

Oberleutnant Paul Bohn, Staffelkapitän of the hard hit 4th Staffel, had already made three claims in June when he took off on the 26th.

At 00.15 hours he approached to eighty metres behind what he identified as a Whitley. A burst of fire hit the Whitley in its fuselage and its right wing and a small blue flame appeared. Bohn made his second attack but the perspex of the Ju 88's cockpit splintered as a burst of return fire from the Whitley struck home. The Ju 88 turned to port and its nose dropped. A fierce blast of icy wind ripped through the shattered perspex. Bohn made no attempt to pull out. Lindner, the Bordmechaniker, got to the pilot and there was little doubt in his voice as he shouted, 'Sepp is dead!'

Taking the control column, Lindner began to pull the Ju 88 out of the dive. Being dark, there was no horizon to fly by, only the dimly lit instruments. Despite the odds Lindner straightened the aircraft out. Once again they were on an even keel, the rate of descent slowed and order was restored. Now the body of Paul Bohn had to be lifted out of his seat, with Lindner taking his place. Unteroffizier Walter Lindner was not a pilot. Although he had flown a Messerschmitt Me 108, his request for pilot training had been turned down as he was, they said, unsuitable. Even so, there had been occasions when Paul Bohn had let him fly back across the North Sea. Now he would have to return on his own. The Bordfunker, Feldwebel Hans Engmann, sent his second message – the first having been to report the attack on the Whitley. The second read: 'Pilot dead. Attempting to return to base.'

Engmann's message was heard at Gilze-Rijen. Hauptmann Karl Hülshoff informed the neighlbouring bases that one of his aircraft was trying to return and asked for the landing lights to be switched on. At

Gilze-Rijen a vertical searchlight acted as a signpost for Lindner and they waited. The time when the Ju 88's fuel would have finally been exhausted came and went – hope faded.

It was not until 8 o'clock the following morning that news came of Bohn's machine. Both Lindner and Engmann had baled out and had been found near Charleville, France. Before they jumped they had attached a static line to Paul Bohn's parachute and pushed him out. His body was not found for twelve days. The aircraft flew on across France, over the Alps and finally ran out of fuel near Mailen, in Northern Italy.

Later Unteroffizier Lindner, on the orders of Göring, was put forward for pilot training. Hans Engmann, however, failed to return from an operation on September 2nd. Command of the 4th Staffel passed to Hauptmann Schütze.

Shortly before midnight on June 27th, Oberfeldwebel Herrmann Sommer reported an encounter with a Wellington in area 2345 East. This was his eighth victory claim, the hundredth claim by I/NJG2 and a greater total than all the other night fighter units operating over Europe put together. Coming the day after Paul Bohn's death, this news did something to lighten the hearts of the Geschwader crews. The news was even announced over the German radio and the crews

The tail of Oberleutnant Paul Bohn's Ju 88, R4 + GM, which crashed after the crew had baled out on 26th June, 1941.

celebrated. The victim of I/NJG2's 100th claim will never be known but it was one of the seventeen bombers which failed to return out of the 150 aircraft that attacked Bremen. Feldwebel Lüddeke also submitted a claim for a Wellington, but as this was received shortly before Sommer's, it fails for some reason to make the same impact as the hundredth and is usually referred to only as a footnote in any survey of I/NJG2.

During the following month, July, an estimated 270 sorties were made by I/NJG2 on twenty-eight nights. Fifty-eight airfields were attacked and nineteen aircraft claimed destroyed, nine of which were over the North Sea. Four of NJG2's aircraft were lost during these raids.

Oberfeldwebel Laufs was the first successful pilot in July. Early in the morning of the 5th he sighted a single engined aircraft, which he identified as a Defiant, preparing to land at North Coates. It was in fact Sergeant Costello's No. 452 Squadron Spitfire which crashed short of the runway. The following night, the 6th, five more claims were made no less than four of which were submitted by Oberfeldwebel Wilhelm Beier, the last coming from Oberfeldwebel Bussmann. Only one aircraft fell in Britain, a No. 500 Squadron Blenheim which crashed and exploded near Docking killing all four of those on board.

Leutnant Rudolf Stradner's Bordfunker, Wilhelm Krieg, sent a message at 03.18 hours on July 9th. 'Emergency – flying east on one engine.'

Soon after this SOS was received, the aircraft crashed. The following morning, Hauptmann Jung found a wheel floating off the Dutch coast. Later the bodies of Krieg and Max Oswald were washed up, but the body of Stradner was never found.

Tiger Moths were the intended target of a pilot on the 15th, when a Ju 88 circled Cambridge and made for the flare path of the tiny airstrip of Caxton Gibbet. No aircraft was hit but on the following night the Ju 88 returned. Flying over Honington, Newmarket, Mildenhall and Waterbeach, it again made for Caxton Gibbett. This time the entire tail section of a Tiger Moth was shot off, the pilot baling out safely. Only one crew claimed to have attacked anything on those nights. Feldwebel Alfons Köster claimed two Blenheims at Wyton.

Although the prime targets for NJG2 were operational bombers, it seems that more often than not, aircraft on training flights became the targets. On the 18th, Sergeant Neighbour, a New Zealander training with No. 54 OTU, was making his first night solo flight. This time it was known that intruders were active near his base of Church Fenton and he was ordered to orbit a flashing beacon near the airfield until the danger had passed. As the Blenheim circled, it began to lose height but this went unnoticed by the inexperienced pilot who was flying on instruments alone. Eventually Neighbour's aircraft flew into the ground and he was killed in the crash. That same night a No. 11 OTU Wellington returned with damage inflicted by a Ju 88.

No. 11 OTU had lost four aircraft to I/NJG2 and its airfield of Bassingbourne had been attacked on eight occasions. No less than three pilots, four wireless operators and an observer were packed into Wellington R1334 as it came in to land at 01.30 hours on July 22nd. Flying through slight rain in total darkness at 600 feet, the Wellington collided with Leutnant Völker's Ju 88. Both aircraft fell in balls of flame and all were killed as the two 'planes crashed into neighbouring fields near Ashwell. Both aircraft had disintegrated, but an AI1(g) officer was able to note that the armament had been increased. Three MG 17s and a 20mm cannon were in the nose but two more 20mm cannon were found mounted on a frame fitted to the lower gondola. This was a similar configuration to that fitted to Johann Feuerbaum's Ju 88 which had flown into the moors near Whitby. Once again a canvas satchel was found, marked with RAF roundels, in which were seven different recognition flares. AI1(k) were at the site as well. On a clothing tag was the date 12/10/39 and the name 'Oberfähnrich H. Völker.' It did not take long for them to realise that this was Leutnant Heinz Völker, the expert of 3/NJG2 with seven claims to his credit – the Wellington would have been his eighth. Feldwebel Andreas Würstl and Unteroffizier Herbert Indenbirken were buried along with their pilot at Bassingbourne.

At 00.42 hours on July 24th 1941, ten 50kg bombs fell near the airfield at Elsham, Lincolnshire. Eight minutes later a further ten bombs fell. Two of I/NJG2's aircraft were in the vicinity. Then at 01.10 hours, the Humber Anti-Aircraft batteries began firing. Villagers at Bonby heard machine gun fire and saw an aircraft burst into flames. Moments later an explosion shook the village as a plane crashed 100 yards away from the school, making a crater forty feet across. Pieces of the aircraft were strewn over a wide area, leaving little for the two air intelligence departments to examine. But a few fragments of maps were found and on a piece of metal were parts of two figures that could have been 'R4'. To this were added parts familiar as the nose armament of a Ju 88 and they reasoned that the aircraft had been a Ju 88C from I/NJG2 based at Gilze-Rijen. They were correct, as 4/NJG2 had suffered another loss. The cause was, and still is, a mystery although it was concluded that it had been brought down by the other aircraft which had bombed Elsham. Machine gun bullet strikes were found on part of a crank case which ruled out the possibility that anti-aircraft fire had brought it down and no claims were submitted by British fighter units. The remains of the Ju 88s crew, Heinrich Ladiges, Friedrich Heinemann and Josef Beblo, were all interred at Kirton Lindsay.

The fragments of maps found in R4 + LM contained another piece of information which was noted by AI1(k). A new area had been marked which covered central England. The area was bounded by Leicester, Woburn, Reading, Salisbury, Trowbridge and Gloucester. This new area was the home for many training units which had previously escaped the attentions of I/NJG2.

Pilot Officer Nick Carter was an instructor on Oxfords with No. 2 FTS. At just twenty years of age he admits that he was hardly one of the more experienced pilots, but typical.

'I had made my first solo in a Magister on Novembr 8th 1940, with just eight-and-a-half hours in my log book. Then I moved on to No. 12 FTS at Grantham where, due to the very bad weather, it took me two months to put in fifty-two hours on Battles. I well remember my first night solo here. I had twenty hours on Battles by day and so on March 23rd 1941, I was told that I was proficient to fly solo at night. I sat in Battle K9296 behind an Anson that I was to follow. As I opened the throttle, a shower of sparks came from the Merlin's exhausts. Instinctively I ducked my head down and tore off between the goose neck flares that marked out the landing strip. Flying on instruments alone it soon dawned that I could see some lights outside, which made things much easier.

One day I was asked if I would like to become an instructor. I had always fancied being a bomber pilot, but I agreed and before long I was posted to No. 2 CFS at Cranwell. By May 28th I was 'Qualified to instruct on multi-engined and elementary types on probation.'

With this I moved to Brize Norton and, on June 3rd, I took up my first pupil whose name was Caplan. By this time I had picked up a few clues on night flying which, in the circumstances, was just as well.

Akeman Street was a small grass strip that we used as a relief landing ground when night flying. On July 27th, I flew an Oxford there to instruct on. My first pupil that night was Caplan and we performed six night landings together. Then I took up Smith. After two circuits and landings, I felt confident that he could perform his first night solo. I got out of the Oxford and made my way to the aircraft control point, 100 yards to the right of the flare path and watched Smith take off. By watching his navigation lights I could follow him as he climbed away from the airfield. Then another aircraft, also with its lights on, came across the airfield at about 1,000 feet. It turned in behind my pupil and a burst of tracer, like a red hose-pipe, engulfed the Oxford. It did not catch fire, but nosed down and slipped into the ground. There had been no raid warning and we were left in a state of shock. One pupil sat in the hangar and cried, we knew that Smith was dead.'

Leutnant Dr Lothar Bisang's Bordfunker, Werner Ulbricht, sent a message to Gilze-Rijen which read, 'Aircraft destroyed. Raum C.' This was Bisang's first victory and he sped away from Akeman Street towards the Essex coast. At Wivenhoe, near Colchester, Lothar Bisang's Ju 88 dived almost vertically into the ground. Again the cause of this crash is a mystery was recorded by the RAF as being 'due to other causes.' As usual it was concluded that, due to the armament, this had been a night fighter. For some reason the bodies of the three crew were never identified and they remain posted as missing, there being no known grave.

That same night another Oxford, this time from No. 54 OTU, fell to the guns of Feldwebel Arnold at Starston Grange, near Church Fenton. Again no enemy aircraft were known to be in the area at that time and so Sergeant Woodward flew with his navigation lights on. A burst of fire hit the Oxford which was totally destroyed and its pilot killed.

The all black Ju 88s of I/NJG2 had only ever been intended to operate at night, but on August 12th, I/NJG2 was ordered up at midday. Fifty-four Blenheims had made a daring daylight raid on the Quadratfortuna power station near Cologne. The Luftwaffe put up every fighter they had, including the black Ju 88s which had been fuelled and armed in readiness for the coming night's operations.

The Blenheims had gone in at low level and it was assumed that they would come out just as low as they had gone in. Thus, whilst course and speed were given to NJG2, they were at low level when the Blenheims went out high above them. No interception was made by NJG2, but Me 109s and flak accounted for twelve of the bombers.

Hauptmann Karl Hülshoff, I/NJG2's Gruppenkommandeur, was patrolling off the Dutch coast when he met an aircraft which he mistook for an Me 109F. It was Squadron Leader H. M. Stephen, in a No. 234 Squadron Spitfire. His fire put both of the Ju 88's engines out of action, injured Oberfeldwebel Mayer, the Bordfunker and hit

Unteroffizier Licht in the arm. Hülshoff was just able to reach land and crash landed at Steenbergen safely.

The following week, beginning on August 13th, saw NJG2's last sustained effort over England. Oberfeldwebel Rolf Bussmann found his way to the small airfield of Weston-on-the-Green, where the pupils of course number 24 at No. 15 Service Flying Training School were just three days away from its completion. Within minutes, two Ansons had been shot down and both the pilots killed. Bussmann then put down the nose of the Ju 88 and roared across the airfield, using his forward armament and releasing six bombs which damaged seven of the Oxfords parked there. Then he was gone, heading for the east coast. Near Ely he spotted a Blenheim and shot it down at Wilburton. Its three crew from No. 17 OTU were all killed in the crash. Bussmann and his crew returned triumphant to Gilze-Rijen, but landed heavily. The undercarriage of the Ju 88 collapsed and the machine slid off the runway. As it came to rest the three men scrambled out before fire engulfed the wreck.

Also on August 13th, No. 11 OTU, based at Bassingbourne, was paid another visit by the aircraft of NJG2. Four bombs fell from a Ju 88 as it strafed the airfield. One of these bombs fell in the wing of a barrack block which collapsed as it exploded and trapped many of the airmen billeted there. Ten men were found dead and a further twelve were injured. Another night fighter attacked the airfield at Upwood at less than 2,000 feet firing at the Ansons and Blenheims of No. 17 OTU. A Wellington was attacked in the circuit of Marham after the fighter had first fired the colours of the day. Before it could damage the Wellington, searchlights illuminated the fighter and it flew off. Another Wellington was attacked at 1,000 feet as it was landing at Wretham. Seven Wellingtons of No. 115 Squadron, returning from Essen, arrived in the midst of this activity. The plotting table at Coltishall showed no enemy aircraft, only a Beaufighter returning from patrol, so Pilot Officer Woods switched on his navigation lights to avoid a collision with his fellow squadron aircraft. At 3,000 feet what was taken to be the Beaufighter approached the Wellington. Four bursts of fire were heard before the Wellington caught fire and crashed three miles from the airfield. The rear gunner, Sergeant Evans, was killed but the other five crew men escaped with bruises.

The following morning, Oberfeldwebel Robert Lüddeke was flying over Binbrook when a No. 12 Squadron Wellington, returning from an abortive raid on Rotterdam, came in to land. Sergeant Cameran, the captain, opened the throttles and turned away but Lüddeke had already seen him, although he missed with his first burst of fire. Believing that the danger had passed, Cameran brought the Wellington back to Binbrook but, in his haste to land, overshot. At 600 feet Lüddeke attacked again and this time the Wellington was hit. Cameran jettisoned the bomb load and took violent evasive action, during which he succeeded in shaking off his attacker. The Wellington, which had been badly damaged in the attack, was later crash landed at Little Coates.

Hahn, now promoted to the rank of Leutnant, returned from leave and brought down a Wellington at about midnight on August 16th. Part of the Wellington hit Hahn's Ju 88 and he returned to Gilze-Rijen on one engine. Leutnant Rudolf Pfeffer and his crew failed to return from a sortie on the night of August 17th. His loss was yet another blow for the hard hit 4th Staffel who were never to know what had become of him. A ship of the Royal Navy found a body floating in the North Sea on August 26th, which was identified as that of Otto Schierling, the Bordfunker in Pfeffer's crew. His body was buried at sea, but those of Pfeffer and Alfred Ranke were never found.

This brief burst of activity ended early in the morning of August 20th, when No. 11 OTU lost its seventh Wellington to NJG2. Flight Sergeant Andrews switched on his machine's landing lights and was instantly shot down. All but one of the crew were killed. The Ju 88 circled Bassingbourne and strafed a stationary Wellington before Feldwebel Köster made off into the night.

Ten days after this attack, on the night of August 29th – 30th, a Wellington of No. 115 Squadron was shot down over Martlesham Heath by an unidentified assailant. Sergeant Murdoch, pilot of 'D Dog' had been part of an attack on Mannheim and was returning to Waddington when he was brought down in flames. Only one man, the wireless operator, was found alive but he died the next day.

I/NJG2's activity had passed its peak. In August an estimated 257 sorties had been made on twenty-six nights, no less than ninety-four attacks had been made on airfields. In September, NJG2 were over Britain on sixteen nights and in October just ten nights. There was still opportunity for some of the old hands to make their mark.

Alfons Köster was back on August 31st. Shortly before midnight Flight Sergeant Maries saw tracers flashing past the starboard wing of his Anson as he circled Croughton, a satellite of Upper Heyford. His pupil, Pilot Officer Bosch, was hit and killed instantly. Three passengers were injured and the aircraft went into a dive. Maries pulled the Anson out but the Ju 88 attacked again. Maries then tried what evasive manoeuvres he could and lost his attacker. Eventually he succeeded in landing safely. An hour later Köster was over Mildenhall where four of No. 99 Squadron's Wellingtons had been diverted, after bad visibility had closed their base at Waterbeach. The pilot of one of these, Pilot Officer Eccles, was a freshman on his first mission who had been given Boulogne as an 'easy target.' After overshooting Mildenhall on his first attempt he came round again and was at just 150 feet when his Wellington was hit by a hail of fire. The aircraft crashed and only the rear gunner got out of the wreck alive.

Feldwebel Walter Kleine was lost on September 2nd after his aircraft crashed into the sea off the Dutch coast. His Bordfunker was Hans Engmann, who had been in Paul Bohn's crew when he had been killed. The luck of the 4th Staffel had not changed.

With the high losses that NJG2 had been sustaining they were constantly seeking to recruit new crews, either from Ergänzungs (training) or operational units. During the summer a circular had been sent out by the RLM to all units asking for volunteers, as all of NJG2's crews were. Hauptmann Rolf Jung had also toured many Ergänzungs units giving lectures. There was a lot to attract crews to I/NJG2, even though it was considered more dangerous than night bombing. The chances of promotion were greater and the food and accommodation better than those of other units. Twice a year crews were sent on a month's leave, either home or to visit a rest home. For most units these were situated at resorts on the Dutch coast, but crews from NJG2 were allowed to take their wives or girl friends to the ski resort of Kitzbühl in the Austrian Tyrol.

One of the new crews who had been attracted to NJG2 by the perks offered was Oberfeldwebel Erwin Veil, along with his Bordfunker and Bordschütze. Before the war Veil had been an instructor at a blind flying school and had then joined KG51 who flew Ju 88 bombers. He and his crew had flown through the Battle of France attacking the Maginot Line, Paris, Calais, Marseilles and Dunkirk. Then came the Battle of Britain. They continued together into the night Blitz on Britain in early 1941, and by April had made about sixty flights over Britain.

On April 6th, Veil's was one of the hundreds of aircraft that fulfilled Hitler's threat to 'destroy Belgrade from the air.' That day they made three flights against the city. After the Yugoslavian campaign came Greece. A rest and a period of re-equipping was followed by a move to Krosno in Poland. Perhaps, they thought, they would pass through

Russia to Turkey or Iraq? Their question was answered early in the morning of June 22nd, the attack on Russia had begun.

The first attack took the Russians totally by surprise, but by the time the second wave flew over the lines, the defences were more organised. Veil's Ju 88 was hit in the radiator and he limped back to base. KG51 lost about sixteen aircraft on the first day and, by the end of the fourth day, one Staffel had only two of its aircraft remaining. Both its Staffelkapitän and the Gruppenkommandeur were missing. Veil and his crew did not fly on the second day as there were no aircraft available. On the third day Veil received a signal posting him and two of his crew to NJG2 at Gilze-Rijen, they were to move immediately. In view of the losses Veil's Staffel had suffered, they were asked to stay but they refused and left amidst much ill-feeling.

After travelling across Germany they arrived at Gilze-Rijen on June 29th, to be met by no less than Karl Hülshoff in person. Compared to the conditions they had lived in on the Russian front, Gilze-Rijen was most impressive and soon, with their considerable experience, they were made operational with the first Staffel. On one of their first flights over Britain, they became completely lost when their direction finding equipment failed due to, what they believed to have been, the effects of an electric storm. It is equally possible that a British 'electronic counter measure', Meacon, had caused the discrepancy. This apparatus caused incorrect bearings to be obtained by falsifying the transmissions of the German radio navigation beacons. Veil brought his Ju 88 down through the cloud to pinpoint his position and was held by searchlights. These soon went out when one of the German signal flares was fired. This was encouraging, they assumed that they were over Holland and began to seek an airfield at which to land. It was only when a landmark was recognised, that the crew realised they were in fact just south of Clacton-on-Sea. Having obtained their location they set their course once more for Gilze-Rijen.

By September 16th, Veil and his crew had made about twenty sorties over England with I/NJG2. They had fired at three aircraft and considered that they had damaged a Wellington. At 20.30 hours on September 16th, they left Gilze-Rijen in R4 + NH, a Ju 88C-4. On board were eight 50kg bombs and two incendiary bomb containers, each of which held thirty-six 1kg bombs. These they released over an airfield they assumed to have been Stradishall.

Erwin Veil cruised around East Anglia at 6,000 feet hoping to catch a glimpse of a British bomber, but all Bordmechaniker Heinrich Welker could see were searchlights. Bordfunker, Engelbert Wegener, received a message from Gilze-Rijen that fighters were known to be in their area and passed this information on to Erwin. The message was correct, for Squadron Leader Raphael DFC and bar was trying very hard to find the Ju 88.

Gordon Raphael was no newcomer to night fighting. As the pilot of a Whitley he had been shot down by an Me 110 and had been forced to ditch into the sea. He was rescued and became a night fighter pilot with No. 85 Squadron in early 1941. By September, he was a flight commander and had five aircraft destroyed to his credit. For fifteen minutes Raphael chased Veil. Twice Raphael's aircraft was illuminated by searchlights and each time Welker opened fire but missed. Veil hurled the Ju 88 around in an attempt to shake off his attacker but each time Sergeant Addison, the Havoc's AI operator, brought them back into contact. Finally, the Havoc closed to 100 yards and Raphael opened fire with a burst of just one-and-a-half seconds. The burst was short, but in that time the Havoc's twelve machine guns fired 330 rounds and hit the Ju 88 in its starboard wing. Immediately the engine caught fire. All three of the crew managed to bale out before their aircraft crashed into the sea off Clacton-on-Sea. They were all later captured by the police.

Paul Semrau made another sortie on September 20th and chose Upper Heyford upon which to release his bombs. They fell in a line across the airfield. Sergeant Van der Merwe was preparing to land at the satellite airfield of Croughton when Semrau was making his attack. Witnesses on the ground heard bursts of cannon and machine gun fire, before they saw a Hampden catch fire in the air. It crashed near the airfield where it was smashed to pieces, killing all four crew.

CHAPTER SEVEN

'Die Experten', October 1941

By October 1941 the most successful pilots in I/NJG2 were Oberfeldwebel Wilhelm Beier (with fourteen claims), Leutnant Hans Hahn (with eleven claims) and Feldwebel Alfons Köster (with eleven claims). All three pilots were held in great esteem by the Luftwaffe's High Command.

Wilhelm Beier

Wilhelm Beier was born on November 11th 1913, at Homberg in Niederrheim. At the age of twenty-seven he made his first claim for an aircraft destroyed when, on December 18th 1940, he reported the destruction of a Hurricane near Lowestoft at 06.36 hours. In the following six months he made five more claims and on July 6th 1941, he claimed four bombers destroyed. These were a Wellington, a Blenheim and two Whitleys, all of which were said to have fallen into the North Sea. On August 8th 1941, he claimed to have destroyed three more bombers: a Blenheim, a Halifax and a Wellington.

Unlike his fellow pilots, Beier seemed not to venture over the British coast, preferring to stay over the North Sea. Nevertheless, he had some close calls. On one occasion, the right main-wheel tyre of his Ju 88 burst when he was taking off and caused the undercarriage to collapse. The aircraft slid to a halt in front of the control tower at Gilze-Rijen and all three crew were able to escape unhurt.

Beier's reputation as a night fighter pilot was rapidly established and with a total of fourteen claims, he was awarded the Ritterkreuz on October 11th 1941.

Alfons Köster

Feldwebel Alfons Köster had been born in Hüingen on February 6th 1919. He was the son of a woodsman and one of ten children. His career with I/NJG2 had begun in 1941 and he made his first claim on April 9th near Coltishall when he brought down Sergeant Truman. His score mounted steadily and stood at ten victory claims by October 3rd 1941. On that night he patrolled 'Raum C.' No. 7 Squadron, based at Oakington, had sent nine of their Stirlings to Brest, but none had been able to locate the port due to the thick cloud which obscured the ground. In the rear turret of Stirling N6085 was Flight Lieutenant George Stock who had been one of the first commissioned air gunners. He had flown in Whitleys and had won the DFC in early 1941. At 22.30 hours on October 3rd, his pilot, Squadron Leader McLeod, ordered him to leave his turret and to take up his landing station.

The Royal Observer Corps had been tracking a raid, numbered 'Raid 475', which had crossed the coast at Southwold at 6,000 feet and had passed over Brandon and Feltwell. The flare path at Oakington had been lit, awaiting the return of the Stirlings, but it also attracted Alfons Köster – 'Raid 475.' As Köster approached the airfield, Mcleod's Stirling crossed his path, flying with all its lights on. Observer Mr D Roe of ROC Post 'D3' looked on as an extraordinary fight ensued. He later reported:

> 'At 22.40 hours a Stirling came down to us from the direction of L7985 (a grid reference) with full lights and turned north west, at the same time another Stirling was travelling towards Oakington from the south west. At about 22.45 hours the Stirling with lights came back again with a Ju 88 on its tail, which was firing bursts every few seconds. At intervals the rear gunner of the Stirling was returning fire.
>
> After turning and twisting around the post for about five minutes the Stirling gave the Junkers the slip and then turned east but the Junkers picked him up again in about another two or three minutes.
>
> At 22.50 hours the Stirling again came overhead at about 100 feet, with the Junkers firing at him from a range of about 50 yards. As they passed overhead, another Stirling came across and turned in behind the Junkers and then gave it a long burst from about 100 yards.
>
> The three planes circled the post, firing at intervals and both Stirlings got in at least two good bursts into the Junkers' fuselage, but the first Stirling caught a heavy burst of fire on L7379. The first Stirling caught fire on about L7581 at about 23.00 hours.'

The observer of the crashed Stirling, Pilot Officer Alverson and the second pilot, Sergeant Hunter, had jumped out at 700 feet – barely sufficient height for them to parachute down safely. They were lucky enough to escape unhurt. However, the remaining five, including McLeod and George Stock, all died when their aircraft crashed near Caxton Gibbet. Köster then went to Upwood, but ten minutes after his first attack he returned to Oakington where he released ten bombs which fell on the airfield and damaged a Wellington of No. 101 Squadron. This was Alfons Köster's eleventh and final claim.

Hans Hahn

Hans Hahn is the best known of the I/NJG2 pilots. His fame however,

78

Leutnant Hans Hahn (left) with Generalmajor Kammhuber after Hahn had been presented with the Ritterkreuz.

Leutnant Hans Hahn.

Oberfeldwebel Wilhelm Beier – 14 claims.

was not due entirely to his ability as a flyer but to his untimely death which no mention of intruders lets pass. Hans was born in Rheydt only three days after Köster, on February 9th 1919. He was the only child of the family.

Hahn joined NJG2 as a Feldwebel on its formation and was quick to make his first claim on October 24th 1940, when he shot down Pilot Officer Davies's No. 102 Squadron Whitley as it took off from Linton-on-Ouse. Early in the new year he claimed another Whitley over the North Sea. Over two months elapsed before he submitted his next claim, for a Blenheim. At midnight on March 12th, he set fire to a No. 54 OTU Blenheim near Church Fenton. As its pilot, Pilot Officer Calvert, tried to land his blazing aircraft, fellow No. 54 OTU pilot, Pilot Officer Babbington, dived on the Ju 88 from 2,500 feet attacking from just fifty yards. Hahn escaped to return the following night when he brought down the Manchester of Flying Officer Mathews DFC, near Waddington.

During the night of April 7th, Hahn attacked a No. 14 OTU Hampden over Little Blytham. The rear gunner opened fire but it was too late to drive off Hahn and the Hampden crashed. One of Hahn's few claims that cannot be verified was a Wellington which he believed he had destroyed in 'Raum C' on April 8th – one such aircraft was, however, damaged.

Hahn's next success occurred on April 17th. Despite a warning that enemy aircraft were operating in his vicinity, Sergeant Kirby continued to fly his Hampden with its lights on. Four minutes after take off he was shot down by Hahn. The fourth claim submitted by Hahn in April was made on the 21st. A Battle of No. 12 FTS fell to his guns near the small airfield of Harlaxton, killing both pupil and instructor.

Whilst most of NJG2's victims were twin engined aircraft, Hahn seemed to specialise in single engined machines. On May 4th he flew low across Coltishall in moonlight and dropped four bombs. Two Spitfires of No. 222 Squadron were on his tail, but suddenly Pilot Officer Klee's machine, 'Zanzibar III', caught fire and crashed just outside the airfield perimeter. Hahn claimed a Fairy Fulmer.

The following night, it was a No. 257 Squadron Hurricane which fell victim as it landed at Duxford. Sergeant Parrott, flying on a weather test, had been diverted from Coltishall after it had been bombed. Although he had escaped the raid on his base, his luck did not hold. His aircraft was shot down in flames and crashed at Royston, short of Duxford's runway.

Hans Hahn himself, had not escaped from his combats over England unscathed. On four occasions he had returned to Gilze-Rijen with his Ju 88 flying on one engine. Once he even brought back a souvenir – a British balloon cable wrapped around one wing. He had had a lucky escape and the balloon cable was ceremoniously hung in the mess as a trophy.

The strain of continual operations began to tell on Hahn and his crew. They were given a month's leave and Hahn spent this in Bad Kudowa. On July 9th he was awarded the Ritterkreuz, the coveted Knight's Cross. This was the first time that this singular honour had been given to a night fighter pilot and he was promoted to the rank of Leutnant. July 31st Hahn was taking off from Gilze-Rijen in a Ju 88 when he crashed. His aircraft was damaged and Hahn along with his Bordmechaniker, Unteroffizier Scheidt, were slightly injured.

On August 16th Hahn returned to active service. Over Scunthorpe he destroyed a Wellington from No. 104 Squadron. Unfortunately part of the wreckage from the bomber hit one of the Ju 88's engines and once more he limped back on one. Police Constable Hollingsworth, of the East Retford Police witnessed the destruction of the Wellington.

'At 00.01 hours on the night of 16th–17th August, I heard machine gun fire to the north-east of South Leverton and I observed tracer bullets. A minute later I saw an aircraft falling in flames. At 00.02 hours I heard the aircraft hit the ground and explode. I proceeded to the spot as quickly as possible and took charge. I was unable to approach the burning aircraft owing to the fierce heat of the fire. However, I remained in close proximity. At 00.30 hours there was a terrific explosion caused by the bombs exploding and I was hurled seventy yards by the blast. I suffered no serious injuries.'

Neither the pilot, Sergeant Stephenson, nor any of his five crew had been able to escape before their Wellington crashed and was consumed by the flames.

The next occasion that Hahn was in combat with an enemy aircraft was on October 11th. Sergeant Tom Graham was an instructor with No. 12 FTS and on the night of the 11th he was instructing Corporal Edwards in Oxford AB767. They had taken off from Harlaxton and were flying steadily over the town of Grantham. It was 21.00 hours, the town was blacked out and local Air Raid Wardens and Home Guard members were patrolling when a short burst of gun fire rent the still night air. A bright streak of flame illuminated the sky as two aircraft plummeted to the ground. Rumours quickly spread around

Oberfeldwebel Heinz Strüning who had 3 claims

Flight Lieutenant Stock, DFC, rear gunner of the No. 7 Squadron Stirling shot down on 3rd October, 1941.

town that one plane was an Oxford with its two pilots dead, while the other was a Jerry which our plane had rammed. The truth, however, was different – Hans Hahn's luck had finally ran out. After firing at his target he had collided with it and both aircraft had fallen.

Local diarist and photographer, Walter Lee, made the following entry:

'Even later in the day the correct solution to the dramatic happenings in the night was still difficult to piece together, but the following was eventually authenticated. The burnt out plane was a German one and there were sufficient human remains to prove that three young Germans had lost their lives. The German plane had somehow come into contact with one of our trainers which had also come down near Neal's works in Dysart Road, one of the engines falling into a front garden without doing any damage.'

Unusually, the BBC radio news reported the incident in one of its bulletins.

At Gilze-Rijen they waited for the aircraft to return. First back that night was Oberfeldwebel Jung, flying his Ju 88 on only one engine, after the crank shaft of the other failed. Ambulance and fire services went out to meet the aircraft as it landed but all three of the crew were safe. Then came the rest, Beier, Köster, Herrmann and Sommer, but of Hahn there was no sign. Nothing had been heard from him since a

82

radio message at 20.45 hours. By the following morning it was clear that Hans Hahn would not return this time. His good luck had finally deserted him. Hauptmann Hülshoff and Hauptmann Semrau took upon themselves the sad task of breaking the news of Hahn's death to his father who lived in Berlin. At this time his wife was seriously ill in hospital and now his only child was dead. The old man sat alone in his room with his grief. There was no one who could console or comfort him.

On October 12th 1941, the very morning that Hahn was reported missing and the day after Wilhelm Beier had been awarded the Ritterkreuz, Kammhuber had the personnel of the Gruppe parade on the runway at Gilze-Rijen. Rumour had begun to spread even before the official announcement but to some members of the unit the news came as a complete shock. I/NJG2 was to move immediately to Sicily for operations over the Mediterranean. They would fly no more operations over Britain.

In fact at least one more operation was flown, for on that evening Oberfeldwebel Strüning attacked and brought down a Blenheim of No. 51 OTU, over Buckinghamshire. It would be over two years before another aircraft was brought down over Britain by intruders.

Many years later Dr Otto Moehlenbeck, the medical officer attached to I/NJG2, described his comrade's reaction to the order to stop operations over Britain. The personnel of I/NJG2 felt betrayed. Had they not proved their worth? Had not the hundreds of sorties flown in all weather been enough? Were the deaths of so many comrades to be considered in vain?

The reasoning behind the order was not open to question – it was Hitler's personal command. It would seem, however, that Kammhuber's attempt to build the intruder force into a truly effective unit had finally succumbed to the mounting opposition of the Luftwaffe Chief of Staff. I/NJG2 had never had more than thirty aircraft made available for their operations. It was constantly refused reinforcements even after it had been agreed, in principle, to create an intruder Geschwader in December 1940. Hitler, it would seem, had ordered that the 'Terror Flieger' (as the RAF became known to the German public) should be brought down beside the houses, factories and towns which they were decimating. It was believed that this would boost morale and provide useful propaganda material which was not really effective when success was achieved over Britain. As it could not be seen, it did not seem to matter what chaos or destruction could be caused at the 'Terror Flieger's' home bases. Whilst this policy may

Above: Leutnant Heinz Völker and Leutnant Johannes Feuerbaum in the cockpit of a Ju 88C. (Möhlenbeck).

Left: Oberleutnant Paul Semrau – 9 claims.

have been immediately expedient, the posting of I/NJG2 to the Mediterranean hardly seemed to aid Hitler's desire to bring down enemy aircraft over the Reich.

With the abandonment of intruder sorties over Britain, General Josef Kammhuber concentrated, as Hitler had ordered, on building up the defences of the Reich. In July 1941, Kammhuber had been charged with the expansion of the night fighter force along with searchlight batteries, the Anti-Aircraft belt and ground control systems.

The almost nightly battles between Bomber Command and the Luftwaffe were only just beginning. Over the next four years, they would consume an enormous amount of the resources of both sides, yet without the decisive results that were hoped for.

Part II

CHAPTER EIGHT

The intruders return. August 1943 – April 1944

In the two and a half years which elapsed before intruders again operated over Britain, many things changed. The aircraft which had been the prey of the old I/NJG2 had been replaced, relegated to training and other duties more suited to their limited performance. Wellingtons, Hampdens and Whitleys had given way to the famous four-engined 'heavies'. The Halifaxes and Lancasters that were now the mainstay of Bomber Command carried their heavier loads further, faster and delivered them more accurately than had been possible in 1941. Not only had the capacity of each aircraft increased, but so had the scale of operations. In October 1941, 2,501 sorties had been launched, but by May 1944 the total had reached 11,353 and for each sortie the bomb load had roughly tripled. Destruction of German cities was on an unparalleled scale.

In addition to the RAF's efforts by night, B17s and B24s of the USAAF's 8th Air Force bombed by day. Pressure on the Reich's defences was enormous. The emphasis of Germany's armament production had turned from attack to defence. Allied casualties rose accordingly to a point in early 1944, where the continual losses sustained in attacks on Germany could scarcely be tolerated.

Throughout the latter part of 1941, the whole of 1942 and the greater part of 1943, the skies over Britain had been clear of intruder activity. Even though the Allied bombing offensive had escalated to an enormous scale, Hitler's decision to make all interceptions over Europe and not to send intruders to Britain, stood. This, whilst indeed

Me 410 as flown by V/KG2 and II/KG51

The Ju 88R-2 flown by Schmidt and Rosenberger to Dyce on 9th May, 1943.

fortunate for the allies, is almost incomprehensible in view of the almost continuous intruder operations flown by the RAF over the Luftwaffe's own airfields. Although losses may have been high, had full scale intruder tactics been employed by the Luftwaffe over Britain, the effect upon the allied bombing effort would have been considerable.

Although no intruder missions were flown during this period there is one event which few works on Luftwaffe night fighters let pass. This is the arrival of Ju 88 R1, D5 + EV of IV/NJG3 at Dyce, near

Aberdeen, on May 9th 1943. This delivery of an intact example of one of the latest night fighters was no accident, rather a planned defection by its crew.

An interesting link between this incident and the intruders which flew over Britain is that two of its crew had flown with 2/NJG2 during 1940 and 1941. On November 9th 1940, Oberfeldwebel Herbert Schmidt and Oberfeldwebel Paul Rosenberger had been attacked by a British night fighter when they were over Lincolnshire. Schmidt flew the damaged Do 17Z-10 back to Gilze-Rijen on one engine and made a crash landing. According to published reports Schmidt was in fact pro-British and, despite the number of flights he made, he never shot an aircraft down. By 1943 Schmidt had risen to the rank of Oberleutnant and this lamentable lack of success by a high ranking officer aroused the suspicion of his superiors. If questioned, he reminded them of his loyalty by recounting the time when he and Rosenberger had struggled to bring their crippled Dornier back safely.

In the face of the large scale losses suffered over Europe by the RAF and USAAF during this period, the damage inflicted by I/NJG2 paled into insignificance. The lessons learned in the early days had been forgotten and hardly any crews flying in 1943 had any experience of intruders over their bases. In the Luftwaffe some were still very much aware of the effect that intruders could have, as they had been subjected to the RAF's intruders ever since late 1940, and their operations had suffered accordingly.

In mid 1943, Generalmajor Josef Kammhuber, who had organised the defence of Germany since 1940 and had established the 'Kammhuber Line' of searchlights, ground control interception stations and fighters across the low countries, was replaced. His successor was Generalmajor Josef Schmid who, as the new General der Nachtjagd, began to toy with the idea of re-starting the intruder operations which his predecessor had been forced to abandon. The first experiments conducted off the West Frisian Islands were, as Schmidt admitted after the war, 'uneconomical' but aid was to come from the RAF itself. In late 1943, Bomber Command begun to use H2S Centimetric Radar operationally over Europe to assist its aircraft to find their targets. H2S enabled a very shadowy image of the ground below to be displayed on a cathode ray tube fitted in the aircraft, thus providing a superb aid to navigation. The heart of the equipment was a device known as the Cavity Magnetron. So great was the advantage of this over previous radars and AI equipment that it could not be allowed to fall into enemy hands. For this reason it was not used over

Europe for some time. When at last its secrets did fall into enemy hands and its method of operation was divined, it was discovered that it was possible to 'home in' on its emissions. The FuG 350 Naxos Z equipment, which was fitted to some night fighters, enabled them to follow a bomber stream with little difficulty so long as the H2S was operating.

With this new approach, Schmid prepared his plans. Intruders, he proposed, would be used en masse on carefully chosen occasions when weather and surprise would be to the fighter's advantage. Intruding was not to become a routine measure, as it had been in I/NJG2's days, because the British defences would soon become accustomed to them.

In December 1943, Generalmajor Schmid laid his proposals before Reichsmarschall Göring. As before, the bomber stream was to be attacked on its way back and whilst landing by several waves of night fighters. The operation was to proceed as follows:

First Wave: Pursuit night fighting on the bombers' return flight, up to the extreme range of the Me 110 Units.

Second Wave: Me 410 units of Fliegerkorps IX to start from Northern France simultaneously with the first wave, to attack bomber bases in West and South West England as a deceptive manoeuvre to elicit 'Bandit' warnings and split up the British night fighter effort.

Third Wave: Ju 88 units to take off as soon as the last bomber elements had crossed the European Coast for intruder activity in landing areas specified by British 'Bandit' reports, and for low level attacks on airfields using small bombs, aircraft armament and iron spikes which were calculated to cause damage to taxiing aircraft.

Fourth Wave: Ju 88 units to take off fifty minutes later for activities similar to the above against newly recognised and diversionary landing areas.

These operations would be assisted by the employment of special duty radio operators flying with Ju 88 crews to listen-in to British landing instructions and to issue false orders. For this enterprise some 600 to 700 aircraft would be put into operation.

Schmid considered that in taking by surprise any enemy accustomed to landing without intruder precautions on fully lit bases, one outstandingly successful operation at least could be expected. Furthermore, such an operation must henceforth result in stronger

Allied night fighter forces being tied down in Britain for the defence of the bomber units.

Göring turned these proposals down flat. Fernenachtjagd (Long range night fighting), he said, was the province of Generalmajor Dietrich Peltz, head of Fliegerkorps IX and Angriffsführer England. Undaunted by this rejection Schmid submitted his plans to Generalmajor Hans Stumpff, of Luftflotte Reich, in February 1944. Once again his suggestion was turned down. The reasons offered were two fold:

(1) FuG 220 Lichtenstein SN-2 Radar could not be allowed to fall into enemy hands as this was the only German airborne radar to be unaffected by the 'window' metal strips that disabled other equipment.

(2) Hitler was, quite simply, opposed to Fernnachtjagd operations on principle.

Generalmajor Schmid shelved his plans, for the time being at least. Peltz, on the other hand, who in Göring's view was responsible for intruder missions, was none too enthusiastic about the idea. Since being appointed Angriffsführer England in August 1943, twenty-nine year old Generalmajor Peltz, an expert on bomber operations, had striven to increase the effectiveness of Fliegerkorps IX. With limited resources in manpower and equipment at his disposal he could make little progress in his task to attack Britain. Intruders, therefore, did not feature greatly in his plans.

Amongst the arsenal available to Peltz for attacks against Britain was the latest in a line of derivitives of the Me 110 – the Me 410. The Me 110 had made its first flight in 1936 and was, in various guises, to continue in service throughout the war. Its design concept was that of a 'Zerstörer', a long range fighter that could clear a way for and protect the more vulnerable aircraft that followed in its path. Later adaptations turned the aircraft into a bomber and a highly successful night fighter, but even in 1938 plans were afoot to develop the design further. The result of this development, known as the Me 210, was not the success of its predecessor. It was unstable around all three axes, stalled and spun in an alarming way and its handling was, to say the least, unpredictable. Three years after the prototype Me 210's first flight the Messerschmitt design team finally overcame their difficulties, but by this time the aircraft had gathered such a reputation that it was decided to allot it the new type number, Me 410. The machine retained many components designed for the Me 210 and was virtually identical in appearance to the later prototypes save for more powerful, DB 603, engines. The standard armament of the Me 410A-1 consisted of two 7.92mm MG 17s with two 20mm MG 151s, all fitted in the nose and two 13mm MG 131s controlled from the cockpit and fitted in barbettes in the rear fuselage. In May 1943, the first bomber and Zerstörer variants began to enter service with II/KG2 replacing their Do 217s. This new unit, known as V/KG2, was one of the units in Fliegerkorps IX under the command of Deitrich Peltz.

In addition to their bombing role, some elements of V/KG2 began to intercept bombers over England and from late August to October 1943, intruders once more presented a threat to Bomber Command.

Oberleutnant Wilhelm Schmitter, Stafelkapitän of 15/KG2, was a very experienced bomber pilot and a holder of the Ritterkreuz. At 02.52 hours (German time) on August 24th 1943, he took off for an intruder sortie over East Anglia in Me 410 U5 + CF. At this time many RAF bombers were returning to their bases after a raid on Berlin. One of these aircraft was Sergeant Chatten's Lancaster, 'Q – Queenie' of No. 97 Squadron. Unnoticed by the crew of the Lancaster, Schmitter closed in on his target and his Bordfunker opened fire with the twin 13mm remotely controlled guns fitted in the fuselage barbettes. Shells exploded in the Lancaster's fuselage and starboard wing. Immediately the order to abandon the aircraft was given. Six of the crew, including Sergeant Chatten who had been wounded in his legs and chest, baled out successfully but the body of the the the mid-upper gunner, Flight Sergeant Kraemer, was later found in the wreck of 'Q – Queenie.'

Just four minutes after his attack on Sergeant Chatten's aircraft, Schmitter dropped eight bombs on an airfield 'west of Cambridge' and headed for home. Over the North Sea his Me 410 became the target for a British night fighter and was so damaged in its fuselage and one of its engines that both the crew were forced to bale out into the sea. Schmitter's Bordfunker was unlucky and hit the aircraft's tail as he jumped clear, breaking both his legs. Exhausted and unable to climb into their dinghies, the two men fired flares into the sky in the hope that someone would spot them. They were fortunate that a flak post at Zeebrugge spotted them and they were picked up by a rescue boat from the Marine Untergruppe Zeebrugge 1½ hours later.

The next aircraft to fall to the guns of an Me 410 over Britain was a Stirling of No. 1657 CU which was engaged on a training flight from its base of Stradishall. The instructor, Pilot Officer Smith, was flying the Stirling when the attack occured and was able to make a crash landing in a corn field at Great Thurlow, enabling the crew to escape before fire consumed the wreck. Three of the crew received only minor injuries but five were more seriously injured and were admitted to White Lodge Hospital, Newmarket where Pilot Officer Smith died of his injuries the following day.

The Stirling's assailant is unkown, but Major Meister submitted a claim for an aircraft destroyed near Lincoln on the night of September 23rd–24th. His victim was Lancaster I W4948 of No. 57 Squadron. The squadron had sent twenty-one aircraft to Hannover and they were returning to East Kirkby when Meister attacked at 00.43 hours. Pilot Officer Duff's aircraft was set on fire in the air whilst in the circuit of the airfield. Only two men were able to bale out before the machine crashed on the outskirts of Spilsby, killing the remaining five crew.

Five nights later, on September 27th–28th, another Lancaster returning from Hannover was brought down. Pilot Officer Skipper was flying Lancaster III ED410 of No. 101 Squadron and had safely returned to his base of Ludford Magna at 01.10 hours. Skipper was refused permission to land there as the base had become unserviceable and was told to divert to Lindholm. Ten minutes later, whilst over the airfield of Wickenby, Oberleutnant Abrahamczik shot the Lancaster down. None of the eight crew had time to escape before the aircraft crashed and exploded in flames.

Claims made by 14/KG2

Lt.	Baak	Two motor	3–4/9/43	Lincoln.
Maj.	Meister	Four motor	22–23/9/43	Lincoln.
Oblt.	Abrahamczik	Four motor	27–28/9/43	Cromer.
Uffz.	Holzmann	Four motor	2–3/10/43	Bedford.
Uffz.	Holzmann	Four motor	2–3/10/43	Bedford.
Maj.	Meister	Four motor	9–10/10/43	Röm.
Uffz.	Holzmann	Four motor	9–10/10/43	North Sea.
Maj.	Meister	Four motor	14/10/43	Saarbrücken.
Fw.	Bolten	Four motor	14/10/43	Bruchsaal.
Uffz.	Holzmann	Four motor	14/10/43	Hagenau.

Another unit to fly the Me 410 was I/KG51. They had begun operations with Me 410s in the home defence role on September 9th 1943, when they intercepted 157 B-17s of the USAAF 3rd Bomb Division attacking Stuttgart. Heavy cloud broke up the American formation as it approached the target and at 16,500 feet above the

Schwarzwald, I/KG51 made their attack. One B-17 went down in flames and one Me 410 was damaged beyond repair by the return fire. Despite their efforts against the American bombers, success was limited and in October, Major Klaus Haeberlen (Kommandeur of I/KG51) attempted to explain this to the visiting Reichmarschall Göring. Haeberlen told Göring that the Daimler-Benz DB 603 engines of the Me 410s were not sufficiently powerful at high altitudes to catch the bombers and an argument ensued. The outcome of this most unfortunate meeting was that the Reichmarschall accused Haerberlen, an experienced combat pilot and holder of the Ritterkreuz, of cowardice and ordered Peltz to relieve him of his command. Almost simultaneously, it seems, Peltz halted the intruder operations of V/KG2 and the unit reverted exclusively to the role of bombers.

During these hazardous bombing operations, several of the crews who had brought down bombers in intruder operations were lost. Schmitter, who by this time had been promoted to the rank of Hauptmann, was killed on November 8th 1943, when he was shot down in another Me 410 near Eastbourne, Sussex. He was posthumously promoted to Major and awarded the Oakleaves to his Ritterkrauz. On this same night, Unteroffizier Holzmann was also shot down and his aircraft crashed into the sea off Beachy Head. Leutnant Heinz-Günter Baak was shot down over Sussex on December 20th 1943, and was killed when he attempted to make a forced landing.

In January 1944, V/KG2 began to prepare for operations against Britain in Operation Steinbock. Orders for this operation had been issued by Reichmarshall Göring in December 1943, as a reprisal for the Allied attacks on Germany. Over 500 aircraft were assembled for the new bomber offensive, in January 1944. Between January 21st and May 15th, raids took place against Britain with what, in the face of Allied attacks, must be regarded as disastrous results. Some 300 German aircraft were lost in the attacks, yet it was not uncommon for the entire force to miss their target completely. On occasion the British only became aware of the intended target upon the interrogation of downed crews or by listening to German propaganda broadcasts.

In March 1944, V/KG2 formed the nucleus of II/KG51, the Gruppenkommandeur of which was Major Dietrich Puttfarken, a twenty-three year old from Hamburg. Puttfarken was a pilot of immense experience with over 250 war flights to his credit when he was awarded the Ritterkreuz on October 7th 1942. In late March

1944, II/KG51 moved from Hildesheim to Soesterberg from where they began intruder operations again.

In the early hours of March 31st 1944, an aircraft swept over the airfield of Swanton Morley, unseen by ground staff but firing its cannon. The civil air-raid warning had been sounded in Norwich and a Lancaster was attacked near the city. At Coltishall a Mosquito had landed and was taxiing towards its dispersal when it was hit by cannon fire. Over Metheringham an aircraft had turned in to join the landing circuit when another aircraft flashed by below, just above the runway, firing its cannon as it went. As the intruder screamed past the control tower its staff identified the attacker as an Me 410. II/KG51's intruders had arrived.

Two aircraft were damaged in this attack – a Mosquitto of No. 25 Squadron and a Lancaster of No. 12 Squadron. The No. 25 Squadron Mosquito had returned to Coltishall from an anti-intruder patrol and was attacked as it taxied across the airfield. The port engine and both the coolant systems were holed but both crew members escaped uninjured. The Lancaster was returning from Nuremburg when it was badly damaged in the fuselage. Its starboard outer engine and the hydraulics were put out of action and the rear gunner injured, but its pilot landed safely at Wickenby. It was not an auspicious debut, but this was after all a comparatively new venture for most of the crews and they would learn quickly.

Ten enemy aircraft were reported crossing the English coast at Cromer, just after midnight on April 11th–12th 1944. For the next hour intruders roamed over Norfolk, Lincolnshire and the Wash. The airfield at Seething was bombed and there were wide spread strafing incidents reported in the Wells area. This time KG51's intruder pilots had followed a returning bomber stream and four Mosquitos of No. 25 Squadron, the old adversary of I/NJG2, were scrambled. One intruder located Coltishall where two aircraft were in the landing pattern. These were Flight Sergeant Maunders's Spitfire, which was returning from a night flight and Squadron Leader Keillor's No. 415 Squadron Wellington, which he was attempting to bring back from a North Sea patrol after suffering engine failure. Without warning, Maunders's Spitfire shook violently as cannon shells hit the machine. The needle of the engine temperature gauge swung across the dial as sparks and flame sprung from beneath the cowlings. The pilot rolled the Spitfire on to its back and tried to get out of the cockpit as the plane went into a left hand spin but he succeeded in throwing himself out of the right hand side and pulled his rip-cord. The parachute opened shortly before the aircraft exploded on the ground two miles from the airfield. A few minutes later Squadron Leader Keillor, who had watched the attack, landed safely.

Also at this time, Lieutenant Donald M. MacGregor was ferrying a B17 'pathfinder' of the 96th Bomb Group to Framlington. From here he was to lead the 390th Bomb Group on that morning's mission to Leipzig. The runway lights were switched on as the B17 circled the airfield and almost immediately a wing exploded into flame and it was hit by cannon shells. The bomber sank to the ground and landed in Great Glemham Park. British soldiers billeted nearby raced to the scene and got MacGregor and eight of his crew clear before two 500 pound bombs and two sky markers blew the plane and the three remaining crew members to pieces. A pillar of flame shot 300 feet into the night sky and shock waves blew out many of the windows in the village.

Unaware of any intruder activity, Stirling 'F – Freddy' of No. 1654 Conversion Unit was making its way to the Bassingham Bombing Range. As its pilot, Sergeant Nicholson, brought the bomber around for a second run over the target the mid-upper gunner spotted another aircraft, flying with its navigation lights on, in the same circuit. Fearing a collision Nicholson switched on his aircraft's navigation lights and carried on. In the nose of the Stirling the bomb aimer, Sergeant Lewis, released a single bomb whilst Sergeant McFarlane in the rear turret followed their companion's lights as they closed in from behind. Suddenly, tracers came rushing towards him. The Stirling's fuselage and port wing burst into flame as McFarlane screamed the instruction 'Corkscrew port' over the intercom. Nicholson flung the four engined bomber into the manoeuvre but the fire was already beyond control. Clipping on his parachute, the mid upper gunner struggled back to help McFarlane from his turret but he waved that he was all right. As the valiant gunner made his way back along the fuselage to the escape hatch in the floor, the order to bale out came. The flaming bomber plunged down 10,000 feet to earth as he and three others baled out. The bodies of the pilot, navigator, bomb aimer and Sergeant McFarlane were all found in the wreckage of the crashed Stirling.

The night's final victim was a Mosquito from No. 60 OTU. Its two crew were engaged on a night cross country navigation exercise from High Ercall when they were attacked over Grantham. Both of the crew, from No. 16 course, were able to bale out before their machine crashed to the ground.

On Tuesday April 18th 1944, the skies over Europe were filled with aircraft both of the Allies and Germans. American forces began the day by sending 500 B17s and 275 B24s to the Heinkel works at Oranienburg and other targets, mostly near Berlin. At night a large Bomber Command force dropped 4,000 tons of bombs on communications targets in France, whilst Mosquitos attacked Berlin and smaller forces attacked cities such as Cologne. The Luftwaffe were also active and in addition to their usual defensive operations, sent 125 bombers to London. Here they dropped fifty-three tons of bombs in what was the last air raid on London. The Me 410s of II/KG51 were also airborne with the intention of pursuing Bomber Command's aircraft back to their bases.

No. 115 Squadron had sent 26 Lancasters to attack Rouen and, in the early hours of April 19th, the force began to return to their base at Witchford, near Ely. At 02.09 hours the undercarriage of Sergeant Lemoine's Lancaster collapsed when it was three quarters of the way along the runway and temporarily prevented other machines landing. Pilot Officer Burnie was the pilot of one of the circling aircraft and, just one minute after Lemoine's machine had come to grief, his Lancaster was shot down by an intruder. Later, at 03.48 hours, another No. 115 Squadron Lancaster met a similar fate. Both aircraft fell close to the airfield giving none of the crew members time to escape.

A third Lancaster to be brought down that night was Pilot Officer Cosgrove's No. 625 Squadron machine, which was one of thirteen the Squadron had sent to Cologne. Cosgrove was completing his landing circuit when his Lancaster was seen to burst into flames and crash close to his base killing all seven crew.

Two nights later, in the early morning of April 21st, an Me 410 pilot found the Miles Master of Flying Officer Banister. The single engined, advanced training machine had taken off shortly after 05.00 hours on a local flight from No. 7 (P)AFU and was shot down one and a half miles from its base at Peterborough. The body of its unfortunate pilot was found later in the crumpled wreckage.

CHAPTER NINE

Target Hamm

The city of Hamm, in Germany's Ruhr, was the target for USAAF Air Force Operation No. 311, to be conducted on April 22nd 1944. Hamm's marshalling yards were the largest in Germany and formed one of the key centres for railway traffic to and from the Low Countries. This fact, combined with the need to disrupt communications in Europe prior to the coming invasion, made Hamm an important target.

Instructions for the day's mission began to be received at 8th Air Force bases throughout East Anglia during the morning of April 22nd 1944. A strike force of 804 bombers would make the attack. These comprised of 526 B-17s from 1st and 3rd Bomb Divisions and 278 B-24s from the 2nd Bomb Division. In support of the bombers were the fighters; 485 forming a close escort with a further 370 making sweeps over Germany, attacking air or ground targets as opportunity presented itself. The force totalled 1,659 aircraft. This mission was unique in the history of the 8th Air Force as it was the first time that a force of this magnitude would make its return to England, in darkness. This was due to the weather conditions prevailing over Europe, which steadily improved through the day to make visual bombing possible only after 19.00 hours.

By 17.00 hours the first of the three waves of bombers, consisting of 248 B-17s of the 3rd Bomb Division, was assembling. They were followed by the remaining 278 B-17s of the 1st Bomb Division. Twenty minutes later the aircraft of the eleven Bomb Groups, which made up the 2nd Bomb Division, began to take to the air. With the 278 dark green B-24 Liberators went the gaily coloured assembly ships, more B-24s painted with huge patterns of checkerboards, stripes, circles or dots. Each could be readily identified by the group's pilots as they made up their formations from the milling bombers. When the formation was complete the strangely colourful formation ships returned to base.

No sooner had the first bombers left the coast near Lowestoft than the German fighter units were alerted to the incoming threat. Stand by orders were given to the units in Jafue 4 and 5 who moved their fighters eastward. The first combat occurred when P-51 Mustang pilots of the 4th Fighter Group spotted twenty Me 109s making a

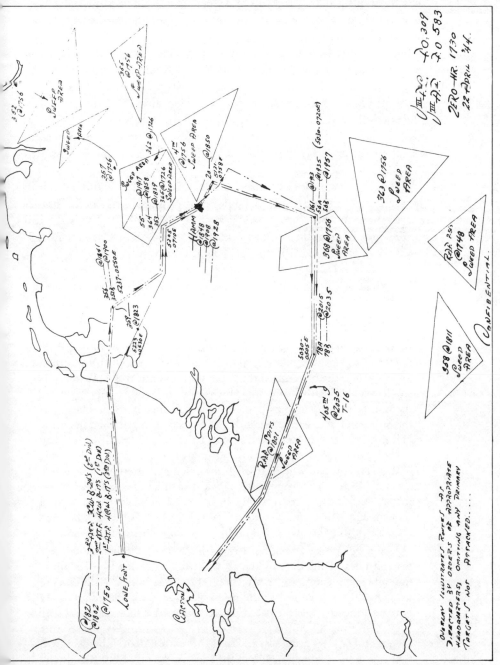

h *Air Force plan of operations for the raid on Hamm. (Crown Copyright).*

D

formation at 4,000 feet over Kassel. The fighters 'bounced' the formation from above and in a furious dog fight, claimed seventeen of the Me 109s destroyed.

The first bombers to reach the enemy coast near Amsterdam, at 18.23 hours, were the 248 B-17s of the 3rd Bomb Division. Here the P-47Ds of the 359th and 353rd Fighter Groups joined the B-17s as escort and headed towards Hamm. The lead aircraft of the 1st Bomb Division followed fifteen minutes after the 3rd Bomb Division with the 364th Fighter Group as escort. Then came the 2nd Bomb Division with their escort P-47s from the 352nd Fighter Group and P-38s from the 55th Fighter Group.

The three formations cruised across occupied Holland and into Germany unmolested until, just before the target was reached, fighters rose to meet the 3rd Bomb Division. Sergeant Bob Peel was the tail gunner in a B-17 of the 385th Bomb Group, based at Great Ashfield. For Peel and his crew 'Mission 311' was their tenth raid.

'Our aircraft was flying 'tail-end Charlie' for the 385th Group and the Wing, but it might have been the whole of the Air Force as far as I knew!

The Channel crossing was uneventful, we cleared our guns and ducked the usual coastal flak.

Approaching the target we were attacked by fighters coming from the 9 o'clock position, directly at our new waist gunner. The new man panicked and ran back and forth as far as his oxygen and intercom lines would allow, at least this is what I was told. A 20mm cannon shell hit the port side of my tail position. It blew a big hole in the fuselage, put the port gun out of commission, knocked out my oxygen and intercom and wounded me. I was too tall to wear a flak suit in the tail, so I spread the sections of it out inside the fuselage in front of me. That shell hit one of them and probably saved my life. Fragments splattered my right side and one deep wound went into my waist. I think the explosion threw me up into the tail controls above my head because I now have a semicircular scar across the top of my head. Over twenty stitches and concussion were involved. Naturally I was knocked out.

When I came to, I remember reporting to the pilot that the tail was hit, but I doubt that my sending set was working. Then I backed up to the tail escape hatch where my chest 'chute was stored. Again, being tall, I could not wear the 'chute in my position. I snapped it on to my harness and jettisoned the hatch cover. I remember looking down; way way down from 20,000 feet.

I saw other crew members waiting by the waist door. The Fort' was flying level but there was a fire in the starboard wing. I returned to my position to learn if we were going to abandon ship. That look down from the tail hatch no doubt encouraged me to hope that we could still get back to England; we really weren't too far into the continent. At this time and at every subsequent moment in the aircraft, I believe that I was acting very irrationally. I had been without Oxygen for some time. I liken it to being drunk; doing some things by reflex and others with no sense at all. That must be why I returned to the tail and fired away at the incoming fighters queued up there. The crew had all jumped, when they saw me at the hatch, putting on my 'chute, they thought that I had received the order.

The fighters saw the parachutes and as the 'plane was on automatic pilot, they poured in for target practice. I sprayed away at them. Others in the air at the time said that I hit some of them, but I doubt it. Then the Fort' blew up. I guess that I was thrown out and automatically pulled the rip cord.

A full day later I opened my eyes and saw a man in a brown uniform offering me a cigarette and a Catholic Sister was bent over me. 'Is this England?' I asked. 'Nein Deutschland' she answered.'

Bob Peel had landed in the courtyard of the Meiningen Hospital on the edge of Werl in Westphalia, near Dortmund. His injuries included a fractured skull, two breaks in his upper left arm, a broken left wrist, a smashed nose, torn ligaments in the right knee and a deep wound in his right side. All the other crew members from his aircraft had baled out successfully.

The 359th Fighter Group, acting as escort, engaged the attacking fighters which they identified as between 20 and 30 Fw 190s. However, the German fighters pressed home their attacks. 1st Lieutenant H. E. Reich's aircraft fell back from the formation, with one of its inner engines in flames. Two P-47s went to its aid in an attempt to protect it from further attacks but eventually it became the 3rd Bomb Division's second casualty. Another B-17 fell victim to flak and many more crews had close shaves. Lieutenant Schmidt reported:

'Twenty-five to thirty Fw 109s hit us head-on, cannon blazing. One shell got an engine, another blew up in the radio room and a third exploded when it hit the windshield in front of my face. A fragment went through the left lapel of my battle jacket; but a strap of my 'chute harness stopped it from going through me. Flying glass caught me in the face and broke my glasses, but I got away with no more than a bloody nose.'

Sergeant Bogner, a waist gunner, reported:

'The fighters hit us twice, hard. The other waist gunner was wounded in the first attack. The radio operator took him to the radio room for first aid and from then on I manned both waist guns.'

The 1st Bomb Division followed the 3rd over the target, avoiding the fighters, as they did for the entire mission. Three of their aircraft however, went down to flak. Last over the main target were the B-24s of the 2nd Bomb Division, who arrived forty minutes after the first bombers had appeared over the marshalling yards. In that time, 1,308 tons of high explosive and 243 tons of incendiary bombs had fallen on the yards. The first bombs had started fires among the rolling stock and adjacent buildings, the smoke from which made subsequent attacks more difficult. Most of the tracks and a large locomotive and wagon repair shop received direct hits. The engine works of Vereinigte Stahlwerke were 'well covered' with hits and left on fire.

In addition to the tonnage dropped on the marshalling yards, fifteen B-17s of the 1st Bomb Division dropped forty-four tons of high explosive on the city of Hamm, causing severe damage and numerous fires in an industrial and residential area. 1.3 million propaganda leaflets also fluttered the 23,000 feet to earth as the bombers left Hamm to recover as best it could. For the 2nd Bomb Division there was a secondary target, Coblenz. Seeing that Hamm had been 'saturated', fifty B-24s kept their bombs for this target.

As the aircraft flew south from the target, numerous crews watched aircraft form up on them. In their concern they reported Fw 190s, painted like P-51s and with fake air scoops, flying simulated escort tactics. These aircraft passed along the leading sections and then turned, coming head-on, attacking aircraft as they went in. In all probability these were P-51s and the firing came from trigger happy gunners! This is not to say that there were no enemy fighters, for the 55th Fighter Group became involved in two combats south of Hamm and claimed six enemy aircraft destroyed. They 'bounced' the 364th Fighter Group who hit the deck and escaped. Four B-24s went down to the fighters.

Soest was bombed, as was Offen, Swevelelle, Niederfeld, Chievres and the airfields of Ahaus, Kobern and Ijmuiden. To add to the confusion, fighter sweeps and returning escort fighters bombed and strafed whatever they came upon; trains, barges, tanks, bridges and airfields.

By the time the aircraft headed back across the North Sea after three hours in enemy airspace the losses were; six bombers in fighter combat, twelve bombers to flak and other causes, five escort fighters and eight fighters on sweeps. All that remained now was the flight home and a landing to be made in darkness.

CHAPTER TEN

Disaster for the 2nd Bomb Division, April 22nd, 1944

By 22.00 hours on April 22nd 1944, almost all the B-17s belonging to the 1st and 3rd Bomb Divisions had landed on their darkened runways. There had been no incidents worth noting, even though some 500 bombers had stumbled through the darkness relying on their navigation lights and airfield lighting to avoid collisions and find their homes.

Approaching the Suffolk coast near Orford Ness after the B-17s were the 270 B-24s of the 2nd Bomb Division, the crews unaware of the presence of anyone but their comrades. The East Anglian country side was dotted with runway and airfield lights to mark the many bases, which often lay only a few miles apart. Whilst captains and pilots strained their eyes to pick out their own airfield and keep a constant watch for other aircraft, the remaining crew men began to relax from the tension of battle. As the aircraft descended through 6,000 feet, oxygen masks were taken off and gunners left their cramped turrets.

The unusual move on the part of the Americans to launch an operation that would return at night had not gone unnoticed by the Luftwaffe. Dietrich Puttfarken's II/KG51 had left Soesterberg and were shadowing the B-24s, only a few miles off the English coast. At 22.07 hours the Me 410s struck and for the next half-an-hour there would be total chaos in the skies over Norfolk and Suffolk.

The first aircraft to be attacked was that of Lieutenant Cherry C. Pitts, the 1st pilot of B-24H 42-52608 of the 715th Squadron, 448th Bomb Group, Seething. Crews of accompanying B-24s saw his aircraft burst into flames and fall, a flaming mass, into the sea one mile off Hopton. No one escaped from the 'plane.

Fifteen miles off the Suffolk coast another Me 410 opened fire on Lieutenant James S. Munsey's B-24, nicknamed 'Cee-Gee II.' A long burst of cannon fire from the 8 o'clock position racked the port side of the ship. Sergeant Ralph McClure was physically blown out of his tail turret into the fuselage. Waist gunner Sergeant John F. McKinney was hit in the chest and head by shrapnel and the 'plane's port fuel tank caught fire. Lieutenant Arthur Orlowski, the bombardier, recalled:

'We couldn't open the bomb bay door. No 2 gas tank and the

101

hydraulic systems were shot out. A fire was burning just in the back of the wing. Conway kicked out the bomb bay doors but Munsey told me to keep him in while he made a run for the coast. Crale, the second pilot stayed with Munsey. The discipline was perfect. The radio operator said that he was hit in the eyes by some debris. Munsey then called Helfand (the navigator) and Laux (the front gunner) up on to the flight deck. McClure was hit on the head and came forward to tell us that McKinney was hit. We went back and found Brown jacking up his ball turret. McClure and Brown attempted to attach the static line to the rip cord of McKinney's parachute, but they couldn't break it loose. The gas tank then exploded and blew all three of them out of the tail hatch. We were over land at this time and the interior of the 'plane was in flames. I shoved Grady ahead of me, then looked back and saw Crale starting to get out of his seat. I don't think that Munsey had his parachute pack snapped on to his harness at that time. Conway, Helfand, Laux, Grady and I jumped through the bomb bay in that order. We were at about 4,000 feet.'

Orlowski, Laux, Brown and McClure landed near Southwold. Top turret gunner, Sergeant Grover Conway, fell in the water only fifty feet from the shore and twenty feet from Leon Helfand. In the freezing water Helfand could do nothing to help the top gunner who slowly drifted out to sea, his body was never found. Both pilots went down in the blazing aircraft which plunged into Reydon Marsh and sank into the sponge-like ground.

Minutes later Lieutenant Teague Gray Harris of the 458th Bomb Group was preparing to land at Horsham St. Faith. Already an attack had alerted the gunners but they failed to see the Me 410 that set their aircraft on fire. The B-24 crashed in flames on to a playing field near the Tuckswood Public House, in Daniel's Road, Lakenham. Only two of the ten man crew survived.

A 93rd Bomb Group B-24, landing at Hardwick, had a narrow escape when an Me 410 strafed it on landing but by now the defences were on the alert. Anti-aircraft gunners fired indiscriminitely, air gunners did little better. Airfield landing and identification lights were switched off as aircraft came in to land. Some aircraft, now being fired at from the ground, risked opening illuminated bomb bays in an attempt to identify themselves. Still not all crews knew what was happening. 1,000 feet above their airfield of Rackheath, 1st Lieutenant Stalie C. Reid Junior's crew of the 467th Bomb Group were in the traffic pattern. Turrets had been vacated, wheels were down and landing lights switched on when an attack was made from just sixty yards immediately behind the B-24 which then spun into the ground near Barsham. Three of the crew baled out but ball gunner, Technical Sergeant Edward Hoke, fell to his death when his parachute failed. The remaining six crew died in the burning wreck.

A 389th Bomb Group watched another aircraft move along side their's noticeable only by its navigation lights. The other aircraft slowly edged ahead, watched by the nose gunner of Lieutenant Wilkerson's B-24. A stream of bright tracers from an Me 410's twin 13mm machine guns slammed into the B-24 as the nose gunner returned the fire and both aircraft began to go down in flames. Only Wilkerson and one waist gunner were able to escape before the B-24 crashed near Cantley. Oberleutnant Klaus Kruger (pilot of the Me 410) and Micheal Reichardt (his Beobachter) were able to jettison their canopy but were unable to escape before the 'plane, enveloped in flame, dived into the ground at Ashby St. Mary. The two machines fell three miles away from each other.

The 715th Squadron, 448th Bomb Group, based at Seething had already lost one aircraft when Lieutenant Cherry C. Pitts had been shot down off Hopton. The fellow 715th Squadron crew of 2nd Lieutenant Eugene V. Pulcipher now went down in flames and crashed into a flooded marsh near Kessingland. Again all ten on board were killed.

Another 448th Bomber Group crew, this time from the 714th Squadron, were on their second mission. 1st Lieutenant Melvin L. Alspaugh and second pilot Dick Watters had seen another aircraft go down and the fires burning on the ground. Suddenly the right inboard engine burst into flames and the whole of the right side of the B-24 rapidly caught fire. On this occasion there was sufficient time for all ten of the crew to bale out. The aircraft went steadily into a steep dive and crashed into a railway embankment near Worlingham. The remaining aircraft of the 448th Bomb Group continued on towards Seething where Captain Alvin D. Skaggs was on his final approach when his left inboard engine caught fire. Petrol from a fractured pipe was fuelling a fire which had started in the bomb bay but Skaggs managed to put the flaming bomber down on the runway. As the aircraft touched down, two gunners jumped clear and Sergeant George Glevanic fell out through the bomb bay, the power line of his heated suit snagged and he was dragged along under the machine. The B-24 eventually slowed to a halt but the fire had taken a firm hold. The remaining crew members scrambled out, releasing Glevanic as they went. No sooner had the crew got clear than a second B-24 overshot the runway. This 'plane was then hit by another B-24 which sliced off

The original caption to this photograph read: Staff Sergeant Eugene Gaskins of Jacksonville, Florida, peers into the twisted hulk of the nose turret of the consolidated B-24 Liberator 'Vadie Raye'. The twenty year old gunner baled out of the burning aircraft at a height of 800 feet after it had been set on fire by shells from enemy fighters, following the attack on Hamm, Germany, on 22nd April, 1944. (USAAF).

42-28240, 41-28595 'Ice-cold Katie' and 42-9575, all from 448th Bomb Group at Seething Airfield on 22nd April, 1944.

its tail. Later a fourth machine contributed to the pile up but escaped destruction.

Ground staff at the 467th Bomb Group base of Rackheath watched three aircraft approach at just 500 feet, their wheels down and landing lights on. Two short bursts of fire shot away the tail section of the middle B-24 which turned upside down and fell to the ground near Mendham police station. The aircraft had been too low to give any of the crew time to escape. Another 467th Bomb Group B-24 was attacked in almost identical circumstances but this time the aircraft made the runway with its number four engine in flames. B-24 52477 was rolling along Rackheath's runway when an aircraft came over at 150 feet with its lights blazing. A series of small bombs then exploded around the taxiing bomber injuring three of its crew. Four ground staff were also injured and another was killed as he cycled across the field. Finally another 467th Bomb Group B-24 taxied into one of the craters left by the bombs and was slightly damaged.

Nearly half an hour after the attack had begun, the intruders of KG51 were still over East Anglia. Lieutenant Stilson of the 458th Bomb Group was still 5,000 feet and ten miles from his base of Horsham St. Faith when his aircraft was attacked from 3 o'clock. As his attacker made a second pass, the gunners returned the fire, hitting the Me 410. Number three and four engines and the bomber's right wing were now in flames. Height was lost rapidly as Stilson held the bomber on an even keel until it hit the ground a mile from base. All the crew were able to escape from the B-24 before it was consumed by the flames.

In the control tower at the 398th Bomb Group base at Hethel were some of the 2nd Bomb Division's 'top brass', Major General James P. Hodges and General Edward (Ted) Timberlake. A B-24 with a collapsed nose wheel already blocked the main runway as Lieutenant Foley came in on the second, shorter, runway. His aircraft had been hit by Anti-Aircraft fire and with its navigation lights on, the B-24 swept over the trees at the end of the runway. As the 'plane touched down its left tyre burst, sending the bomber careering across the grass towards the control tower. Directly in its path lay the airfield's radar hut which was totally demolished by the bomber. Two men working in the hut were killed but the bomber's crew were uninjured.

The B-24s of the 2nd Bomb Division were not the only aircraft to encounter the intruders. An Armstrong-Whitworth Albemarle of No. 42 OTU was engaged on a night navigation exercise that took it over Suffolk. The rather unwieldy twin engined, twin tailed aircraft designed as a bomber but relegated to a glider tug and parachute transport, was flying from its base at Ashbourne and Darley Moor in Derbyshire when attacked. It crashed, killing three of its crew but two were fortunate enough to have time to bale out.

Finally all 270 B-24s were down and KG51 left East Anglia as anonymously as they had come. It was some time before anyone fully appreciated what had happened and even then the identity and number of the attackers was grossly exaggerated. Nine B-24s and one Albermarle had been shot down. Three damaged aircraft had crashed on runways and two had been destroyed in the collision at Seething. A total of sixty-one airmen had been killed.

At Soesterberg, II/KG51 waited for their aircraft to return. The crews recounted the night's success and waited for the return of others. As daylight broke it began to be realised that two crews were not coming back. 9K + HP, the mount of Oberleutnant Kruger was now a smouldering heap of twisted metal in a Norfolk field, but the big shock was that the Gruppenkommandeur was missing. Major Dietrich Puttfarken, Ritterkreuz holder with five aircraft already destroyed to his credit, was missing. His loss remains a mystery to this day and it must be assumed that he and his Beobachter, Oberfeldwebel Willi Lux, had fallen victim to the North Sea.

After the outstanding success of April 22nd, II/KG51 continued their patrols over England and on the night of April 24th–25th, they returned to harass aircraft of Bomber Command returning from Karlsruhe. The Me 410 pilots roamed widely over Britain in search of targets and found their first, a Lancaster of No. 626 Squadron, over Colchester. Warrant Officer McPherson's aircraft was seen to catch fire in the air and fall, like a torch, to the ground. No one got out alive. Ten minutes later, over Ely, a Halifax of No. 76 Squadron was attacked and heavily damaged. Its pilot, Pilot Officer Dibbins, made to land his machine but crashed in the attempt and only the rear gunner, Flight Sergeant Anderson, escaped alive to be admitted to hospital with injuries.

II/KG51 had suffered its first losses on intruder sorties on the April 22nd raid but the number mounted steadily. At 04.30 hours on April 27th 1944, Leutnant Wolfgang Wenning was flying his Me 410 in the vicinity of Rugby when he spotted another aircraft. What followed will never be known as, before fire was opened, the two machines collided. Both aircraft fell to the ground in flames and all aboard were killed. The RAF machine was an Airspeed Oxford of No. 18 (P)AFU, flown by Pilot Officer Moore, who was in the landing pattern of Church

Lawford airfield. When officers of AI2(g) arrived to inspect the wreckage of the German machine they found several points of interest. The armament had been increased to four MG 151 20mm cannon and two MG 17 machine guns in the nose, keeping another two MG 131 machine guns in the two fuselage barbettes. Two 66 gallon drop tanks were carried to increase the range of the aircraft, the first time that this feature had been seen on an Me 410. Of the crew, only the body of the Bordfunker, Feldwebel Gustav Delp, was immediately identifiable to ADI(k) but there were clues to the identity of the pilot. The second body carried both Iron Cross, 1st and 2nd class, along with the Gold (110) war flights badge. Whoever he may have been, it was assumed that he was a very experienced pilot. In fact he is now known to have been Leutnant Wolfgang Wenning of the Geschwader Stab II/KG51.

Almost a month passed before the next aircraft fell to the guns of an intruder. On May 22nd–23rd 1944, the Lancasters of No. 619 Squadron were returning to Dunholm Lodge from a raid on Duisberg when one of their number was shot down at East Wretham. Only the bomb aimer, Sergeant Leeson, was able to escape before the machine crashed, killing the remaining six men.

A crew that had already had a most eventful night, was that of Squadron Leader Heney of No. 582 Squadron, based at Little Staughton. On their bomb run over Dortmund, an incendiary bomb dropped from another aircraft above them had hit the port rudder and a second lodged in the port outer engine, where it exploded and set the wing on fire. Heney ordered his crew to prepare to bale out as, by this time, flames were trailing back fifty yards. Searchlights then picked them up as they dived 5,000 feet, in the hope of extinguishing the flames. This attempt failed and the Lancaster carried on flying at 13,000 feet with the searchlights following. After seven minutes the flames died away and the fire went out, enabling Heney to set course for base. As the Lancaster crossed the Ruhr, it was hit by flak near Cologne. Again they survived and carried on to the English coast where they began to lose height prior to landing. Near Little Staughton, as they flew at 2,500 feet with their navigation lights on, an intruder attacked from behind and below. The rear turret had already been put out of action, leaving the Lancaster defenceless. Heney put the Lancaster into a corkscrew manoeuvre to starboard and escaped, but not before their aircraft had been raked by cannon fire. Fortunately none of the crew had been injured, but the hydraulics had been shot away. A good landing was made using the emergency undercarriage and flap systems, after which Heney reported:

'Aircraft cat AC as a result of enemy fighters, flak and incendiaries dropped by Main Force. 1 × 500 GP hung up and brought back to base.'

Heney's Lancaster was not the only aircraft to be attacked over Little Staughton, for No. 13 OTU (which was based at Bicester) made the following entry in their Operational Record Book:

Accident to Anson LT. 476 at Little Staughton.

159852 F/O. P.B. Davidson	(Pupil Pilot)	– D.I.
1579629 F/Sgt. Blythe R.N.	(Pupil Nav.)	– D.I.
952558 W/O. Lister G.	(Staff Nav.)	– Uninjured.
1577715 Sgt. McConchie R.F.H.	(Pupil Nav.)	– Uninjured.

The aircraft was engaged on a Navigational exercise on the morning of the 23rd May in the hours of darkness, when it was subjected to an attack from another aircraft. As the aircraft was flying at 2,100 feet with navigational lights it is considered safe to presume that the attack was made by a hostile aircraft and the supposition is supported by the fact that an Alert was received in the vicinity shortly after the attack. The pilot was seriously wounded by a cannon shell which entered his back and passed through the abdomen and F/Sgt. Blythe received a wound in the thigh. W/O. Lister who was unhurt, was at the rear of the aircraft and baled out immediately it went into a steep dive. His parachute functioned perfectly and he landed in a ploughed field without damage to himself, although the aircraft was at a comparatively low height. The fourth member of the crew, Sgt. McConchie, was unhurt and he assisted the pilot to land the aircraft at RAF Little Staughton. The pilot died of wounds on 26th May 1944.

At the American base at Great Ashfield a B-17 parked in a hangar was destroyed along with the building. At 03.10 hours the Lancasters of No. 105 Squadron were arriving back at Bourne when the airfield was attacked. Several bombs exploded but did no damage. Two Lancasters were, however, hit by cannon fire.

Following this burst of activity there was a lull of a week before the intruders returned. At 02.39 hours on May 29th, Flying Officer Yates was carrying out circuits and landings at Stradishall in Stirling R9298 of No. 1657 Conversion Unit. As the aircraft made its approach, an intruder opened fire on the Stirling which crashed on to the airfield killing all six on board. Two other Stirlings parked on the airfield were damaged by the crashing machine. One was so severely damaged that it was written off as being damaged beyond repair.

The Allied invasion of Europe began on June 6th and many operations were flown in the role of tactical support for the invasion forces. The target for the B-24s of the 34th Bomb Group on the

On 8th June, 1944. B-24H, 42-94911, from 34th Bomb Group is shown at Mendlesham Airfield.

B-24J, 44-40085, after it crashed into the signals hut at Hethel Airfield on 22nd April, 1945. (Evans).

Wreckage of the B-17G of the 96th Bomber Group which crashed at Great Glenham on 12th April, 1944. (Evans)

evening of June 7th had been Nantes, but results had been poor. Return to base at Mendlesham was made in darkness at 23.00 hours. Top gunner in one of the B-24s was Technical Sergeant Jack Blackham, who suddenly saw pieces flying off the wing of his aircraft. Releasing himself from his turret, he made his way to the flight deck to find out what was going on, only to be greeted by another burst of fire. Before he finally baled out, Blackham went forward to help the nose gunner from his turret and then returned to the bomb bay, clipping on his parachute as he went. In all, seven left the aircraft but three of his fellow crew members were later found dead in the wreck of the B-24 which crashed at Wetheringsett, a mile short of the airfield. All other 34th Bomb Group aircraft were then ordered to divert to other airfields, away from the intruders, but the pilots of II/KG51 had not finished. Another B-24 of the 34th Bomb Group was actually over Mendlesham when it was shot down and crashed into buildings on the technical site of the airfield, killing most of its crew. The 34th Bomb Group Air Inspector reported:

> 'On 7th June 1944, the office files and records of the Inspection Section were completely destroyed when a B-24 aeroplane crashed and burned during an attack by E/A. M/Sgt's Ward and Arsulich, T/Sgt R Ryan and S/Sgt M Merkley were in the office awaiting return of our A/C at the time of the crash. These men managed to get out of the building but very narrowly escaped death or serious injury. M/Sgt Merkley was slightly burned when the gas tanks exploded and Sgts Ward, Arsulich and Ryan were blown through a partially constructed building 20 feet away by the force of the crash.'

A third B-24 of the 34th Bomb Group crashed near Ipswich and a fourth made a crash landing at Eye. In all a total of thirteen men had been killed and four aircraft destroyed.

The next aircraft to fall to the guns of II/KG51's Me 410s were on the night of June 27th–28th, when fourteen of No. 90 Squadron's Lancasters were returning to Tuddenham from a raid on Biennais. As the bombers were approaching their airfield, situated just south of Mildenhall, an intruder opened fire on Lancaster NE145, which immediately crashed to the ground at Icklingham. The aircraft had been so low that none of the seven man crew had time to escape before the aircraft crashed and exploded. Flight Lieutenant Burton DFC was flying another Lancaster of No. 90 Squadron when it was attacked over base. A hail of fire hit the Lancaster which escaped to land safely, but its rear gunner, Sergeant Smith, had been killed in his turret by the cannon fire. Also on this night a B-24 of the 801st Bomb Group was shot down at Eaton Socon. Seven of its crew baled out but three more were killed. An unusual occurrence during the crew's escape was that two men baled sharing one parachute – one of the few authenticated occasions when this has been successful.

This was the last attack recorded on bombers over Britain for nearly nine months. II/KG51 was withdrawn for attacks against the invasion beach-head and the last loss of a KG51 intruder occurred on July 25th 1944. Twelve aircraft and their crews had been lost whilst engaged on intruder sorties in the three months they had been operating, but their effect upon the Allies had been considerable.

Part III

CHAPTER ELEVEN

Of Zeppelin and Gisela

After Operation Steinbock, Generalmajor Dietrich Peltz (head of Fliegerkorps IX and Angriffsführer England) had little interest in operations over Britain. In June 1944, the Allies invaded Europe at Normandy and Peltz's forces were fully employed in attacks against the Allied beach-head. Further attacks on Britain were now to be made by the V-1 flying bombs and V-2 rockets. Intruder operations by II/KG51 had tailed off and all but ceased by mid-June, leaving the skies over Britain once more free from intruders.

Generalmajor Josef Schmid, whose plans for large scale intruder operations had been so conclusively turned down in December 1943, once more put forward his ideas. In October 1944, as General der Nachtjagd, Schmid was given the go-ahead and began detailed preparations with the full support of Oberstleutnant Streib, Inspeckteur der Nachtjagd.

The basis of Schmid's plan remained unchanged from that of late 1943 – a 'knock-out blow' which would have a devastating effect on Bomber Command. To deliver this blow, an intruder force of unparalleled size would have to be assembled from the existing night fighter units which could scarcely provide sufficient cover for the defence of the Reich. The attack would have to be carefully co-ordinated and take place on a night when the bombers were operating in weather conditions that favoured the night fighters.

One of the first moves was the expansion of III/NJG2 by the addition of IV/NJG3. The new II/NJG2 would, it was hoped, achieve what the original I/NJG2 had been prevented in doing in 1941.

The task of preparing such a large number of crews posed a problem, as they would have to be fully briefed prior to the attack – the date of which could not be known. In late November 1943, crews of the units to be involved were warned that they would soon take part in a special operation, but that was all.

On December 1st 1944, Unteroffizier Rudolf Woblik and his crew, consisting of Unteroffizier Herbert Latoch and Obergefrieter Norbert Kolodziej, were called to a briefing with other crews of 9/NJG3. Behind locked and guarded doors they were told that the whole of the night fighter force would be employed in intruder attacks on Bomber Command bases in England. Specially prepared maps were issued to each pilot of the Staffel and these were marked with the airfields to be attacked as well as all known defences, such as Anti-Aircraft sites and balloons. It was emphasised at the conference that, as a security measure in case of maps falling into enemy hands, these maps were deliberately incorrectly marked in all areas with the exception of the area of operation and routes of entry allotted to the 9th Staffel.

Two routes of entry were laid down for the Staffel, both of which were in the neighbourhood of Hull; the intruders were to cross the North Sea at minimum altitude and climb to cross the coast by the given routes at a height of 4,500 metres, which was believed to be the height at which the RAF bombers returned. Once in the area of operations, the night fighters were to operate as low level intruders.

In order to familiarise crews with the British system of airfield lighting and night landing procedure, a special edition of the Einzelnachrichten des Ic Dienstes West der Luftwaffe (Luftwaffe Western Front Intelligence Summary) had been prepared and was given to crews for study. This publication gave sketches and descriptions of typical British airfield lighting systems, such as the Drem system with funnel lights and angle of glide indicators.

Other instructions were given, such as how best to approach RAF bases in order to converge upon landing bombers from behind. They were told that a red light on top of the control tower meant that an intruder warning was in progress and that airfield installations would probably be easily identified.

Finally there were two code names; 'Zeppelin' was an indication that the operation was imminent and 'Gisela' would mean that the operation would take place that night. The crews were dismissed and before long the details and code names began to fade from their memories.

A German technical illustration of the Ju 88G-6.

On January 1st 1945, whilst engaged on a night fighter mission, Ju 88G D5 + PT landed in Luxembourg. On board was Unteroffizier Lattoch, who had been present at the briefing of 9/NJG3 on December 1st. He was then passed to the intelligence branch of the USAAF 9th Air Force and elicited the fact that a large scale intruder operation would take place shortly. Details were signalled to the Air Ministry on January 5th and the next day Lattoch was flown to England for further interrogation by ADI(K), Wing Commander Felkin's department, which had kept a close watch on the development of I/NJG2 in 1941.

Details of ADI(K)'s report were distributed immediately to thirty-four different bodies and alerted all concerned to the impending danger. Both Bomber and Fighter Commands issued special warnings to all Squadrons that their airfields were likely to be subject to attack. Bomber Command sent a copy of the ADI(K) report to all its units and warned crews to maintain a particularly sharp look out for intruders. Diversion schemes were devised to divert bombers to alternative airfields should an attack take place on their own base.

An intruder warning system had in past years been devised which linked all bomber stations by telephone lines to Fighter Groups. Immediately an intruder was reported, all bomber stations were advised and given all known plots of the intruders, with their headings and heights. Station Commanders would then organise the blackout and airfield lighting precautions. Pilots were informed that intruders were operating and could be ordered to douse their navigation lights at any time.

Only three Mosquito squadrons remained to provide defence as most Squadrons were operating in Europe or in support of the bombers. The home defence Mosquito squadron's usual role was to intercept the V-1 launching He 111s then operating over the North Sea, but they could be diverted for use against any intruder force.

The Anti-Aircraft organisation in Britain had, by this time, been deployed almost exclusively against the V-1 attacks. Under this scheme, code named 'Diver', restrictions were placed on Anti-Aircraft guns in an attempt to prevent them firing upon friendly aircraft. The 'Diver' defences consisted in the main of four areas: the 'Gate', an eleven mile wide searchlight belt along the coast between Yarmouth and Skegness; the 'Gun Box' in the Thames Estuary; the 'Gun Strip' between Clacton and Yarmouth and the 'Gun Fringe' stretching from Ingoldmells Point to Filey.

Although there were no organised intruder sorties taking place in early 1945, occasionally a determined night fighter crew had been known to pursue its prey far over the North Sea towards Britain. This seems to have been the case on the evening of February 21st, when a Stirling of No. 195 Squadron was attacked as it landed at Shepherd's Grove. The Stirling had returned from Rees, in Germany after what is believed to have been a supply dropping mission. The aircraft was set on fire as it made its final approach but the pilot, Flight Lieutenant Campbell, brought the blazing machine down on the runway safely. As the fire took hold, its crew which included Captain George Slater G.3.Air, SAS Troops No. 38 Group HQ, scrambled clear. Only one man, the rear gunner, failed to escape and was burnt to death.

In the knowledge that intruder operations were likely to take place in the near future, Fighter Command, in consultation with other RAF commands, devised a plan code named 'Trigger'. The basis of this plan was to give Anti-Aircraft defences greater freedom to engage targets by keeping friendly aircraft clear of the East Coast and by restricting essential night flying to the area of the 'Gate' where no Anti-Aircraft guns were deployed. It was also intended that whenever possible, Bomber Command should route their bomber stream to the west of London both on the outward and return flights. Bomber Command reserved the right to suspend both 'Trigger' and 'Diver' as and when operational requirement dictated, as restrictions could not be allowed to interfere with operations.

CHAPTER TWELVE

March 3rd 1945

At midday on March 3rd 1945, messages from Bomber Command Headquarters were printed out on teletype machines at bases across Eastern England. Now in its sixth year of war, Bomber Command had come a long way since the days when a handful of Hampdens and Wellingtons groped their way to Germany. On this night, a 'moderate' force of four engined 'heavies' would take part in a complex plan, with feint attacks and diversions, countermeasures and deceptions to protect the main force.

The 'Main Force' for the night would be split into two separate raids on targets near Münster. No. 4 Group were to complete the destruction of the synthetic oil installation at Kamen and No. 5 Group would attempt to destroy the aqueduct, safety gates and canal boats on the Dortmund Ems Canal at Ladbergen.

At each Bomber Command base involved, details for the coming operation were received and instructions issued to the appropriate personnel. This, as with every operation of this nature, would run to precise details which covered every facet: fuel loads, course, height, speed, bomb load, bomb fuse settings, 'Window' discharge rates, target indicators, signals and flight plan restrictions. Nearly 5,000 airmen were briefed for their various tasks and 817 aircraft fueled and armed. In addition to these aircraft and crews, both Training and Coastal Command aircraft were operating over Eastern England and the North Sea.

As usual, the 'Trigger' plan was scheduled to be in force, but Bomber Command decided to exercise their right to suspend the plan on this occasion. Restrictions were lifted to allow flying over the 'Diver Gun Fringe' area from Ingoldmells Point to Filey and aircraft would not be using the 'Gate', where there were no guns stationed. The bombers' route took them out over Southern England, via Reading and the English Channel as per the 'Trigger' plan, but they were to return over the North Sea. The reasoning behind this was that the low cloud which extended over the continent, would make it difficult for the returning bombers to steer clear of the friendly artillery zones in Allied occupied territory. This would mean that the bombers would run the risk of being engaged by the Allied Anti-Aircraft defences.

These routing instructions were all contained in the flight plans received at the bomber bases.

Forces scheduled to take part in operations 3rd March 1945

Main Force

No. 4 Group	Kamen	201 Halifaxes
No. 8 Group	Kamen	21 Lancasters (Pathfinders)
No. 8 Group	Kamen	12 Mosquitoes (Pathfinders)
No. 5 Group	Ladbergen	212 Lancasters
No. 5 Group	Ladbergen	12 Mosquitoes

Support and diversions

No. 8 Group	Berlin	64 Mosquitoes
No. 8 Group	Wurzburg	32 Mosquitoes
No. 5 Group	Oslo Harbour	16 Lancasters (Mine-Laying)
No. 1 Group	Kattegat	15 Lancasters (Mine-Laying)
No. 7 Group	Frisians	40 Lancasters
No. 7 Group	Frisians	19 Halifaxes
No. 7 Group	Frisians	39 Wellingtons
No. 100 Group	Mepen	10 Halifaxes
No. 100 Group	Mepen	7 Mosquitoes
No. 100 Group		12 Halifaxes (Mandrel)
No. 100 Group		4 Stirlings (Mandrel)
No. 100 Group		7 Halifaxes (Signal Investigation)
No. 100 Group		1 Mosquito (Signal Investigation)
No. 100 Group		5 Halifaxes (Window/Jamming)
No. 100 Group		3 Liberators (Window/Jamming)
No. 100 Group		8 Fortresses (Window/Jamming)

Weather reconnaissance 1 Mosquito

USAAF 8th Air Force
492nd Bomb Group Emden 24 B-24s

At around 18.00 hours, aircraft began to take to the air from their bases and set course for Europe. The first aircraft over Germany were the 89 Mosquitoes of No. 8 Group, bound for Berlin and Wurzburg. On route to Berlin, one of the Mosquito pilots became ill and decided to turn back. 23,000 feet over Bremen, a single 4,000 pound, high capacity Minatol 'Cookie' was released at 19.51 hours. The first bomb of the night had fallen and the remaining Mosquitoes carried on their targets.

Berlin was first 'marked' by three H2S equipped Mosquitoes at 20.27 hours. Six red and six green, 250 pound target indicators were dropped in three clusters which fell in a line from the north-east to the south-west across the target. Sixty-four other Mosquitoes then made their way through the searchlights and flak to drop 59 tons of bombs on the target indicators.

Wurzberg was bombed at the same time as Berlin. Six 'Oboe' Mosquitoes marked the target with fifteen, 250 pound, red target indicators. These dropped through heavy cloud cover, illuminating the river which ran through the target below. The following 24 Mosquitoes each dropped their single, 4,000 pound 'Cookies' in a concentrated area on the east bank of the river. A large fire was still visible when the bombers were fifty miles away. None of the crews noticed any defences.

Sixteen Lancasters of No. 5 Group and fifteen Lancasters of No. 1 Group set about sowing their 'vegetables' in their appropriate 'gardens' between 20.15 and 21.08 hours. One of the No. 5 Group Lancasters aborted the mission, leaving fifteen to drop 36 Mark IV and 54 Mark VI mines in Oslo Harbour. The fifteen Lancasters of No. 1 Group made their way over the North Sea above low 10/10ths cloud to Denmark, where the weather cleared. Major Werner Husemann in a Ju 88G of I/NJG3, was on patrol east of Aarhus and close to the area in the Kattegat where the No. 1 Group Lancasters were to lay their mines. At 20.29 hours, Husemann shot down his 33rd aircraft, a Lancaster. Flying Officer Gregoire DFC and his crew went down into the Kattegat in Lancaster 'R – Robert' of No. 153 Squadron and became the night's first victim. The remaining fourteen Lancasters 'planted' 47 Mark IV and 36 Mark VI 'vegetables' and one crew claimed to have shot down a Ju 88.

Perhaps the most unusual of the sorties flown were those flown by the various aircraft of No. 100 Group. Although comparatively few in number, they performed a vital role in confusing the Luftwaffe's defences.

Twelve Halifaxes and four Stirlings took up positions in a line across the bomber route and at 20.45 hours switched on their 'Mandrel' equipment. This effectively shielded the incoming force by jamming the long range German ground based 'Freya' radar equipment. The sixteen aircraft orbited their positions for 45 minutes and then flew on a bearing of 060 degrees for eight minutes, where they again orbited for 50 minutes before returning to their original stations for another 25 minutes.

One Mosquito and seven Halifaxes from No. 192 Squadron flew a signal investigation patrol to monitor enemy radio transmissions. Although one Halifax returned early, when its undercarriage became unserviceable, the remaining aircraft accompanied the No. 4 Group Halifaxes to Kamen.

Five Halifaxes, three Liberators and eight Fortresses set out on other jamming missions, but three aircraft returned early due to mechanical failures. The remaining thirteen aircraft operated 'Pipe Rack', 'Carpet' and 'Jostle' to confuse the defences whilst accompanying the bombers.

From various operational conversion units of No. 7 Group, 40 Lancasters, 19 Halifaxes and 35 Wellingtons were detailed to fly a 'Sweepstake' diversionary flight towards the Frisian Islands. Three Halifaxes cancelled after mechanical failures but the remaining 91 aircraft spent an hour throwing 3,721 bundles of 'Window' out over the North Sea.

The American contribution to the night consisted of 24 B-24s. Six of these returned early, leaving eighteen aircraft to drop 183 500 pound bombs on Emden.

The final preamble to the main attacks came again from No. 100 Group with a feint attack on Mepen. Ten Halifaxes and six Mosquitoes successfully dropped nothing but flares and target indicators over the town in an attempt to mislead the fighter controllers into diverting their night fighters from the main force.

Just one minute after the target indicators were released over Mepen, the first main attack began on the canal at Ladbergen. The first markers to fall over the canal were eight, 1,000 pound, green target indicators. Then came 305 flares to illuminate the target and finally Mosquitoes dropped ten, 1,000 pound, red target indicators. This main group of markers fell just 300 yards to the north-west of the aiming point and the 'Master Bomber', orbiting over the target, began to issue instructions to the 118 Lancasters of the main force. Sergeant Harper was the flight engineer in Lancaster OL-C of No. 83 Pathfinder Squadron and was on his twenty-eighth operation. On this flight it was his task to orbit the target while the main force attacked, in case the 'Master Bomber' required further illumination during the attack.

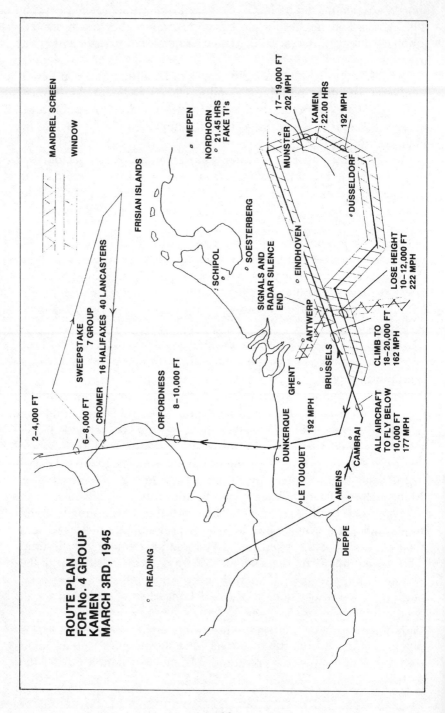

ROUTE PLAN
FOR No. 4 GROUP
KAMEN
MARCH 3RD, 1945

'We were orbiting when one of the engines vibrated badly and the revolutions went up well over the 3,000 mark. It was obvious we had a propeller trying to run away. This could have rapidly lead to the engine seizing up, or even smashing itself to pieces, so we feathered it and continued on three engines. We stayed over the target until the controller came over the VHF: 'Thank you Marker Force, that's enough, go home and good luck'. It was then a routine, but lonely and dark flight back to base.'

Among the squadrons taking part in this attack was No. 467 (RCAF) Squadron based at Waddington, who had visited the Dortmund Ems Canal several times in the past months. They had bombed it twice in November 1944, and on New Year's Day 1945, they had bombarded Ladbergen. The squadron returned to Ladbergen on the night of February 7th–8th when they lost their newly appointed leader, Wing Commander Douglas, who had held the post for just one week since replacing Squadron Leader Ellis, who had been shot down on February 1st. They bombed the canal again on February 20th and returned on February 21st, but 10/10 cloud over the target prevented them making a daylight attack. An attack on February 28th was cancelled. March brought no better luck when early morning attacks were cancelled on March 1st and 2nd. When bomb and fuel loads similar to those of the previous days were prepared, it was obvious to all what the target would be. The crews had been up early in preparation for a daylight operation, but this was cancelled in favour of the night attack, for which fifteen of the Squadron's Lancasters took off. Newly promoted Wing Commander Langlois, whose promotion from Flight Lieutenant had come through only that morning, lead the squadron on the eighteenth trip of his second tour. With him was the new gunnery leader, Flying Officer Taylor, who had only just joined the squadron.

Eighteen, 12,000 pound, 'Tallboy' bombs were dropped by No. 9 Squadron's Lancasters and the remainder of the tonnage came in the form of over two thousand, 2,000 pound bombs fitted with half and one hour delay fuses. Under this weight of explosives the canal burst its banks on both sides of the safety gates, flooding the surrounding area and leaving many canal boats stranded. The attack lasted for slightly over twenty-five minutes.

As the Lancasters left the target area, some of the Luftwaffe's leading night fighter pilots were being directed on to the bomber-stream by their ground control stations. Whilst the 'Window' and other devices made detecting the bombers a difficult task, the large number of four engined aircraft in the comparatively small air space formed by the bomber stream made it almost inevitable that any fighter in the area would be able to locate an aircraft. Four fighter pilots claimed to have brought down eight of the 203 Lancasters in the space of eighteen minutes. All fell in the vicinity of Münster. The first claim to be made was by Major Heinz-Wolfgang Schnaufer, Geschwaderkommodore of NJG4 and holder of the Ritterkreuz with Diamonds, the highest award ever given to a German night fighter pilot. At 21.55 hours he brought down a Lancaster between Münster and Osnabrück – his 117th claim. Nine minutes later another Lancaster became his 118th victim. Hauptmann Hermann Greiner, Gruppenkommandeur of IV/NJG1, claimed to have brought down three Lancasters – his forty-ninth, fiftieth and fifty-first claims. Hauptmann Joseph Kraft, also from IV/NJG1 made his fifty-third and fifty-fourth claims whilst Major Martin Drews, Gruppenkommandeur of III/NJG1 made his forty-ninth claim. All three of these pilots were holders of the Ritterkreuz with Oakleaves.

Losses over Europe 3rd – 4th March 1945

Lancaster LM750 of No. 15 Sqn.	F/O. Gregoire and five crew missing. Shot down into the Kattegat.
Mosquito TA404 of No. 157 Sqn.	F/Sgt. Leigh and one other Missing.
Lancaster PA197 of No. 189 Sqn.	F/O. Dykins and three crew prisoner, three killed. Crashed at Bevergen, Germany.
Lancaster NG254 of No. 207 Sqn.	F/O. Miller and five crew killed, one prisoner. Crashed at Tillbeck, Germany.
Lancaster NG170 of No. 227 Sqn.	F/O. Johnston and crew. Crashed at Altenberge, Germany.
Lancaster NG469 of No. 463 Sqn.	F/O. Howells and four crew killed, two prisoners. Crashed at Hesum, Germany.
Lancaster PB806 of No. 467 Sqn.	Sqn/Ldr. Langlois and five crew missing.
Lancaster PB808 of No. 467 Sqn.	F/O. Reid and five crew missing.

Lancaster R5868 'S Sugar' of No. 467 Squadron which is now at The RAF Museum, Hendon.

Lancaster LM677 of No. 467 Sqn. F/O. Eggins and five crew killed, one prisoner. Crashed at Havixbeck, Germany.

Lancaster ME453 of No. 467 Sqn. F/O. Ward and six crew killed. Crashed at Pentrup, Germany.

Of the seven Lancasters lost in this raid, three came from No. 467 Squadron, amongst which was the aircraft of their new commanding officer, Wing Commander Langlois.

Whilst Germany's night fighter 'Experten' wrought havoc among the Lancasters of No. 5 Group, the Halifaxes of No. 4 Group approached their target at Kamen. As before the attack was opened with markers, this time dropped from between 28,000 and 35,000 feet by eight 'Oboe' Mosquitoes from No. 8 Group. Twenty-one Lancasters also from No. 8 Group, followed the red target indicators with green target indicators and nearly 98 tons of high explosives which effectively illuminated the synthetic oil plant for the following 181 Halifaxes. A total of 690 tons of bombs fell on the target in the space of ten minutes.

Although several night fighters were seen by the Halifax crews, none were attacked. Only searchlights and flak met the bombers who left continuing explosions and spreading fires in their wake.

Fighter Command had sent twenty-nine Mosquito night fighters in

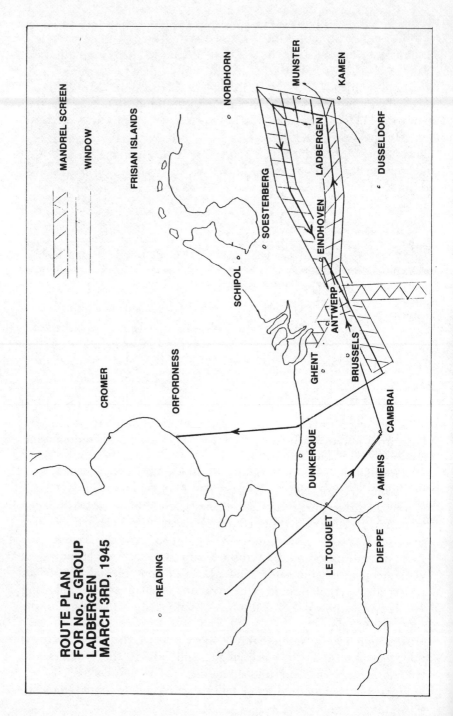

ROUTE PLAN
FOR No. 5 GROUP
LADBERGEN
MARCH 3RD, 1945

the intruder role to intercept the Luftwaffe fighters, either on patrol or with the bomber stream. One of these obtained a contact on its ASH equipment near Münster, but lost it in 'Window' after a five minute chase. Another Mosquito returned to base with a wire cable and parachute embedded in its tailplane. Eleven more Mosquitoes patrolled various airfields in Germany in the hope of catching a fighter unawares. Flight Lieutenant MacKenzie and Warrant Officer Muir in a Mosquito Mk. XXX of No. 406 Squadron were on such a 'Flower' operation to the Rhein-Twente area. Away to the south they could see the bombing of Ladbergen in progress as they began to orbit one of the revolving coloured beacons flashing red and white. A contact was obtained on the Mk.X AI equipment, which was eventually caught and identified as a Ju 88. From 400 feet behind the Ju 88 MacKenzie opened fire, hitting the Ju 88's port engine and causing pieces to break off. The aircraft then peeled away to starboard and exploded on the ground by the side of a road. Another No. 406 Squadron crew, Flight Lieutenant Croone and Flying Officer Johnstone, damaged an aircraft on the airfield of Handorf before attacking and destroying a locomotive on their return.

Flight Lieutenant Tarkowski and Flying Officer Taylor from No. 307 Squadron were on a high level patrol in support of the bombers and saw target indicators falling over both the main targets. Shortly after this they watched an aircraft falling in flames and exploding south of Münster. They continued their patrol for nearly an hour before a Ju 88 was identified, fifteen miles west-north-west of Bonn. After a four-and-a-half second burst the aircraft exploded with a vivid white flash and went down in flames.

By midnight few aircraft remained over Europe, the 'Sweepstake' had stopped 'Windowing', the 'Mandrel' screen, 'Carpet', 'Jostle' and 'Pipe Rack' jamming were switched off and the air armada withdrew from Germany across the North Sea to home.

CHAPTER THIRTEEN

Operation Gisela

Long before any of the bombers had taken off for their targets, the Luftwaffe listening services had intercepted Allied radio traffic which indicated that some 500 aircraft would operate that night. The code word 'Fasan' (Pheasant) was passed to the Luftwaffe's night fighter units bringing them to the alert. Shortly after this came another code word 'Gisela' and the messages were passed on to the crews. Some heard the announcement in the officers' mess, very informal and given with no sense of urgency. Many crews did not even remember the significance of the girl's name but soon it struck a chord in the minds of the crews – tonight was 'Gisela', the big blow.

Many things had happened in the three months since crews were gathered together for the special briefings. Crews had gone and new ones had arrived in their place. In addition to their normal night defence tasks some crews had begun to strafe ground targets, vehicles and trains, in an attempt to hinder the Allied advance across Europe.

The crews due to participate in the operation gathered for briefing and were reminded of the many details of which they had already been informed. Lights, landing systems, searchlight locations, return courses, flak and barrage balloons. The meteorological report contained nothing unusual. A strong front moving across the North Sea meant that the bombers would fly above this on the way back and that the fighters would be forced to fly under the cloud in heavy rain to keep below the radar defences. Wind was northerly at 50 km/hr. and a half moon was rising.

Flying kit and survival equipment were donned. For most, this consisted of a flying suit, life jacket and dinghy, under which were foam lined underclothes. Should anyone have the misfortune to come down in the North Sea they would only survive for about half an hour before hypothermia set in and death would almost certainly follow. The foam underclothes helped to insulate the body from the cold but were bulky to wear within the confines of a Ju 88s cockpit. As conditions were so cramped some crews elected to leave their radar operator behind as they would not be required to use the equipment over England. The majority of crews however, chose to fly with their usual four man crew.

According to Luftwaffe records, 142 Ju 88Gs took part in Operation

Gisela from the following units: I/NJG2, II/NJG2, III/NJG2, III/NJG3, IV/NJG3, III/NJG4, III/NJG5. British reports would lead one to believe that some seventy to eighty aircraft operated over Britain.

The first waves of Ju 88s began to take off at 23.00 hours and for the next hour a steady stream of fighters made their way to the Dutch coast where the pilots dived to sea level. To keep below British coastal radar, the fighters had to stay below fifty metres. In the rain and darkness the wave tops flashing below could just be discerned but, as the pilots knew, to rely on judgement alone would have been foolhardy. Instead trust was placed in the FuG 101 radio altimeter which was extremely accurate, as were all the night fighter's blind flying instruments. For over an hour the pilots stared, almost hypnotized, at the small dial upon which all their lives depended. The strain was enormous but at last the English coast was reached. Shortly before the coast was crossed the Ju 88s climbed steeply to a height similar to that of the bombers.

The night fighters began to cross the coast on a wide front which stretched from Essex to Yorkshire but were greeted by nothing more lethal than searchlight beams wavering in the clear skies behind the weather front. At first many of the Luftwaffe crews found little as they flew over the brightly moonlit countryside, but the main bomber force soon returned from Ladbergen and Kamen. Just after midnight a Ju 88 opened fire on a Fortress III off the Suffolk coast – the first shots of Operation Gisela had been fired.

The Fortress which had been fired on was from No. 214 Squadron and had been returning from a 'Window' patrol when the controls of its No. 1 engine were shot away. Flight Sergeant Kingdon managed to land safely at Woodbridge even though most of the perspex had been knocked out of the cockpit and the No. 1 fuel tank holed.

Shortly before this, the station commander at Oulton Airfield near Lowestoft had reported a 'suspect aircraft' over his station and almost immediately 'Hostiles' began to be reported at the headquarters of No. 100 Group. From here the 'Scram' order was given to its aircraft. 'Scram' was the code word for pilots to divert to alternative airfields, usually in the south or west of England, away from the intruders. The next aircraft to be attacked was another No. 100 Group machine, a Mosquito of No. 169 Squadron returning from an intruder sortie in support of the Kamen raid. Its pilot, Squadron Leader Fenwick, had received the 'Scram' order but was shot down en route to his diversion airfield.

Reports of intruders had been received by Nos. 7 and 12 Groups by

00.10 hours. Six minutes later another Fortress of No. 214 Squadron was attacked, but this time the crew were not as lucky as their fellows and crashed on approach to Oulton. Soon after yet another No. 214 Squadron Fortress was attacked over Peterborough but the pilot escaped his attacker to land at Brawdy.

As the official Bomber Command intruder warning was received at bases all over Eastern England, a Halifax of No. 640 Squadron crashed into a wood near Woodbridge Airfield as it attempted to land on three engines. The Halifax had returned early from Kamen and it is not clear whether this loss was due to an accident or intruder damage.

Flight Lieutenant Errington was the wireless operator in a No. 171 Squadron Halifax returning from a 'Mandrel' operation when his aircraft was attacked. West of Norwich, at 3,000 feet and heading for base at North Creake, he takes up the story:

> 'I was receiving an urgent radio message "Scram diversion – land at Tangmere" and had just passed this to the skipper when he shouted "Good God Norman, don't you know what's just happened?" to which I replied, "I have a jolly good idea."
>
> Cannon shells came whizzing right through the aircraft in a head-on attack. A burst of fire hit the starboard side of the aircraft, set fire to the wing and inner engine, shot away the leading edge of the wing, damaged the elevator and caused an explosion in the flight engineer's, department. Squadron Leader Procter, the pilot, gave the order to bale out as the Halifax was becoming uncontrollable and all eight of us landed safely near Knettisall Airfield. The only injury was suffered by the rear gunner, F/O Stephenson, who broke his ankle when he landed on top of a petrol bowser.'

At 00.29 hours Lancaster 'Y' of No. 12 Squadron, engaged on a cross country navigation exercise, dived almost vertically into the ground near Alford, Lincolnshire. The machine hit the ground with such force that its engines buried themselves ten feet in the ground. One minute later Halifax 'X' of No. 158 Squadron dived into a hill side at Sledmere Grange and disintegrated. So swift were the crashes that no one escaped to relate what had overtaken them.

Unaware that there was any danger, the crew of Halifax 'N' of No. 466 Squadron returned from Kamen to their base at Driffield where other aircraft were already landing. Flight Sergeant Hadlington, the wireless operator, had just received a coded message when the Halifax was attacked. He did not have time to decode the transmission (which would have read, 'Bandits') before tracers were seen flashing past the fuselage. Immediately all the airfield lights were switched off and Pilot Officer Schrank was forced to abandon his landing switching off his lights as he did so. The rear gunner, Flight Sergeant Kernaghan, had been dazzled by the glare of the tail light and had failed to see either the attacking aircraft or the tracer. As Schrank began to climb, there was time to take stock of the damage which had been inflicted on the Halifax. The rear fuselage had been badly damaged and several holes blown in its floor and sides, the hydraulics had been hit and the undercarriage dropped down, the compass, H2S and radio equipment had all failed. The only casualty was Sergeant Stewart, the mid-upper gunner, who had been injured in the leg by cannon shell splinters. But most seriously, a fire had been started in the rear fuselage. Flight Sergeant Tobin, the navigator, went with the flight engineer to tackle the blaze and found the rear gunner already there. The engine covers, which were carried should the aircraft land away from base, had caught fire and were burning fiercely. All seven fire extinguishers were used but to no great effect and the rear exit door had been buckled by the heat of the fire which prevented it from opening. Finally, Tobin used a fire axe to drag the covers to one of the holes blown into the floor by the cannon shells and pushed them out. The fuselage itself was now well alight however and all the extinguishers were empty. Three minutes after the first attack the fighter approached again but was spotted. Schrank threw his machine into a dive to starboard and escaped once more. By now there was an estimated ten minutes of fuel remaining and with full power, the Halifax was taken up to 6,000 feet where the crew baled out. All seven landed safely north of Waddington Airfield with little incident. Tobin landed in a five feet deep lake and waded ashore, whilst Hadlington landed in a paddock with three bulls but escaped unscathed. Before Schrank had baled out he put in 'George', the auto pilot and headed the Halifax east, to the coast. The aircraft flew on unmanned and eventually crashed at Friskney where it demolished a cottage.

Only now, at around 00.45 hours, was the intruder warning changed from 'purple' to 'red' and 'Scram' orders issued to the Halifaxes of No. 4 Group. Halifax 'E' of No. 76 Squadron was in the landing circuit of Holm Airfield when it was attacked and damaged. Although only six cannon shells hit the aircraft, one had exploded in the mid-upper turret, mortally wounding Flying Officer MacDougal. The pilot, Pilot Officer Oleynik, brought the damaged bomber down on to the runway at Carnaby, but the port tyre burst causing the Halifax to swerve into a stationary aircraft and a steam roller. Flying

E

Officer MacDougal succumbed to injuries and died in the airfield's sick bay later that day. A similar fate befell Halifax 'R' of No. 158 Squadron which was hit by 25 cannon shells. The aircraft was eventually landed safely at Lissett, its rear gunner, Sergeant Tait, having been wounded in the chest.

A particularly vigilant crew was that of Lancaster 'Q' of No. 1654 CU, who were carrying out bombing practice over the Bassingham ranges after participating in the 'Sweepstake' diversion. The crew, who had not yet flown an operational sortie, had seen an aircraft shot down (which was probably Pilot Officer Schrank's No. 466 Squadron machine) and were very much on the look-out for fighters. Whilst over the ranges at 00.45 hours, Sergeant Morgan, the rear gunner, spotted a Ju 88 150 yards away on the starboard quarter. The pilot, Flight Sergeant Pinkstone, put the Lancaster into a corkscrew manoeuvre and a burst of cannon fire went over the port wing. The persistent Ju 88 pilot followed the Lancaster into its dive. The rear gunner, Sergeant Morgan, returned the Ju 88's fire before the intruder broke off the attack. The Lancaster then headed west in accordance with the 'Scram' instructions, but five minutes later Sergeant Campbell in the mid-upper turret saw another Ju 88. Again Pinkstone evaded the fighter with another corkscrew and escaped damage. At 00.57 hours, over Worksop, the Lancaster was hit in the starboard inner engine. This time no one had seen their attacker. As Pinkstone put the Lancaster into another corkscrew it was raked by cannon fire from stem to stern and went out of control as Pinkstone ordered, 'Jump! Jump!'. All the crew, with the exception of the mid-upper gunner, who had been killed by cannon fire, abandoned the aircraft before it crashed. On the ground near Church Worsop, Police Sergeant Hancock saw three of the parachutes open as the blazing aircraft described a large arc until its fuel tanks exploded and the Lancaster fell to the ground.

Among the night fighter pilots who had already brought down aircraft was Oberleutnant Walter Briegleb, the Staffelkapitän of 7/NJG2. He had taken off from the airfield of Marx, near Wittmundhafen in a Ju 88G-6 with his usual crew. Unteroffizier Brant, the Bordfunker, Feldwebel Weilbaucher, the Bordwart (radar operator) and Unteroffizier Bräunlich, the Bordmechaniker. Although Walter Briegleb had already been credited with 23 victories over Europe, when he flew past the searchlight belt it was the first time that he had flown over England:

'We were all very tense and our nerves were on the edge, our minds filled with all the familiar dark thoughts. After a short time we saw something that was almost unbelievable – four engined bombers, flying with all their lights on – the dream of my life had come true!

Actually I felt almost sorry for the bomber crews who were obviously unaware of our presence and probably preparing to land. I could imagine the pilots as they made their approaches, the radio chatter with the ground, the navigators packing their maps, the rear gunners getting out of their cramped turrets to stretch their legs, all were probably happy to be home again. Then I thought of my hard working ground crew and of making my combat report after we had landed. Talking with other pilots of my Staffel, such as Heinz Koppe, with his twelve claims.

Meanwhile, I had taken my Ju 88 into the attack position for the Schrägen Musik. The Lancaster was about 150 metres above me. Now the moment to fire – pressure on the gun button – and nothing, just the sound of compressed air escaping! 'Arming switch on!' I screamed and pressed the gun button again – still nothing. Next I moved behind the Tommy, checked my course and speed and fired my four MG151 20mm cannon in the nose. The Lancaster immediately burst into flames and fell like a comet to earth.

Now I had little time to get away from the area as the combat had doubtless been seen from the ground. Then another aircraft appeared with its navigation lights on and at the same height as myself. As I got nearer to the aircraft its navigation lights went out and also those on the airfield, they knew that we were in the area. I could still see the shape of the aircraft straight ahead of me and began my attack. The bomber was weaving from side to side in a regular swing (right, left, up, right, down) over and over again. With great difficulty, I got into my firing position and followed. Probably they thought that they had lost me, as after ten minutes the Lancaster flew steadily on in straight and level flight. I flew straight towards him at the same height (about 400 metres) and dived 200 metres below, pulled up behind and fired. The Lancaster flew through my cannon fire and caught fire before it crashed to the ground. Many burning pieces paid testament to the effect of my attack. This was my 25th night victory in fourteen months and it was also my last.'

Walter Briegleb submitted two claims for aircraft destroyed. The first, at 00.36 hours, for a Lancaster south of Waddington and a second, at 00.56 hours, for another Lancaster west of Lincoln.

Hauptmann Kurt Fladrich, of III/NJG4, also submitted a claim for a Lancaster at about this time. The combat was reported as being at 00.33 hours, north-east of Cambridge. This was Fladrich's fifteenth and last claim.

Flying Officer 'Robbie' Roberts was the pilot of Halifax 'G' of No.

192 (Special Duties) Squadron and has cause to remember this night well.

'My crew and I were briefed to carry out a lone electronic intelligence mission which involved a patrol over the North Sea to search for possible navigational aids which were thought to be associated with the 'V' bombs and their guidance to targets in the UK. We had taken off at around 20.00 hours and on completion of the patrol, we headed back across the North Sea to our base at Foulsham.

When we arrived, flak was firing and I told the crew to keep a sharp look-out. The airfield lighting was on and after calling the tower for permission to land, I began to lose height down into the circuit, having been given the OK to 'Pancake'. My navigation lights were on as I selected wheels down to lose height as quickly as possible. At 2,000 feet I received a message that 'Bandits' were overhead and then all the lighting on the ground went out. I was told to turn right, so I selected wheels up and hit the switch to turn off the navigation lights as I turned away from the circuit.

At 1,200 feet an attack was made which appeared to come from below us, it looked like that from the tracer. The aircraft was hit and both inner engines were put out of action and the aircraft caught fire. The mid-upper gunner reported streams of flame ripping past as the wing tanks ignited. As the height was 1,200 feet, I thought that there would be a chance for some of the crew to escape by parachute and gave the order for an emergency parachute escape – provided that I could keep the aircraft under some sort of control. The special operator, Flying Officer Todd, made his escape in this way. The aircraft became more difficult to conrol and at 1,000 feet I ordered all the crew back to their normal crash positions and told them to sit tight as it was too low for them to attempt any further parachute escapes. We suffered a further attack and this resulted in the extremely messy death of the wireless operator, who was in his crash position on the step beside me and also the disintegration of the instrument panel. The cockpit began to fill with smoke and I saw both the navigator and the bomb aimer, who had gone forward prior to baling out, lying on the floor in the nose.

Beyond this point things are a bit hazy. I can remember grappling with the controls to try and maintain some sort of stability and heading for a field in which to make a crash landing. I can remember passing over some trees on the boundary of a field and pulling everything back into my lap in an endeavour to make a belly landing which apparently did come off.'

'Robbie' Roberts made a wheels up landing on a poultry farm in the village of Fulmodestone. The aircraft came to a rest not far from several houses and burst into flames. From its crew, Flying Officer

The crew of Flying Officer Roberts' Halifax. Back row, left to right – Sgt. Grapes (rear gunner), Sgt. Anderson (flight engineer), W/O. Clementson (wireless operator), Sgt. Sutcliffe (mid-upper gunner). Front row, Left to Right – F/Sgt. Holmes (bomb aimer), F/O. Roberts (pilot), F/O. Darlington (navigator). (Roberts).

The wreckage of Halifax LV255 at Fulmudston. (Roberts).

Todd had baled out safely but Sergeant Grapes, the rear gunner, was found dead with an unopened parachute. Either he had baled out when the aircraft had been too low or, as was suggested at the time, he had been hit by gun fire as he baled out. 'Robbie' Roberts and the mid-upper gunner, Sergeant Sutcliffe, were dragged from the burning wreckage by locals but suffered burns to their bodies and faces. 'Robbie' also had a crush fractured spine and remained unconscious for two weeks. The bodies of the remaining four crew were found later in the burnt out wreck of the Halifax.

In addition to the many operational aircraft in the air, still more were engaged on cross country navigational exercises. The crew of Lancaster 'J' of No. 460 Squadron were returning from a flight over France and were approaching their base at Binbrook. It was obvious that all was not well as the airfields were blacked out and a fire was seen burning on the ground. No intruder warning had been received, but even so the pilot, Flying Officer Warren, decided to fly west. Bursts of Anti-Aircraft fire were then seen in the vicinity and Warren left his aircraft's lights on until he was clear of the danger. No sooner had the westerly course been set then a burst of cannon fire rocked the aircraft. The flight engineer and wireless operator were killed instantly, the mid-upper gunner was wounded, the rear turret put out of action and the starboard inner engine set on fire. Despite the damage, the aircraft was still under control and Warren went into a corkscrew as he put out the lights. During the next few minutes tracers were seen on several occasions close to the aircraft but no more hits were made. The fire however had begun to take hold. Speed and height were now being lost and the surviving crew members were ordered to take up their crash stations. The only man capable of this was Flying Officer Cannon, the navigator, as the path of Flying Officer Kelly, the bomb aimer, was blocked by the body of the dead flight engineer. The Lancaster was brought into a good crash landing in a field at Barfield House, near Langworth, Lincolnshire and the crew scrambled out of the burning wreck. Flight Lieutenant Grinter, the mid-upper gunner, was still trapped in his turret and the rest of the crew began a race to free him before the fire spread to his position. The fuselage door however was jammed and an axe was searched for, but an iron bar sufficed to force it open. The gunner was brought out of the wreck with severe multiple injuries. Still the crew's ordeal was not over as a fighter made three strafing runs over the Lancaster, forcing them to fling themselves to the ground.

Two more Lancasters returning from navigation exercises were 'M' of No. 1654 HCU and 'F' from No. 1662 HCU which had two attacks made on it over Doncaster. Lancaster 'M' was attacked over Wigsley airfield when its starboard wing, inner engine and undercarriage were damaged. Its pilot, Flying Officer Mosby, dived his machine from 5,000 feet to 500 feet and lost his attacker, but his rear gunner, Warrant Officer Kann, baled out in the confusion. Kann later reported by telephone from Sutton-on-Trent whilst the damaged aircraft was landed some three hours later at High Ercall.

The bulk of the bombers were now returning from their targets and in the space of the next ten minutes, between 01.05 hours and 01.15 hours, nine more four engine bombers were brought down.

CHAPTER FOURTEEN

Ten minutes of destruction

At 01.05 hours, witnesses on the ground near Newark saw an aircraft catch fire in the air and dive into the ground with great force. A crash ambulance and a medical officer from RAF Winthorpe arrived at the scene of the crash near Stapleford Village. There was little to be seen, save for a twelve feet deep hole, small pieces of an aircraft scattered by the crash and the remains of three charred bodies. Later it was established that this was all that remained of Lancaster III LM748 'H' of No. 1654 CU and its seven crew.

Jack 'Ginger' Wilson had had an eventful career in the RAF as Flight Sergeant 1030488 Wilson J., a ginger haired, Geordie, flight engineer.

'I had already nearly completed a tour of operations in No. 4 Group with No. 51 Squadron at RAF Snaith under 'Big Larry Ling', a massive Wing Commander who always carried a riding whip. He had me Court Martialed for striking the Station Warrant Officer at Snaith. I was reduced to the rank of Leading Aircraftsman and sentenced to eighty-four days in the 'glass house'. On release, I went back to my ground trade as an engine fitter and served with No. 102 Squadron at Pocklington under Air Commodore Gus Walker.

On November 11th 1944, I returned to the rank of Flight Sergeant and was posted to No. 6 (Canadian) Group. After weeks of hanging around at RCAF Walton and Topcliffe, I was posted to RCAF Dishforth where I met my crew.'

'Ginger Wilson's new crew were all Canadians and were flying Halifax 'R' of No. 1664 HCU.

'I had barely got to know my crew before the incident happened. I remember the pilot was a ginger haired Flying Officer by the name of John Maunders, from St. John's Newfoundland. The navigator was Flying Officer Cruikshank and the bomb aimer was a ginger haired Sergeant from Montreal. The wireless operator was Sergeant Pete something and I, as the flight engineer, was the only member of the crew with any operational experience.

We had called up base and I was acting as co-pilot. Suddenly, after we had made all preparations for landing at Dishforth, all hell let loose. Blue sparks and smoked filled the cockpit, the accumulators behind the engineer's panel flew through the roof, the intercom went dead. Flying Officer Maunders was struggling to keep control and yelling "Get out!''.

I saw the front hatch open beneath my feet and someone leaving, so I clipped on my 'chute and followed suit.

God! It was like jumping into a frozen lake. I pulled my rip cord and seemed to rise towards the propeller blades, then descended. I saw another Halifax pass by in a mass of flames, crash and then explode.

Then I saw what I think was a Junkers 88, all guns firing, whether at me I'm not sure. I could not see the parachutes of the other crew members who left the aircraft and wondered why there were no other 'chutes. The Junkers 88 returned, firing madly, which distracted me from my approach to the ground. I hit the deck with a wallop and as I did so an aircraft circled around in flames and exploded a few fields away. I naturally thought that it was our aircraft.

I managed to unclip my 'chute, but could not rise from the ground. I must have injured my back. My 'chute floated away. Suddenly a figure loomed over me with what I thought was a game keeper's gun. 'Get up, you German So and So', he demanded. 'German be blowed, I'm a Geordie', I replied. 'You're not, are you?' He went on, 'are you hurt?. 'Yes, I think I have hurt my back,' I said, at which he went off to a nearby farm house having told me to stay where I was. He returned with a woman in a nightdress covered by an overcoat and carrying a trestle type table top. They gently got me on to this and carried me to the house. Then an RAF medical officer and orderlies came on the scene and I was put in a blood wagon and driven off. Suddenly the ambulance braked and I was carried out and placed at the side of the road with the medical officer lying over me to protect me. 'What's up, Sir?' I enquired. 'You'll see,' he retorted as a Junkers 88 flew along the the roadway firing on the ambulance. This happened three times before we eventually took refuge in an oxygen depot, staffed entirely by WAAFs who gave us a cup of tea. We remained there until the all clear sounded.

Eventually I arrived at Dishforth where, the following morning, I was told by a medical officer that my spine was broken. Later the navigator and mid-upper gunner came to see me and related what had happened after I had left the aircraft. The wireless operator had been hit and was in hospital with bad shrapnel wounds in his back. The men I had seen baling out were the bomb aimer, who broke a toe on landing and the wireless operator who had been wounded in his left arm. The skipper did not come to see me as he felt responsible for us baling out unnecessarily. It seems that after we had baled out, he made a heroic effort to regain control of the aircraft and landed it about ten minutes later with the remaining four members. I believe that he was to be recommended for a DFC but refused to fly again and returned home under a cloud.'

137

The aircraft that 'Ginger' Wilson had seen crashing nearby was a fellow No. 1664 HCU machine, ZU-S, that had been following his aircraft on the approach to Dishforth. Mr Scaife, who operated the railway level crossing at Burton Grange, saw two burst of cannon fire set fire to the aircraft which stalled, rolled on to its back and exploded as it hit the ground.

Leutnant Arnold Döring of IV/NJG3 had left the airfield of Jever and had flown over the North Sea to Scarborough in his Ju 88G-6. After flying to and fro for some time, an illuminated airfield was spotted which flashed the morse code letters 'DH', the code for Dishforth. Forty years later Arnold Döring can still recall his experiences:

'As we flew over the airfield we saw a flashing red light, which we took to be the night fighter warning signal, yet still there was a bomber pilot carelessly flying with his navigation lights on. It was a stupid and tremendously pig-headed thing to do, as only a bomber pilot could. I know, for I had been a bomber pilot and had made over 350 flights over Russia. This machine was now not far from becoming a burning heap on the ground. I had caught him during his approach to the Drem landing system, and as the Tommy sank lower, I quickly closed in to attack with my Schrägen Musik cannon. The airfield was very active and many aircraft were flying around with their lights on. I sat about fifty metres beneath the Tommy and fired a long burst into the fuselage, cockpit, two motors and the fuel tanks in the right wing. The aircraft caught fire and crashed near the airfield, then all the lights went out. Walter Hoyer, my Bordfunker noted the time as 01.05 hours.

Then I caught another four engined bomber and fired my Schrägen Musik into its left wing, between the engines where the main fuel tanks were. After about fifteen rounds the aircraft caught fire, flew on for one or two minutes and then slid on to its right wing. At about 01.15 hours there was a big explosion and the wreckage burnt on the ground below me. I could not see any parachutes in the light of the half moon.

The other Tommies then put their lights out but my Bordmechaniker, Paul Unger, saw a target with its lights still on and I made a head-on attack. The bomber came towards me quickly, then a hundred things happened at once before I could fire. This was stupid of me. I pulled up and by a hair's breadth the Tommy passed below. For an instant I had been a little out in my reckoning, the Tommy put out his lights and disappeared into the darkness.

My fuel supply was getting low and I decided to start the flight back. I was still over the airfield flashing 'DH' and had eighty kilometres to go to reach the coast. We were not expected to return home with any ammunition left in our nose guns and we were free to attack any targets, on the ground or in the air. The Tommies did this in the day, shooting at vehicles, trains and men in fields, villages and towns. Now we would fight back and repay like for like. A light briefly illuminated a train travelling north, a long burst of my fire set fire to a wagon and the train let out a lot of steam as I shot it full of holes. I fired the last of my ammunition into the streets of the harbour town of Scarborough, jumped over the coast and out to sea. A searchlight illuminated a barrage balloon which we were able to fly over, thanks to the Lord, and we went down to only a few metres above the sea and headed for home.'

Despite the combats which had taken place near Driffield there was still considerable activity. Halifax 'C' of No. 466 Squadron was one of the aircraft attempting to land there. Flying Officer Shelton, its pilot, had overshot when refused permission to land but had gone around again and was given permission. When at just 150 feet, all the airfield lights went out and he was told to go on a dog-leg. As the Halifax headed towards Pocklington, Sergeant Welsh, the flight engineer, reported that there was only fifteen minutes fuel remaining so Shelton began a climb to 4,000 feet which would give them a chance to bale out, should the need arise. Flight Sergeant Johnson, the bomb aimer, was in the nose position when he saw a fighter approaching from port. The mid-upper gunner swung his guns in that general direction only to see the two port engines burst into flame in front of him. The port side of the fuselage, foreward of the rear exit, caught fire and the navigator, sitting at his table, saw a strike on the fuselage just above it. The aircraft quickly went into a dive to port and Shelton gave the order to bale out. The mid-upper gunner dived out of the rear exit, followed by the navigator who passed Sergeant Welsh who was hesitating at the door way. Flight Sergeant Bullen, in the rear turret, opened the doors but as he made his way out his size ten right boot jammed under his seat. With the aircraft in a steep dive and flames lapping around the turret he pulled his foot out of the boot and left. Pulling the parachute release quickly he landed heavily and knocked himself out. Sergeant Welsh was the last man to leave the aircraft but he had hesitated at the hatch too long and hit the ground before his parachute had time to open.

Flying Officer Shelton's Halifax crashed near Elvington, the base for the French No. 347 Squadron. Halifax 'O' of No. 347 Squadron flown by Squadron Leader Terrien, neared Elvington as Shelton's aircraft was shot down and its crew saw it go down in flames. They had already evaded one fighter attack and all the crew were maintaining a

139

Above: The crash of Halifax NR235 'O' of No. 347 Squadron at Sutton-on-Derwent.

Below: Remains of Halifax NR235 'O' of No. 347 Squadron at Sutton-on-Derwent.

Below: Remains of Halifax PN437 'X' of No. 158 Squadron at Sledmere Grange, near Driffield.

140

particularly good look out. Despite their alertness and the clear moonlit night, no one saw the fighter which set fire to their starboard wing. Both engines soon became engulfed in flames but Squadron Leader Terrien held the Halifax level as the crew made their escapes. Four of the crew had already made good their escapes by the time Adjutant Puthier, the flight engineer, secured one of the hooks of the pilot's parachute to Terrien and left the aircraft. Sergeant Dunand, the rear gunner, was the last to leave the Halifax which was now in a steep dive. Only the pilot was still in the aircraft when it crashed and all six survivors stated in their reports that they were convinced that his actions in holding the Halifax level for so long saved their lives.

Terrien's entire crew were on their 28th mission but their fellow squadron crew, in Halifax 'H', were returning from their first. They had successfully reached Kamen but the fuselage bomb doors had failed to open and it was not until twenty minutes later that they discovered that the entire fuselage load was still in place. The fault, it seemed, had been caused by flak damage on the bomb run. The bomber was by now over France and a return to the bomb jettisoning area in the Wash was decided upon. Here, in an operation which lasted twenty minutes, the load was released by hand. The 'Bandit' warning had been received and as fuel was running low, the pilot made for the diversion airfield of Long Marston. All the crew were at their action stations but they were surprised by an attack from below which damaged the Halifax's nose slightly. Captain Laucou, the pilot, put the bomber into a corkscrew and executed other evasive actions for two or three minutes, by the end of which they had succeeded in losing their attacker. A few minutes later they were attacked again and once more escaped. Then a third attack was made, but this time the Halifax was hit badly. The starboard inner engine caught fire and the engine covers in the rear fuselage were set ablaze. Laucou and the flight engineer, Sergeant Le Masson, held the bomber steady as five of the crew baled out, but seconds after the last men left, the aircraft crashed and its fuel tanks exploded.

Mrs Nelson, wife of the Station Commander at RAF Blyton, was outside when she saw a fire overhead. There were two explosions as the aircraft began to disintegrate in the air and a third as it hit the ground. When the station's crash crew appeared at the site they found the remains of a No. 12 Squadron Lancaster scattered over the ground and among the wreckage, the bodies of its seven crew. They were later identified as Flying Officer Thomas and crew who were overdue from a cross country navigation exercise.

Not far from its base of Woolfox Lodge, Lancaster 'K' of No. 1651 CU crashed and burst into flames. Its crew had been over base when both the port engines had been set on fire. They had been at 4,000 feet, but none of the crew had baled out before the aircraft crashed. Miraculously the rear gunner, Sergeant Thompson, found himself half out of his turret, trapped by his foot. Although burnt, he undid his boot and scrambled out of the wreckage, but the six others were dead.

By about 01.05 hours, all but sixty of No. 5 Group's Lancasters had landed and these did not escape the attentions of the intruders. Leutnant Gunther Wolf had left Wittmundhafen in Ju 88G-6 C9 + CT of 9/NJG5 at 23.21 hours and had arrived safely over the Wash after his low level North Sea crossing.

'In my crew I had Hein Schmitz, my Bordfunker, Jupp Horosiewicz, my Bordschutze and a man whose name I can't remember, stood in for Hein Kay who was grounded. Flying over the English coast was an experience. All along the Wash and the Humber were searchlights, some swinging wildly, others standing in vertical beams marking all sorts of lanes. As we passed these lights one held us momentarily and was so bright that we could have read by it, but we left it behind. After a short time I saw the blue exhaust flames of a Lancaster ahead of me. It seemed to be in its landing circuit on approach to an airfield. I put my undercarriage down to reduce my speed and manoeuvred towards my target. I followed the Lancaster and slowly came into position, with the landing light of the bomber above me. The shells of my Schrägen Musik set fire to the fuel tanks near the right motors. I saw the rear gunner firing wildly – they obviously had not been expecting night fighters. The fire in the wing spread to the fuselage and started an even bigger fire. The Lancaster then went into a steep right hand turn and dropped to the ground.'

Mr Smith, a worker on the Earl of Yarborough's Brocklesby Estate, near Grimsby, heard the sound of aircraft engines and gun fire over his house and ran outside. He was just in time to see a Lancaster on approach to RAF Kirmington, fall in a mass of flames and explode in the woods of the estate. Workers quickly reached the place where the bomber had exploded but there were no survivors to be found amongst the splintered trees and scattered wreckage. Eventually RAF personnel identified the aircraft as Lancaster III ME442 of No. 44 Squadrron, which had been attempting to land on its return from Ladbergen. Flying Officer Ryan and his crew were, as the estate workers suspected, all killed.

In the space of ten minutes (assuming the report times are of reasonable accuracy) nine four engined bombers had been destroyed when moments from safety. Yet still the Luftwaffe's intruders were roaming the skies over eastern England.

CHAPTER FIFTEEN

A long night ends

By 01.30 hours, the intruders had been operating for an hour-an-a-half. Most of the returning bombers had landed, but 'Gisela' was far from over.

Staff in the control tower at West Raynham saw another of No. 5 Group's Lancasters, with its navigation lights still on, flying over their airfield at 800 feet. The lights suddenly went out and the colours of the day were fired into the air. Then four streams of cannon fire were seen to have been fired from immediately behind. The aircraft nosed towards the ground and disintegrated in a field north of East Raynham railway station. All the crew were found dead in the wreckage of Lancaster 'H' of No. 189 Squadron.

At 01.35 hours, Lancaster 'F' of No. 1651 HCU was shot down over Cottesmore airfield and crashed vertically into a field only 450 yards from the control tower, killing its entire crew. Not a piece larger than four feet by six feet was found.

Pilot Officer Bertenshaw had been flying in the midst of the intruder activity for over an hour in Halifax 'R' of No. 76 Squadron. He and his crew had returned from Kamen to their base of Holme but their approach had been baulked and as they went round again, instructions to dog-leg were issued. As the Halifax flew on over the Wash, combats were seen all around them but eventually flying control called their aircraft and Bertenshaw made for Holme again. Despite their vigilance, none of the crew saw the attacking fighter whose cannon shells exploded in the starboard wing, blowing two large holes between the engines and causing a fire. The bomber began a spiral dive towards the damaged wing. Bertenshaw and Flight Sergeant French between them managed to control this, levelling off the aircraft just above the tree tops. The starboard outer engine began to fail and the flames grew around the two gaping holes in the wing. A crash landing, Bertenshaw decided, would be too dangerous so he climbed, using maximum power from the inner engines, to 600 feet when the abandon aircraft order was given. The pilot continued to climb as the crew made good their escapes and levelled out at 800 feet but then the starboard wing tanks exploded. With the whole of the wing's upper surface ablaze, the bomber dived to starboard, but as the pilot attempted to pull it out of the dive, the aileron control snapped.

Bertenshaw now had to get out.

With difficulty, the pilot pulled the pin from his Sutton harness (which now had the parachute resting on top) and broke the oxygen and intercom leads to his helmet. He then jumped out of the front hatch, but the slipstream momentarily held his legs to the underside of the fuselage. Although he pulled his 'D' ring release quickly his parachute barely had time to open before he landed on the edge of a ditch, fell backwards and sprained his ankle.

Mr Scaife, the level crossing keeper, who had been watching the activity over Dishforth, had already seen one aircraft go down and now saw another crash some distance away. This was another Halifax, 'V' of No. 10 Squadron, which had been attempting for some time to land on return from Kamen. Flight Lieutenant Laffoley and five of his usual crew were on their 33rd mission, whilst the navigator, Flight Sergeant Hamilton, was on his twentieth and the last trip of his second tour. Pilot Officer Palmer, acting as second pilot, was on his very first sortie. This experienced crew had returned to their base at Melbourne at 00.30 hours, but the pilot twice overshot the runway. On the third attempt to land, the 'Bandit' warning was received and the landing was aborted. Flying control then told the crew to divert for twenty minutes, but on their return they found the airfield's lights out and they were told to divert to Dishforth. When they arrived however, its lights too had been extinguished and the wireless operator was unable to raise flying control. Once more the pilot began another diversion but a Ju 88 attacked. The attack came from below and set the Halifax's wing on fire. Despite attempts to extinguish the flames with the Graviner extinguisher system, the fire took hold and Flight Lieutenant Laffoley ordered his crew to bale out. The navigator, Flight Sergeant Hamilton, found the mid-upper gunner struggling to open the rear hatch. Hamilton forced his way out and dived headlong from the aircraft, followed by the gunner. Whilst these two were still in the air they saw the Halifax, its wing wreathed in flames, dive steeply to starboard and crash with the remaining five men on board.

The intruder attack had, without doubt, taken the much reduced defences by surprise. The 'Trigger' and 'Diver' measures proved totally useless and even the intruder warning system and pre-arranged diversion plans had not been completely successful. Nos. 125 and 68 Squadrons scrambled Mosquitoes on anti-intruder sorties. From No. 125 Squadron, Squadron Leader White had four contacts. The first two were Mosquitoes and a third was lost. A fourth contact was being chased into cloud when a constant speed unit from one of the

Mosquito's propellers failed and Squadron Leader White was forced to return to base. Warrant Officer Griffiths, also from No. 125 Squadron, had better luck. When on patrol off the Suffolk coast, he was vectored on to his 'Bogey' which was gradually losing height and was finally sighted 700 feet above the sea. Griffiths fired three short bursts from 900 feet which caused smoke to issue from both of the target's engines. The aircraft peeled off to starboard and went down vertically as Griffiths followed, giving one final burst and watching the enemy crash into the sea some forty miles off the Suffolk coast. Later, two more aircraft were chased out to sea, but were lost before contact was made.

Flight Lieutenant Wills in a No. 68 Squadron Mosquito met another enemy aircraft out to sea off Cromer and closed to minimum range on what he identified, by its tapered wings, as a Ju 88. A burst of one or two seconds produced a violent explosion from the target's starboard engine and wing root and it fell into the sea, burning furiously.

The aircraft brought down by Griffiths and Wills are assumed to have been Ju 88G-6s, but as no trace was ever found of airframe or crew, their identitites will remain unknown.

Squadron Leader Woodman DSO DFC was also involved.

'That night I had returned from supporting the bombers of Ladbergen and the Ruhr. I was senior experimental test pilot at the Bomber Support Development Unit, Swanton Morley, Norfolk. My aircraft was a No. 100 Group night fighter, Mosquito MM684, fitted with radar plus other secret electronic devices such as ASH, Centimetric Homer and Perfectos. My radar observer was Squadron Leader Gledhill.

We were warned that German intruders were operating, landed and after de-briefing I had my night flying supper and went off to bed. I was awakened shortly afterwards by Flight Lieutenant Carpenter, another radar specialist, saying that Group wanted me to get airborne in my aircraft again as my radar devices might pick up the German intruders which were still around.

I put on my flying suit over my pyjamas, drove down to the aircraft which had been refuelled and was serviceable. Carpenter came with me. With the airfield blacked out, I took off straight across the grass out of the parking bay. I did not bargain for the USAAF Liberator base some four miles away. I was climbing away at some 2,000 feet when all hell let loose. They threw everything at me. By that time they had manned their aircrafts' guns and, as they fired day tracers, it was a brilliant display but nothing hit me.

146

I stayed up until all the intruders were gone but got no contact on them with any of the electronic devices and so had no joy.'

Although during the initial phase of the attack none of the intruders came to grief, three crashed in quick succession whilst making low level attacks.

Oberfeldwebel Leo Zimmermann and his three-man crew from 5/NJG4 chose to attack an American Air Transport Command B-24 as it came in to land at Metfield, Norfolk. Zimmerman who had been promoted to the rank of Oberfeldwebel on March 1st, flew under the B-24 which was at less than 300 feet in an attempt to use his Schrägen Musik upward firing cannon. The B-24 crew spotted their attacker however, and the pilot began evasive manoeuvres during which he saw the Ju 88 turn steeply and slip towards the ground only a few feet below. A wing tip struck the ground and the Ju 88 cart-wheeled across several fields, disintegrating as it went and killing its four crew instantly. Some eyewitnesses have suggested that a Beaufighter was responsible but no claim was submitted.

Eight minutes after this crash, at 01.45 hours, Observer Mr J P Kelway of the Royal Observer Corps was driving his car along a road near the village of Welton, two-and-a-half miles east of Scampton Airfield. Although the car's lights were blacked out according to regulations, there was just enough light for them to be seen by Feldwebel Heinrich Conze and his crew. Doubtless they were looking for ground targets to attack as they had been briefed and as they had done recently in Liberated Europe. As Conze streaked low over the ground towards Kelway's car, the Ju 88 struck telegraph wires and poles which threw the fighter out of control and into the car. The Ju 88 crashed into Kelway's car and scattered the wreckage of both over a wide area. Kelway and the four crew of the Ju 88 were all killed. Later the markings C9 + RR were found to identify the aircraft as belonging to 7/NJG5 and in confirmation a camp cinema ticket was found in the clothing of one of the bodies which was stamped III/NJG5.

Over Pocklington, a Ju 88 attacked a Halifax which was coming in to land. Then the intruder dived low over the airfield in a strafing run. It was then seen to open fire on a taxi travelling with its headlights on along a road which ran parallel to one of Elvington's runways. As the Ju 88 came lower, its starboard wing clipped a tree and it careered on through another line of trees before it broke up on the ground. So badly were the bodies in the cockpit mutilated that only two could be identified. They were the Bordfunker, Feldwebel Gustav Schmitz, aged 24 and Feldwebel Hugo Böker, aged 28. There was also the body

The Ju 88G-6 of 5/NJG4 which crashed at Linstead Parva, near Metfield, after attacking a B-24.

Hauptman Johann Dreher, Staffelkapitän of 13/NJG3, who crashed near Elvington.

All that was left of Feldwebel Conze's Ju 88G-6 which crashed at Welton, showing the massive destruction left by the impact.

of another Feldwebel and a fourth, whose name and rank could not be found. Although not appreciated at the time, the unidentifiable body was that of Hauptmann Johann Dreher. Dreher, who had been born in München in 1920, achieved fame as a bomber pilot by making over 400 flights and becoming the Staffelkapitän of 5/KG53 in Russia. In recognition of his efforts he was awarded the Ritterkreuz on April 5th 1944. He then requested a move to night fighters and flew with 13/NJG3. He had made only two claims before he crashed.

By 02.00 hours there were few remaining aircraft in the air for the later intruders to hunt. Feldwebel Günter Schmidt, of 12/NJG3 flying a JU 88G-6, crossed the English coast at 01.50 hours and began to search for a target. On his return he was able to file the following report:

Schmidt, Günter, Feldwebel.
12/NJG3.   Base, 4th March 1945

Engagement Report

Referring to the shooting down of a four-engined aircraft on March 4th of 1945 at 02.11 hours over an airfield 10 km south of Darlington.

'On 3rd March 1945, I took off with a Ju 88G-6 at 23.42 hours despatched to perform long distance night fighting over the British mainland. Landfall over the British coast was made 01.50 hours.

At 02.00 hours the Bordfunker, when spotting some Verey pistol shooting, saw an aircraft overhead, which shortly after was identified by the entire crew as a four-engined one with a twin tail fin. My altitude was 200 metres, that of the enemy aircraft about 800–1,000 metres. I managed to approach from below and let the first burst go from about 150–50 metres at 02.05 hours, the enemy aircraft proceeding against the landing direction within the traffic pattern (Drem circuit) altitude 500 metres. Hits were observed in the port wing and some debris was also lost. The aircraft turned to the left. The second attack was started some distance from astern. Hits in the rear turret and fuselage. Small fire in the fuselage with dark red flames. Third attack from the rear, also from a distance of about 150–50 metres. Again hits in the port wing and fuselage. Almost immediately it crashed and exploded north of the airfield, within the traffic circuit. I was in a position to watch the enemy aircraft until it crashed. There was no defence. The airfield where the combat occurred was located roughly 10 km south of the city of Darlington and had, along the west side of its Drem system, the identification letters 'CR' formed by white lamps.'

Gunter Schmidt

The details observed by Schmidt and his crew leave no doubt as to their victim's identity. The all French crew of Captain Notelle, flying Halifax 'D' of No. 346 Squadron, had completed a normal trip to Kamen, their twenty-seventh sortie and had returned to their base of Elvington. By this time, two Halifaxes had already been brought down near the airfield and all aircraft were being sent to diversion airfields or, if low on fuel, to Croft. Notelle set course for Long Marston but shortly after received another signal which read: 'Proceed to diversion airfield, A/C 49 land at 327'.

'327' as Sergeant Santoni, the wireless operator, knew referred to Croft but no one had any idea what 'A/C 49' meant. Notelle changed course for Croft. As the Halifax neared the airfield Schmidt made his attack and set a wing on fire. Sergeant Malia, the rear gunner, attempted to return his fire but the Halifax was already crippled and at only 900 feet, Notelle decided to attempt a forced landing. As the crew went to their crash positions, Schmidt made another attack. Fortunately, the ground below as visible in the moonlight, but the aircraft flew into a slight rise in the ground at ninety miles-per-hour after first slicing through a copse of small saplings. The aircraft caught fire as the crew scrambled out, carrying their unconscious pilot with them and watched the fire consume the Halifax. Only later was it found that 'A/C 49' was an error and should have read 'aircraft low on fuel'.

By 02.15 hours, Operation Gisela was almost over. Only one more aircraft, Lancaster 'Z' of No. 1666 HCU, was attacked but its pilot evaded his attacker and escaped damage. The final RAF loss was an accident. Mosquito XX NT357 of No. 68 Squadron was being flown by Flying Officer Aust and Flying Officer Halestrap on an anti-intruder sortie but they returned after an uneventful patrol. Over Coltishall, an engine failed and the undercarriage refused to come down. Aust attempted to fly a circuit of the airfield but the Mosquito crashed and exploded in flames.

The night had brought tragedy for many, yet still others had lucky escapes.

Sergeant Neale was the wireless operator on a No. 640 Squadron Halifax returning from Kamen.

'We crossed the coast in the early hours and were somewhat pleased that luck was on our side, but very fatigued. Everyone was extremely happy that things had gone well. We reached our airfield of Leconfield and having flown down wind turned to port 180 degrees and got the OK to funnel. We were about fifty feet from touch down when flying control gave the 'Bandit' warning. All transmissions ceased and the

Neal and crew of No. 640 Squadron.

landing lights on the airfield were immediately switched off. Our skipper, Flight Lieutenant Van Whiet, made an instant decision to land but kept the engines at full power and raced to the end of the runway, turned as quickly as he could and went into the first available dispersal. We immediately left the aircraft and laid our weary bodies down in the tall grass. Within seconds a Ju 88 attacked the airfield, making straight for us. I lifted my head just after the Ju 88, with all its guns blazing, passed the control tower and flashed by about twenty feet above the ground and fifty yards from us. The Ju 88 then turned to port and disappeared in search of easier prey. Later we collected our flight documents from the aircraft and went to de-briefing where we were met, as always, by the Station Padre. The Commanding Officer, Group Captain Waterhouse, warned us that we should not mention the attack to anyone while we went on our well earned seven days leave.'

Flight Lieutenant Brian Davies of No. 10 Squadron.

'We were returning from our twenty-sixth operation, in Halifax III ZA-J and were perplexed by the number of Verey cartridges being shot over the coast. We decided that we too would join in the display and fired the colours of the day, for no other reason than that we had never done it before. The 'creep back' effect was taking place and Verey signals were being fired well out to sea.

We crossed the coast and turned north towards base at Melbourne, near York. En route the pilot relaxed the hitherto strict no smoking rule as his need was greater than the rest of the crew. We reached base just in time to see the airfield lighting switched off and to receive the 'Bandit' warning. Our diversion drill sent us to Blackpool for as long as our fuel would allow and we returned to base to find it still blacked out. We were ordered to Leeming, which was fully lit and receiving aircraft, and landed safely. Taxiing was done under instructions from airfield control and it seemed a very long way to go. The taxi track skirted what seemed to be a grass area, beyond which were a group of buildings. As we approached these, a twin engined aircraft made a low pass in front of us. It pumped cannon shells into the grass with a sound like a slow running diesel engine and the shells cut across the taxi track. We stopped and switched off our lights which, in the bright moonlight, was a futile gesture.

A WAAF driver came from the opposite direction and as soon as we were parked, she drove us to debriefing. We were delivered to the watch office and left our kit outside the main entrance while our pilot went inside, looking for the usual crowded de-briefing room. He found nothing except for an officer crouching in the knee-hole of his desk. Nervous reaction from the trip and admiration for the unknown girl who had fetched us from the dispersal proved too much and the poor chap under the desk received a vocal blasting. Towards the end of this, realisation dawned that the man's rank was unknown and, having relieved his feelings, our pilot fled down the stairs to mingle with the rest of us to avoid his possible identification!'

In the two-and-a-half hours that the attack had lasted, thirteen Halifaxes, nine Lancasters, a Fortress and a Mosquito had been shot down. In excess of twenty other aircraft had been attacked but had escaped with varying degrees of damage. During the bombing and strafing of ground targets, seventeen civilians had been killed and twelve seriously injured.

As the last of the bombers were landing, the first of the intruders were returning to Europe to locate their bases where a new danger confronted them. The weather front, under which they had flown on the outward journey, had moved eastward and now covered much of western Europe.

Oberleutnant Walter Briegleb was the first of his Gruppe to return.

'When at last we crossed the Dutch coast we could relax a little. We recognised the landmarks around us but the weather had unexpectedly deteriorated. We had to pull ourselves together and concentrate and I had to stay alert. After four hours in the air we found our good old home of Marx again and landed safely, to be greeted by the ground crew who had been waiting for us to return.'

Leutnant Gunther Wolf of 9/NJG5 returned later.

'As I flew back across the North Sea the tension began to lift – it was over. The events, the combat, the tracers, the searchlights and balloons, the whole episode seemed to have lasted just a minute. Then we flew into the thick syrup like cloud, where on the 1:100,000 map would it end? For an hour we flew on and eventually decided that we had drifted to the north of our intended track. From the Humber Estuary we had set an exact course, but what had the wind done? When our calculations indicated that we must be near the coast, the Bordfunker tried to get a QDM from Wittmundhafen but all his attempts failed, anything he got was unintelligable. Now we began to doubt our navigation, was that Borkum below us? Could we possibly have flown that far?

As if in a dream a bright light shone below us, now we would know where we were. The crew began to search the documents to look up this beacon, they searched long, very long and hard and eventually, with doubt in their voices said, 'that is Leewarden'. If that was so then we were a good 120 km from our estimated position. We called Leewarden and confirmed our position, a glance at the fuel gauges showed that we could still reach Wittmundhafen and I set course east-north-east. The weather meanwhile had become even worse. The cloud base was 300 metres and it was raining, but I could just see to land and touched down at 02.56 hours.

I made my report on the operation and learned that many crews had still not returned. Perhaps they had landed at other bases? One crew had flown over the coast and crashed into the ground, another crew reported that they had baled out after running out of fuel west of Berlin! What had happened? The wind had changed direction sharply and

153

A Halifax of No. 347 Squadron at Elvington.

All that was left of Halifax HX322 'V' of No. 10 Squadron after coming down near Knaresborough.

Left: Leutnant Arnold Döring of 10/NJG3.

154

was three times as strong as forecast. No wonder we crossed the coast in Holland and not East Friesland. The rain and cloud did the rest.'

Leutnant Arnold Döring of 10/NJG3 had flown for nearly two hours towards his base at Jever before he entered the cloud.

'The cloud hung only a few metres above the sea and the British had jammed our radio beacons so that we could not get a fix on them. Only the dark earth under me told us that we had crossed the Dutch coast, but I could not orientate myself. Water and then land continued to pass beneath us and we tried to get a fix but all the beacons were being jammed. Eventually, after flying below the cloud, we found an airfield which we thought was Jever as it had about twenty-five aircraft on it. Only after we landed did we discover that we were at Nordholz, the World War 1 Zeppelin base. Thank God, we were on the ground again and in one piece.

We were waved in with torches and I stopped the motors after a five-and-a-half hour flight. I telephoned the Division from the control tower, to inform them of my twentieth and twenty-first claims and was told that I had been awarded the Ritterkreuz. The Division wanted to know everything – weather, flight plans, places we had been in England, times and defences. We got our breakfast and went to bed, but the telephone kept ringing. First it was the Gruppe, then the Geschwader, then it was the Division again and then the Jagdkorps, they all wanted to know. I got no sleep, I was furious. Why hadn't these idiots flown themselves? Then they would have known!

The following morning I had 500 litres of fuel put in the tanks and we flew to Jever where we got a great reception. Our 10th Staffel reported five combats, the Staffelkapitän two, Feldwebel Misch one and I had had two. The crew of Unteroffizier Lohse was missing. Unteroffizer Kowalski crashed in bad weather and was killed. The Gruppen Kommandeur, Major Ney, had been forced to bale out and he had broken his back when he landed. The Staffelkapitän of the 13th Staffel was also missing, he was Hauptmann Dreher.'

The return from the operation showed that it had been a major blow to the Luftwaffe's night fighter force. Although perhaps only five aircraft had been lost in combat over England, eight crews were missing, three had crashed and had been killed, six crews had baled out when lost or short of fuel and eleven aircraft had crashed or had been damaged on landing.

Claims as originally submitted for Operation Gisela

Hptm. Raht	I/NJG2	Two aircraft.
Hptm. Hissbach	II/NJG2	Two aircraft

Oblt. Brinkhaus	II/NJG2	One twin engined aircraft.
Fw. Koppe	III/NJG2	A Lancaster.
Oblt. Briegleb	III/NJG2	A Lancaster, south of Waddington – 00.36 hrs.
Oblt. Briegleb	III/NJG2	A Lancaster, west of Lincoln – 00.56 hrs.
Oblt. Foerster	IV/NJG3	Two four engined aircraft.
Ofw. Misch	IV/NJG3	A four engined aircraft.
Lt. Döring	IV/NJG3	A B-17.
Lt. Döring	IV/NJG3	A Lancaster.
Fw. Schmidt	IV/NJG3	A four engined aircraft near Croft – 02.14 hrs.
Hptm. Fladrich	III/NJG4	A Lancaster, north-east of Cambridge – 00.33 hrs.
Lt. Wolf	III/NJG5	A Lancaster, near the Humber Estuary – 01.08 hrs.

As the number of aircraft brought down in this operation is greater than the number of claims submitted, it seems reasonable to assume that the remainder were brought down by some of the crews who failed to return.

CHAPTER SIXTEEN

The last intruders. March 1945.

By March 1945, very few German aircraft ventured over Britain, but there were still attacks. These came in the form of V-1 (flying bombs) and V-2 rockets, indeed in the week prior to 'Operation Gisela' 79 missiles had exploded, which killed 198 people, injured 501 and 84 were listed as 'missing, presumed killed'.

The night following 'Operation Gisela', March 4th–5th, ten intruders returned to East Anglia and Lincolnshire but found no targets. Only three incidents were reported and one person was seriously injured. Several bombs were dropped and a number of places were machine-gunned, but only a limited number of Allied aircraft were operating. Some Bomber Command Mosquitoes attacked Berlin and other aircraft were minelaying but none were attacked by the intruders.

One of the few night fighter crews to fly over Britain after 'Operation Gisela' was that of Feldwebel Rudi Morenz, from IV/NJG2. His crew had taken off on 'Operation Gisela' but had been forced to return after one engine had failed because of falling oil pressure. On their second sortie (probably on March 4th–5th) they located the airfield at Pocklington. Morenz's Bordfunker, Otto Dombrowsky, takes up their story:

'After our flight across the North Sea, we soon found the airfield beacon of Pocklington and spotted a Halifax flying towards it. We were certain that we had caught him, there were no fighters and the crew were fully occupied in landing. Then the airfield flak started firing at us. We did a steep turn away from the airfield and began to look for another target. We found one, which I believe was a Lancaster, but then the flak started firing again and we saw a Mosquito climbing up to us. It was a relatively bright night so we set course for home.

The third operation (on March 17th–18th) started from Vechta and began exactly as the last one had and again we found a bomber. This time a Lancaster flew straight and level as we came from behind and fired. It soon caught fire and then crashed in flames.'

This had been the Lancaster of Flight Sergeant Lockyer and crew from No. 550 Squadron who were on their first flight since joining the Squadron from No. 1654 HCU. Only one man got out of the Lancaster alive, the flight engineer, Sergeant Ted Drawbridge. Forty years later he recalls the night well:

'We took off from North Killingholme on the afternoon of March 17th when it was still daylight, on a flight that would last well into the night. The flight plan included a cross country navigation exercise, fighter affiliation and bombing practice. The cross country flight was completed but for some reason the fighter affiliation did not take place and we moved on to Wainfleet bombing range.

It had been dark for some time when, with about two-thirds of the practice gone, the range called us up to say, 'return to base'. No other message was received from either the range or our base. At this stage we were cruising home with our lights on and guns unloaded.

On arrival at where the pilot expected North Killingholme to be, he could see no sign of the runway lights or of the Morse beacon. He asked the navigator for confirmation of our position and was told that base should be in sight. The wireless operator was then instructed to call base and ask what was going on.

We were now at 4,000 feet and beginning to realise that something may be amiss. Before the wireless operator could complete his message, the call came back, 'Douse lights – Bandits!' Immediately the lights were switched off and simultaneously the rear gunner called, 'Down port, go'.

We corkscrewed and lost the night fighter, which I believe was a Ju 88. The fighter found us again and we corkscrewed two or three more times before the rear turret was hit by a heavy burst of cannon fire. The turret and the rearmost fuselage became enveloped in flames and it was obvious that the rear gunner could not have survived. The pilot then told us to abandon the aircraft so I got up from my seat and made to get my parachute, which was stored behind the pilot's seat.

At this moment two of the crew (probably the navigator and the wireless operator) approached from the rear and obviously thinking that I had fitted my 'chute on, pulled my helmet off from behind and tried to bundle me through to the bomb aimer's compartment. The act of removing a helmet from behind and pushing a fellow crew member towards the escape hatch was taught as a way of getting a reluctant member out of the aircraft. I believe that these two thought me to be reluctant as, with no 'chute on, indeed I was. Finding the job of either removing or getting past me impossible, the navigator and wireless operator then went towards the rear door to bale out. On trying to struggle to my feet, I found that I could not move and it was only after examining the situation that I found the flight engineer's sliding foot rest protruding through the harness. This had held the other two members up but saved me from being jettisoned from the aircraft 'chute less.'

Standing again, I found the aircraft still to be flying straight and level although the pilot was obviously having some difficulty with the elevator control. As some time had now elapsed since the original order to bale out I thought it sensible to ask the pilot, whom I was standing next to, if we were still high enough to escape or if indeed the pilot was going to attempt a landing. The order came back 'bale out!'. I went. I pulled the rip cord almost immediately and seemed to land within seconds. I sat up in a field and as I did so the aircraft crashed some way behind me, causing a fire-ball.

I could not walk due to straining my side on landing, so I crawled to the roadside where a civvy bus picked me up and took me to a nearby village. After seeing the village doctor I was shown to the police station from where I 'phoned my report through to the airfield. The policemen on duty told me that there were no other survivors.'

An official report on the night's operations stated that some eighteen enemy aircraft had reached the coast at 21.00 hours and mingled with a number of No. 92 Group aircraft which were returning from a training flight which was used as a feint for Bomber Command operations. No radar indication had been received, but the 'Y' (radio interception) service heard six Ju 88s taking off from Twente and ten more from Leuwarden. This news did not reach Fighter Command until 21.30 hours and their Mosquitoes were unable to make any interceptions. The Anti-Aircraft guns were unable to fire as the intruders were mixed with the bombers on the approach and they were flying too fast on their return. Bases at Coltishall and Carnaby were strafed but no damage was caused and anti-personnel bombs together with some high explosive bombs were dropped on Hull, Wisbech, Buxton (north of Norwich) and Wickham Market.

The next intruder operations came on the night of March 20th–21st. The first indication that the RAF received of this came at 20.20 hours, when radar picked up first one then nine more intruders sixty miles east of Orfordness. Twenty-two Mosquitoes were dispatched to meet them which resulted in six contacts on friendly machines and the destruction of one aircraft (reported to have been a Ju 88) ten miles north-east of Cromer.

Despite the efforts of the Mosquitoes, the intruders made their way inland where some aircraft of No. 38 Group were engaged on training flights. No. 38 Group was not one of the usual Bomber Command groups but specialised in providing support for airborne operations such as those at Arnhem. Stirling LK116 of No. 620 Squadron had carried out a container drop at Great Sampford and was returning to base at Great Dunmow when it was shot down in flames. Only the flight engineer escaped by parachute, the remaining six, who included

Squadron Leader Whitty DFC (Officer Commanding 'A' Flight) were killed. The night's other victim was a Halifax from No. 1665 CU which was shot down near Wittering whilst on a cross country exercise from Tilstock. This time six of the crew escaped but three more died in the crash. Information relating to the intruder claims submitted at this time is sketchy but it is believed that a claim made by Oberfeldwebel Hommel of III/NJG2 relates to the loss of one of these aircraft.

In addition to this the airfields at Matlask, Watton, Swanton Morley, West Raynham and Little Snoring were attacked but they did not sustain damage. Three searchlight sites were also machine-gunned before the intruders crossed the English coast. These were the last recorded intruders to have flown over Britain and they ended a story that had begun four-and-a-half years earlier with the flights of I/NJG2 in 1940.

Following these final intruder operations, the Deputy Chief of Air Staff asked the Director of Operations (Air Defence) for a summary of the RAF's own intruder operations. His reply was as follows:

'"Intruder" operations have been carried out by Fighter Command since December 1940. The intention was to intercept and destroy enemy bombers operating against this country. Attacks were carried out upon information obtained from Intelligence as to which enemy bases were being used or likely to be used. 'Intruder' aircraft then patrolled these bases to intercept outgoing or returning enemy bombers or to shoot them up on the ground.

These "Intruder" operations were, therefore, mainly complementary to the defence of the UK by interfering with the enemy's offensive operations against London and other targets. These operations were very successful; they prevented the enemy from using his forward bases for short flights to the UK and from carrying out double sorties by forcing him to locate his bombers further back.

About the end of 1942, the enemy's night attacks decreased and Bomber Command's operations became more extensive. Fighter Command "Intruder" Squadrons then undertook missions which consisted of:

(a) Patrols of the enemy night fighter bases in support of large scale attacks by Bomber Command.

(b) Visits to enemy fighter training areas to disrupt his training.

(c) Attacks on transportation and other targets.

Between March 1943 and February 1944 inclusive, approximately 3,527 offensive sorties were flown which included attacks on 700 trains and 900 other targets including airfields. 90 enemy aircraft were destroyed, seven probably destroyed and 49 damaged.

For the period March 1944 to February 1945 inclusive, 3,650 offensive "Intruder" sorties by Fighter Command have been flown resulting in 110 enemy aircraft destroyed, eleven probably destroyed and 47 damaged. The above figures indicate the extensive "Intruder" operations which have been undertaken by the command during these periods. Our losses for the last two years were 93 aircraft.'

CHAPTER SEVENTEEN

Epilogue

Many books which are written about the Second World War end their story with the war's conclusion. This leaves one wondering what became of the men who featured within their pages. For this reason I am grateful to the following who sent me details so that I could continue their stories.

The members of I/NJG2 who were captured during 1941, were processed through AI1(k) before moving on to Prisoner of War Camps in England, and later Canada. After his interrogation in London, Heinrich Beul was sent to a camp at Windermere in the Lake District. In 1942, he was taken by ship to Canada where he stayed until 1946. He was then brought back to Britain and was not allowed to return to Germany until early 1947 when he was finally reunited with his family.

Herbert Thomas underwent a similar experience but was not sent to Canada due to the severity of his injuries. In late 1943 the Swiss Red Cross arranged an exchange of 1,500 British and German troops in the town of Göteborg. He stayed in Germany where he was rehabilitated and after the war went into the car industry. Thomas continued with his interest in aviation and is the President of the Bochum Flying Club. He is also an active member of the Gemeinschaft der Jagdflieger and often contributes articles to their magazine. As a result of the researches for this book, Herbert Thomas visited Britain in 1986 to view what remained of his Dornier after it had been excavated.

Of the two 'Experten' who survived their time in I/NJG2, Wilhelm Beier continued to fly night fighters throughout the war and eventually began to experiment with the flying of Me 262 jets at night. He had accumulated over 250 missions and is credited with 36 claims. The second 'Experten', Alfons Köster, was awarded the Ritterkreuz on 29th October 1942, but was killed on 7th January 1945, when he crashed into farm buildings while attempting to land in fog.

The creators of the intruder force all survived the war. Josef Kammhuber went on to build the 'Kammhuber Line' of night defences and was made Inspekteur de Nachtjäger in 1943 after which he was posted to command Luftflotte 5 in Norway. After the war he became an Inspekteur der Bundesluftwaffe.

Karl Hülshoff also entered the Bundesluftwaffe, and from 1958 to

Josef Kammhuber (right) in 1961 as Inspekteur der Bundesluftwaffe with Erich Hartmann. (Böttner).

Herbert Thomas (centre) returns to England with colleagues in 1986.

1964, was Oberst American Tactical Air Force at Ramstein Air Force Base.

Wolfgang Falck remained in command of NJG1 until June 1943 after which he held a series of staff positions. He also continued his career in the Bundesluftwaffe. His crest of the diving falcon was used on the F-86K's flown by JG74 when it was created in 1954 and can still be seen in a modified version on the latest jet fighters.

The fate of the crew of the Ju 88 which went missing on 17th April 1941, Ogergefreiter Wilhelm Beetz, Gefreiter Rudolf Kronika and Gefreiter Johann Mittag, was officially unknown. However, aviation enthusiast Andy Saunders and members of what was then the Wealden Aviation Group believed that there was evidence to suggest that an aircraft crash site at Gothic House Farm, Thorney, near Peterborough, was that of their Ju 88. In 1976 the site was excavated and from a depth of up to thirty feet, the remains of the Ju 88 and of its three crew men were unearthed. After being officially identified, their remains were buried with full military honours at the German Military War Cemetery, Cannock Chase, Staffordshire. This is the final resting place of many Luftwaffe crews who fell on British soil.

The careers of pilots who flew with I/NJG2

Name	Last known rank	Claims with I/NJG2	Final Score	Remarks
Arnold	Fw.	4	4	
Barth	Fw.	1	1	
Beier	Oblt.	14	36	Won the Ritterkreuz and survived the war.
Berschwinger	Ofw.	2	12	Killed in action.
Bisang	Lt.	1	1	Killed in action 28/7/41.
Blum	Uffz.	1	1	
Böme	Lt.	1	1	
Bohn	Oblt.	6	6	Killed in action 26/6/41.
Bönsch	Hptm.	6	7	Killed in action 1943.
Bussmann	Hpt.	7	23	Won Deutscheskreuz in Gold and survived the war.
Feuerbaum	Lt.	3	3	Killed in action 4/6/41.
Geissübel	Fw.	1	1	
Hahn	Lt.	12	12	Won the Ritterkreuz but killed in action 11/10/41.

Harmstorf	Hptm.	1	4	Killed in action 23/7/42.
Herrmann	Oblt.	9	9	Won Deutscheskreuz in Gold. Taken prisoner 10/3/41.
Hülshoff	OberstLt.	4	11	Won Deutscheskreuz in Gold. Survived the war.
Jung	Major	3	3	Survived the war.
Köster	Hptm.	11	29	Won Ritterkreuz. Killed in action 7/5/43.
Laufs	Lt.	5	12	Killed in action 27/1/42.
Luddecke	Ofw.	3	7	Won Ehrenpokal.
Merbach	Ofw.	1	1	
Middlestädt	Fw.	1	1	
Pfeiffer	Lt.	2	2	killed in action 17/8/41.
Semrau	Major	9	46	Won Ritterkreuz with Eichenlaub. Killed in action 8/2/45.
Schmidt	Oblt.	0	0	Defected 9/5/43.
Schramm	Fw.	1	1	Missing in action 17/8/40.
Schulz	Hptm.	6	17	Killed in action 31/1/44.
Schütze	Hptm.	1	5	Killed in action.
Sommer	Ofw.	9	19	Killed in action 11/2/44.
Stradner	Lt.	1	1	Killed in action 9/7/41.
Strüning	Hptm.	9	56	Won Ritterkreuz with Eichenlaub. Killed in action 24/12/44.
Völker	Lt.	9	9	Killed in action 22/7/41.
Wiese	Fw.	1	1	Killed in action 21/6/41.
Ziebarth	Fw.	1	1	Killed in action 22/12/41.

Of the Allied crews who were involved during 1940–1941, comparatively few survived the war. Flying Instructor Nick Carter was later posted to a flying school in South Africa. After the war he became a member of the British Aerobatic Team and now flies with the Tiger Club at Redhill, Surrey.

The pilots of the No. 25 Squadron Beaufighters continued to fly on operations throughout the war. Harold Pleasance (who had brought down Hoffmann's Ju 88 on 14th June 1941) became the Squadron's Commanding Officer until the end of the war. Pilot Officer Thompson (who shot down Herbert Thomas's Dornier on 8th May 1941 and Bähner's Ju 88 on 14th June 1941) was killed when his Beaufighter crashed on landing at Wittering on 8th July 1941. New Zealander, Michael Herrick, (who brought down Heinrich Beul's Ju 88 on 22nd June 1941) joined the Royal New Zealand Air Force in 1943 and flew operations against the Japanese. He returned to Britain in December of that year and became a Flight Commander with No. 305 (Polish) Squadron. He was shot down and killed in a Mosquito during an intruder raid over Denmark on 16th June 1944.

The Americans continued their operations but suffered heavy losses. Bob Peel and his crew from the 385th Bomber Group, who had baled out over Germany on 22nd April 1944, spent the remainder of the war in captivity before returning to America. After the war, Bob Peel returned to the hospital where he had landed at Meiningen and was reunited with some of those who had helped him.

As 'Operation Gisela' took place only two months before the end of the war in Europe, the majority of those who survived the attack also survived the war. Jack 'Ginger' Wilson was sent to a rehabilitation centre at Hoylake in the Wirral. He recovered from his injuries and finished the war as an Instructor at No. 7 S of TT at Westwood and Sutton Bridge. He is a member of the Caterpillar Club and now lives in York.

Neal's crew from No. 640 Squadron had a reunion in 1972 but by this time two of their number had died.

'Robbie' Roberts recovered consciousness in an RAF hospital at Ely about two weeks after the crash.

> 'I learned that my mid-upper gunner, Sergeant Sutcliffe, had survived with slight burns and I had survived with serious facial burns and a crush fractured spine. The remainder of the crew perished in the wreck. My recovery was long and somewhat painful. I had operations for bone grafting to the spine and initial grafting for the facial burns at Ely, before going on to East Grinstead for further plastic surgery by Sir Archibald McIndoe and thus became a member of the famous Guinea Pig Club. I was discharged from hospitalization, medical rehabilitation and the Service in June 1947 returning to 'civvy street' to take up occupation in the civil engineering industry. I returned periodically to hospital for cosmetic surgery until 1949. I think it was August 1949 when the last of the plastic surgery operations finished.
>
> Ken Sutcliffe, my mid-upper gunner, returned to Leeds after the war, he sadly died in 1983 after suffering a brain haemorrhage.

Ted Drawbridge, the sole survivor of the Lancaster crash on March 17th 1945, was taken to Raunceby Hospital where he stayed for ten days. When he returned to his base, he was sent on fourteen days sick leave after which he continued operational flying. Several months later he overheard a conversation concerning the retrieval of the mid-upper gunner's body from the Humber. As this was confirmed as being from his aircraft he asked permission from his section to attend the funeral. For reasons that were not explained to him, permission was refused and he was reminded not to contact any relatives of the crew. Ted now lives with his wife in Lincolnshire and is a retired mechanical engineer. He is a member of the Fenland Aircraft Preservation Society and looks after their exhibits.

Of the Luftwaffe crews, Arnold Döring was recommended for the Ritterkreuz in April 1945, but did not receive his award until 1955. He flew with the Bundesluftwaffe and now lives in retirement in Germany. Günther Schmidt, despite the fact that he is now blind, continues his interest in aviation and has helped researchers in Germany. Walter Briegleb, now Doctor Briegleb, is a dentist and has a practice in Köln. Günther Wolf joined Lufthansa, the German national airline, as an airliner captain.

'Often when I have been flying my Jumbo to New York or Chicago, I have seen the lighthouse at Spurn Head flashing out over the North Sea. Whenever I see this, my mind goes back to the events of March 1945 when I had flown back in that terrible weather. When flying from Newcastle to Frankfurt and the flight plan shows that we might be eighteen mimutes late, I have to take the microphone and explain this to my nervous passengers. I tell my crew of a similar situation, but then a man had time to stop and have an hour to himself.'

Claims submitted by pilots of I/NJG2
during operations over Britain

23/7/40		Fw. Wiese	Wellington over the North Sea
23/7/40		Fw. Schramm	Wellington over the North Sea
17/8/40	23.00	Fw. Laufs	Hurricane near Lowestoft
27/8/40	21.30	Ofw. Merbach	Hurricane near Grimsby
7/9/40	23.00	Oblt. Herrmann	Blenheim near Waddington
9/9/40	23.15	Fw. Sommer	Blenheim near Waddington
20/10/40	21.30	Hptm. Hülshoff	Hampden near Dishforth
24/10/40	23.02	Fw. Hahn	Wellington near Linton-on-Ouse
24/10/40	22.05	Oblt. Herrmann	Blenheim near Hemswell
24/10/40	22.10	Oblt. Herrmann	Blenheim near Hemswell
28/10/40	00.30	Lt. Völker	Hampden near Scampton
23/11/40	18.30	Hptm. Hülshoff	Wellington over the North Sea
23/11/40	18.45	Oblt. Herrmann	Hampden over the North Sea
23/11/40	18.40	Fw. Strüning	Wellington over the North Sea
17/12/40	04.00	Oblt. Bohn	Hampden near Scampton
18/12/40	06.36	Ofw. Beier	Hurricane over the North Sea
22/12/40		Lt. Völker	Blenheim near Cranwell
22/12/40	09.00	Uffz. Blum	Blenheim over the North Sea
1/1/41	18.40	Lt. Stradner	Wellington over the North Sea
2/1/41	18.45	Uffz. Arnold	Wellington over the North Sea
2/1/41	19.02	Fw. Hahn	Whitley over the North Sea
3/1/41	18.50	Lt. Böhme	Whitley over the North Sea
16/1/41	02.30	Oblt. Schulz	Blenheim near Church Fenton
16/1/41	02.45	Oblt. Schulz	Blenheim near Church Fenton
11/2/41	01.10	Oblt. Schulz	Blenheim near West Raynham
11/2/41	02.30	Hptm. Jung	Wellington near West Raynham
11/2/41	04.15	Oblt. Semrau	Blenheim near Feltwell
11/2/41	04.20	Oblt. Semrau	Blenheim near Feltwell
11/2/41	06.41	Oblt. Herrmann	Hampden near Waddington
11/2/41	06.58	Oblt. Herrmann	Hampden near Waddington
15/2/41	09.15	Fw. Strüning	Hudson over the North Sea
15/2/41	19.58	Fw. Strüning	Wellington over the North Sea
16/2/41	01.25	Oblt. Bönsch	Blenheim near Waddington

25/2/41	23.40	Fw. Ziebarth	Blenheim near Waddington
27/2/41	00.10	Oblt. Bönsch	Blenheim near Scampton
27/2/41	01.40	Oblt. Herrmann	Blenheim near Waddington
12/3/41		Oblt. Bönsch	Blenheim near Scampton
12/3/41	22.10	Fw. Mittlestädt	Blenheim near Wells
12/3/41	01.15	Fw. Hahn	Blenheim near Leeming
13/3/41	22.00	Fw. Hahn	Manchester near Waddington
18/3/41	06.53	Fw. Laufs	Wellington near Cromer
18/3/41	07.20	Lt. Pfeiffer	Wellington near Mildenhall
4/4/41	01.00	Lt. Völker	Wellington near West Raynham
8/4/41	23.45	Fw. Hahn	Hampden near Upwood
8/4/41	01.20	Lt. Feuerbaum	Hudson near Wells
8/4/41	01.23	Lt. Feuerbaum	Hampden near Wells
8/4/41	22.50	Hptm. Hülshoff	Blenheim over the North Sea
8/4/41	23.00	Hptm. Hülshoff	Hampden over the North Sea
8/4/41	23.45	Fw. Hahn	Wellington in Raun C
9/4/41	23.15	Uffz. Berschwinger	Wellington near Marham
10/4/41		Fw. Laufs	Wellington near Wells
10/4/41	01.30	Oblt. Schulz	Wellington near Cambridge
10/4/41		Ofw. Beier	Whitley over the North Sea
10/4/41		Uffz. Köster	Single engine machine near Upwood
17/4/41		Lt. Völker	Hampden near Finningley
17/4/41		Fw. Hahn	Hampden near Waddington
21/4/41		Fw. Hahn	Hampden near Digby
24/4/41		Fw. Giessübel	Twin engined machine near Marham
24–25/4/41		Lt. Völker	Three Blenheims near Lindholme
25–26/4/41		Fw. Biehne	Blenheim near Lindholme
26/4/41		Lt. Pfeiffer	Single engined machine near Hemswell
30/4/41	00.15	Ofw. Sommer	Blenheim near Tollerton
30/4/41	00.20	Ofw. Sommer	Blenheim near Tollerton
30/4/41	00.50	Ofw. Sommer	Blenheim nar Hucknall
30/4/41	01.30	Ofw. Sommer	Blenheim near Bircham Newton
3/5/41	03.30	Lt. Feuerbaum	Hampden near Church Fenton
4/5/41		Ofw. Hahn	Fulmar near Stoke Holly Cross
5/5/41		Ofw. Hahn	Blenheim near Feltwell
7/5/41		Fw. Strüning	Wellington near Upwood
8/5/41		Uffz. Köster	Wellington over the North Sea
8/5/41		Oblt. Semrau	Wellington near Nottingham
8/5/41		Ofw. Beier	Wellington near Wells
8/5/41		Uffz. Köster	Blenheim over the North Sea

9/5/41	Fw. Strüning	Wellington over the North Sea
10/5/41	Oblt. Harmstorf	Wellington over the North Sea
11/5/41	Ofw. Beier	Blenheim 50km east of Scarborough
16/5/41	Ofw. Sommer	Wellington near Wells
18/5/41	Oblt. Semrau	Blenheim in Raum B
4/6/41	Ofw. Beier	Blenheim near Lowestoft
12/6/41	Uffz. Köster	Hampden location unknown
12/6/41	Oblt. Bohn	Wellington over the North Sea
12/6/41	Oblt. Bohn	Whitley over the North Sea
13/6/41	Ofw. Beier	Defiant near Thornaby
13/6/41	Oblt. Semrau	Four engined machine near Finningley
17/6/41	Ofw. Bussmann	Two Wellingtons over the North Sea
17/6/41	Fw. Arnold	Whitley over the North Sea
17/6/41	Oblt. Bönsch	Two Wellingtons over the North Sea
17/6/41 03.55	Ofw. Sommer	Wellington over the North Sea
17/6/41 04.05	Ofw. Glas	Wellington over the North Sea
19/6/41	Oblt. Semrau	Whitley over the North Sea
22/6/41 00.15	Oblt. Bohn	Wellington over the North Sea
26/6/41	Ofw. Jung	Wellington over the North Sea
23/6/41	Oblt. Bönsch	Wellington over the North Sea
26/6/41	Oblt. Bohn	Wellington over the North Sea
27/6/41	Fw. Lüddeke	Wellington over the North Sea
27/6/41 23.55	Ofw. Sommer	Wellington over the North Sea
30/6/41	Fw. Arnold	Wellington over the North Sea
30/6/41	Ofw. Jung	Wellington over the North Sea
5/7/41	Ofw. Laufs	Defiant Wells
5/7/41	Ofw. Strüning	Wellington near Bircham Newton
6/7/41	Ofw. Bussmann	Wellington over the North Sea
6/7/41	Ofw. Beier	Wellington over the North Sea

6/7/41	Ofw. Beier	Blenheim over the North Sea
6/7/41	Ofw. Beier	Two Whitleys over the North Sea
7/7/41	Fw. Barth	Blenheim over the North Sea
7/7/41	Oblt. Semrau	Blenheim near Wells
8/7/41	Fw. Berschwinger	Whitley over the North Sea
9/7/41	Lt. Schulz	Hampden over the North Sea
15/7/41	Fw. Köster	Two Blenheims near Wyton
18/7/41	Oblt. Semrau	Blenheim near Digby
18/7/41	Ofw. Beier	Blenheim over the North Sea
19/7/41	Oblt. Schütze	Unknown type near Wyton
22/7/41	Lt. Völker	Wellington Ashwell (1)
28/7/41	Lt. Bisang	Unspecified type in Raum C (2)
30/7/41	Fw. Arnold	Whitley near Hemswell
8/8/41	Lt. Schulz	Wellington over the North Sea
8/8/41	Fw. Köster	Whitley near Marham
8/8/41	Ofw. Beier	Blenheim over the North Sea
8/8/41	Ofw. Beier	Halifax over the North Sea
8/8/41	Ofw. Beier	Wellington over the North Sea
13/8/41	Ofw. Laufs	Wellington Coltishall
13/8/41	Ofw. Bussmann	Three Wellingtons near Oxford
15/8/41	Ofw. Lüddeke	Wellington over the Humber Estuary
15/8/41	Ofw. Lüddeke	Whitley over the Humber Estuary
16/8/41	Lt. Hahn	Wellington near Scunthorpe
19/8/41	Ofw. Strüning	Two Blenheims near Grantham
20/8/41	Fw. Köster	Blenheim near Binbrook
1/9/41	Fw. Köster	Halifax near Hatfield
1/9/41	Fw. Köster	Wellington near Upper Heyford
20/9/41	Oblt. Semrau	Unknown type over central England
30/9/41	Ofw. Bussmann	Blenheim near Winthorpe
3/10/41	Fw. Köster	Stirling near Cambridge
12/10/41	Lt. Hahn	Oxford near Grantham (1)
13/10/41	Ofw. Strüning	B-17 near Upwood

(1) These aircraft were involved in mid-air collisions which resulted in the destruction of both machines.

(2) Reported by radio.

It should be noted that these claims are as near as possible to those submitted by the pilots. No attempt has been made to alter or add to the

171

details in the light of information gathered during the research for this book. Any reader wishing to match these claims with losses should bear in mind the conditions under which the claims were made and give considerable latitude to times, locations and type identification. Although the claims may at times appear to bear little relation to the aircraft losses, one factor must be remembered. Many Allied aircraft were brought down by intruders during this period, thus the only reasonable conclusion is that they were brought down by the pilots of I/NJG2.

Losses of RAF aircraft attributable to intruder action

1940

24/10/40 21.30 hrs. Blenheim IV P4858 of No. 17 OTU.
Landed at Docking Airfield, Norfolk after being damaged by cannon fire. No crew casualties sustained.

24/10/40 21.15 hrs. Beaufort.
Attacked and damaged over Docking, Norfolk and landed safely with a holed fuel tank. No crew casualties sustained.

24/10/40 22.10 hrs. Whitley V P5073 'D' of No. 102 Sqn.
Shot down in flames on take off from Linton on Ouse, Yorkshire. P/O. T. R. Murfitt (pilot) and Sgt. I. C. Scoular (observer) killed. P/O. A. G. Davies (pilot), P/O. T. E. Lee and Sgt. A. S. Wilson injured.

28/10/40 00.30 hrs. Hampden I X3027 of No. 49 Sqn.
Crashed into the sea half a mile off Skegness, Lincolnshire. F/O. J. R. Bufton (pilot), F/O. D. M. Robertson (gunner) and Sgt. F. J. W. Bichard (gunner) killed. P/O. K. Ballas-Andersen missing.

28/10/40 Hampden I X3001 of No. 49 Sqn.
Attacked when circling a 'Q' Site. Landed safely at Lindholm with punctured tyres and accumulators shot through. P/O. Green, Sgt. Huggett, Sgt. Turpey and Sgt. McIver all safe.

1941

1/1/41 22.25 hrs. Wellington IC T2517 of No. 301 Sqn.
Crashed in flames near Digby, Lincolnshire. Sqn/Ldr. Floryanowicz, P/O. Olszyna, F/O. Kulbacki, Sgt. Hejnowski, Sgt. Guzowski and Sgt. Gachowski killed.

2/1/41 01.35 hrs. Wellington 1C T2518 of No. 301 Sqn.
Span into the ground when landing at Digby, Lincolnshire. P/O. Murowski, P/O. Dzuibinski, F/O. Sadowski, Sgt. Sawicz and Sgt. Kasianowski killed. Sgt. Wanciziewicz injured.

3/1/41 18.50 hrs. Whitley T4234 of No. 10 Sqn.
Severely damaged but landed safely at Catterick, Yorkshire. P/O. Williams and crew safe.

15–16/1/41 Defiant L7002 of No. 54 OTU.
Attacked and crashed near Church Fenton, Yorkshire. P/O. H. G. S. Wyrill and one other safe.

15–16/1/41. Defiant N1542 of No. 54 OTU.
Damaged and forced to land near Church Fenton, Yorkshire. F/Lt. R. J. B.

Burns and one other safe.

11/2/41 02.00 hrs. Wellington 1C R1084 'Q' of No. 115 Sqn.
Forced down on to a single track railway cutting of the LNER, two and a half miles west of Swaffham, Norfolk and burnt out. Sgt. Rodgers DFM (captain), Sgt. Robson (pilot), Sgt. Benson (navigator), Sgt. Bennett (wireless operator) and Sgt. Baird (front gunner) safe. Sgt. Hill (rear gunner) injured.

11/2/41 03.50 hrs. Blenheim of No. 21 Sqn.
Attacked off the coast and damaged. Force landed at 04.45 hrs. on Bodney Airfield, Norfolk. Sqn/Ldr. Sabine, F/O. Winder and Sgt. Ritson safe.

11/2/41 03.10 hrs. Blenheim IV Z5877 of No. 21 Sqn.
Attacked over Bodney Airfield, Norfolk. Crashed and burnt out attempting to land. Sgt. A. Chattaway (pilot) and P/O. G. E. Sharvell (observer) killed. Sgt. Birch (gunner) safe.

11/2/41 05.40 hrs. Hampden I AD719 'C' of No. 49 Sqn.
Shot down in flames and crashed at Langworth, Lincolnshire. Sgt. J. Butterworth and Sgt. D. A. Caldwell killed. Sgt. Bates and Sgt. Blower baled out with slight injuries.

11/2/41 05.50 hrs. Hampden I P1164 of No. 144 Sqn.
Attacked and damaged in hydraulics, undercarriage and flaps but landed safely at Hemswell, Lincolnshire. Sgt. McVie and crew safe.

11/2/41 Hampden I X3077 of No. 144 Sqn.
Refused permission to land due to intruder action. Sgt. Dainty and crew baled out safely when fuel was exhausted and aircraft crashed near Newton, Lincolnshire.

15/2/41 23.00 hrs. Hampden I P2917 of No. 44 Sqn.
Damaged over Lincoln and landed safely at Waddington, Lincolnshire. F/O. Penman and crew safe.

16/2/41 41.00 hrs. Hampden I X3025 of No. 44 sqn.
Hit in port engine and fuselage. Landed at Waddington, Lincolnshire. Sqn/Ldr. Smalies and crew safe. Aircraft later hit by a Wellington of No. 300 or No. 301 Sqn. on landing.

16/2/41 00.15 hrs. Oxford I R6076 of No. 2 FIS.
Damaged but landed safely at Fulbeck, Lincolnshire. F/O. R. M. Hackney and Sgt. R. L. Earp safe.

16/2/41 hrs. Oxford I V3244 of No. 2 FIS.
Damaged but landed safely at Fulbeck, Lincolnshire. F/O. M. E. Blackstone and P/O. E. J. R. Blezzard safe.

25/2/41 23.00 hrs. Wellington IC R1009 'L' of No. 218 Sqn.
Shot down whilst waiting to land at Marham, Norfolk. Force landed at Red Lodge, two miles south of Swaffham. Sgt. Hoos (captain), Sgt. Brummwell (pilot) and Sgt. Heyward (rear gunner) injured. Sgt. Stanley (front gunner) seriously injured. Sgt. Groves and Sgt. Caswell safe.

26/2/41 23.08 hrs. Oxford I R6107 of No. 2 CFS.
Shot down when landing at Fulbeck, Lincolnshire. F/Lt. D. E. C. Trench

(pupil) killed. A-F/O. D. M. Egan (instructor) safe.

10–11/3/41 Whitley of No. 78 Sqn.
Damaged but landed safely. No crew casualties.

12/3/41 23.59 hrs. Blenheim I L6835 of No. 54 Sqn.
Damaged and made a forced landing at Ulleskelf near Church Fenton, Yorkshire. P/O. M. G. Calvert and Sgt. F. W. Mutton safe.

12–13/3/41 Wellington P9226 of No. 311 Sqn.
Damaged but landed safely. No crew casualties.

12–13/3/41 Blenheim R3753 of No. 21 Sqn.
Damaged but landed safely. Sqn/Ldr. Allen and crew safe.

13/3/41 Manchester I L7319 'C' of No. 207 Sqn.
Shot down shortly after take off from Waddington, at Wisby, Lincolnshire. Aircraft burnt out and some of its bomb load exploded. F/O. H. V. Matthews DFC, (captain), Sgt. H. C. Redgrave (observer), Sgt. R. D. Welch (gunner) and Sgt. H. W. Hemmingway (gunner) killed. Sgt. Cox and Sgt. ·J. Marsden (pilot) thrown clear and taken to Lincoln Hospital where Sgt. Marsden later died.

14–15/3/41 Wellington 'J' of No. 221 Sqn.
Damaged but landed safely. No crew casualties.

18/3/41 06.10 hrs Wellington 1C R1474 'M' of No. 149 Sqn.
Shot down when attempting to land at Mildenhall and crashed at Beck Row, Suffolk. Sgt. R. Warren (captain), Sgt. E. R. Cooke (pilot), Sgt. E. A. Lown (observer), Sgt. H. Chapman (wireless operator), Sgt. W. J. Greaves (gunner) and Sgt. D. J. Capel (gunner) killed.

18/3/41 Wellington 1C of No. 221 Sqn.
Attacked and damaged over Great Yarmouth, Norfolk.

30–31/3/41 Wellington R1444 of No. 150 Sqn.
Damaged but landed safely. Sqn/Ldr. Coleman and crew safe.

4/4/41 00.25 hrs. Wellington 1C R1470 'H' of No. 115 Sqn.
Forced to crash land on a mud bank off King's Lynn, Norfolk. Sgt. C. M. Thompson (captain), Sgt. H. Y. Chard (pilot), P/O. S. S. Barnett (navigator), Sgt. J. S. C. Sherman (wireless operator) and Sgt. E. Keetley (front gunner) killed. Sgt. Russell (rear gunner) injured.

7–8/4/41 Hampden I P2092 of No. 14 OTU.
Shot down at Little Blytham, Lincolnshire. Sgt. R. J. Holborow and two others killed.

7–8/4/41 Whitley V Z6478 of No. 51 Sqn.
Attacked over the Wash and landed safely at Dishforth, Yorkshire. No crew casualties.

7–8/4/41 Hudson 'X' of No. 206 Sqn.
Attacked over Langham at 800 feet but landed safely at West Tofts, Norfolk by P/O. Alexander at 00.30 hrs.

8–9/4/41 Beaufighter of No. 29 Sqn.
Shot at when landing at Wellingore, Lincolnshire, swerved off runway and hit trees. Sqn/Ldr. Guy Gibson safe.

8-9/4/41 Wellington IA P9230 of No. 311 Sqn.
Damaged but landed safely at East Wretham, Norfolk. P/O. Hrncir safe, Sgt. Nyc injured by cannon splinters.

9/4/41 23.25 hrs. Hurricane V6611 of No. 257 Sqn.
Span into the ground in flames and crashed at Duffields Farm, Worstead near Coltishall, Norfolk. Sgt. L. R. Truman killed.

10/4/41 00.35 hrs. Wellington IC R1049 'B' of No. 221 Sqn.
Shot down on take off from Bircham Newton and crashed in flames at Burnham Westgate, Norfolk. P/O. P. C. Brown (captain), Sgt. F. H. Butterworth (gunner) and Sgt. E. R. Owens (rear gunner) killed.

10/4/41 00.40 hrs. Wellington I L4253 of 11 OTU.
Shot down and crashed at Ashwell, Cambridgeshire. Sgt. G. D. H. Dutton and one other safe.

17/4/41 00.15 hrs. Hampden I AD761 of No. 144 Sqn.
Shot down four minutes after take off from Hemswell, Lincolnshire and crashed in flames two miles east-north-east of the airfield. Sgt. H. Kirby (pilot), Sgt. W. A. Tyler (navigator) and Sgt. V. G. Elliot (gunner) killed. Sgt. G. Walsh (gunner) baled out severely wounded.

21/4/41 02.38 hrs. Battle I P6674 of No. 12 FTS.
Shot down whilst attempting to land at Harlaxton, Lincolnshire. Pupil and Instructor killed.

24/4/41 00.50 hrs. Wellington 1C N2912 of No. 11 OTU.
Shot down over Bassingbourne Airfield, Cambridgeshire and crashed on top of Wellington R1404 parked in a dispersal. Sgt. P. H. Nicholls (pilot) injured. Sgt. F. N. Alstram (pilot) and Sgt. R. Wilson (gunner) killed.

24/4/41 23.35 hrs. Blenheim I L1320 of No. 54 OTU.
Crashed on landing at Church Fenton, Yorkshire. Sgt. Spurgin safe.

24/4/41 23.35 hrs. Blenheim I L1478 of No. 54 OTU.
Damaged when landing at Church Fenton, Yorkshire. Sgt. G. W. Attenborough safe.

24/4/41 23.35 hrs. Blenheim I K7132 of No. 54 OTU.
Shot down in flames eight miles north-east of Barnsley, Yorkshire. F/Lt. R. W. Denison baled out safely.

26/4/41 02.08 hrs. Defiant I N1568 of No. 54 OTU.
Flew into the ground during combat with a night fighter near Church Fenton, Yorkshire. Sgt. F. C. Crozier (pilot) and Sgt. G. Bell (gunner) killed.

31/4/41 03.14 hrs. Wellington IC T2721 of No. 99 Sqn.
Believed to have been brought down off the East Coast. Sgt. F. Hewitson, Sgt. Bennet, Sgt. E. C. Stevens, Sgt. S. J. Holt, Sgt. W. P. James and Sgt. R. R. Thomas missing.

1/5/41 02.30 hrs. Oxford L9686 of No. 2 CFS.
Damaged over Fulbeck, Lincolnshire, but landed safely. LAC. Patrick safe.

3/5/41 03.14 hrs. Whitley of No. 77 Sqn.
Attacked and damaged when attempting to land at Topcliffe, Yorkshire. Sgt. Mills and crew safe.

4/5/41 01.45 hrs. Spitfire IIA P7699 'Zanzibar III' of No. 222 Sqn. Shot down near Coltishall, Norfolk. P/O. P. B. Klee killed.

5/5/41 01.15 hrs. Hurricane I P3866 of No. 257 Sqn.
Shot down when attempting to land at Duxford and crashed at Royston, Hertfordshire. Sgt. R. G. Parrott killed.

7/5/41 02.10 hrs. Wellington R3227 of No. 11 OTU.
Set on fire and forced to land at Wendy Village, Cambridgeshire. F/O. T. J. Warner (instructor), P/O. J. McAnally (pilot) and Sgt. L. Stuart (rear gunner) injured.

8/5/41 04.05 hrs. Oxford II W6636 of No. 14 FTS.
Crashed in flames south of Sibson relief landing ground, Leicestershire. Fate of crew not known.

8–9/5/41 Wellington R1397 of No. 103 Sqn.
Damaged but landed safely. P/O. Anderson (pilot) and crew safe.

10–11/5/41 Wellington of No. 103 Sqn.
Damaged but landed safely. P/O. Harper (pilot) and crew safe.

11–12/5/41 Wellington T2911 of No. 40 Sqn.
Damaged but landed safely by P/O. Smith (pilot). One of crew killed.

11–12/5/41 Wellington R1589 of No. 75 Sqn.
Damaged but landed safely by Sqn/Ldr. Widdows (pilot). One of crew killed.

12–13/5/41 Wellington W5354 of No. 142 Sqn.
Damaged during a training flight but landed safely by Sgt. Maize.

16/5/41 05.03 hrs. Wellington IC R1466 of No. 311 Sqn.
Forced to land near Thorpe Rectory, Haddiscoe, Norfolk. Crew of five safe.

18/5/41 02.20 hrs. Battle (T) R7363 of No. 12 FTS. Crashed in flames 3 miles south of Grantham, Lincolnshire. F/O. B. K. Thomas killed.

3/6/41 Hampden I X2912 of No. 144 Sqn.
Damaged over the Wash. Sgt. W. A. Tyler (rear gunner) wounded. Sgt. W. A. Whitmore and crew safe.

12/6/41 02.00 hrs. Hampden I P1341 of No. 16 OTU.
Overshot Akeman Street Landing Ground, Oxfordshire. P/O. L. B. Gunter and crew safe.

12/6/41 02.00 hrs. Anson I N5014 of No. 16 OTU.
Damaged and landed safely at Brackley Airfield, Northants. P/O. D. G. D. Buckley safe.

12/6/41 02.00 hrs. Anson I R9691 of No. 16 OTU.
Damaged and landed safely at Brackley Airfield, Northants. P/O. D. C. Adams safe.

13/6/41 Wellington IC R1708 of No. 25 OTU.
Shot down in the circuit of Finningley, Yorkshire. Sgt. W. R. L. Collyer and five others killed.

5/7/41 01.08 hrs. Spitfire IIA P8085 of No. 452 Sqn.
Shot down when attempting to land at North Coates and crashed at Fen Lane Farm, North Somercoates, Lincolnshire. Sgt. A. G. Costello killed.

7/7/41 03.04 hrs. Blenheim IV Z6041 'O' of No. 500 Sqn.
Shot down near Docking Airfield and crashed near Burnham Market, Norfolk. F/O. A. Leeson, F/O. R. W. V. Smith, Sgt. C. V. Pearce and Sgt. A. N. F. Glide killed.

15–16/7/41 Tiger Moth II R4968 of No. 2 EFTS.
Tail shot off near Caxton Gibbet, Cambridgeshire. Pilot baled out safely.

18/7/41 Blenheim I K7090 of No. 54 OTU.
Flew into the ground half a mile from Church Fenton, Yorkshire, when flying on instruments. Sgt. C. J. Neighbour killed.

18/7/41 01.05 hrs. Wellington IC X3619 of No. 11 OTU.
Damaged but landed safely at Steeple Morden, Cambridgeshire. No crew casualties.

22/7/41 01.30 hrs. Wellington IC R1334 of No. 11 OTU.
Collided with the Ju 88 of Völker and crashed at Ashwell, Hertfordshire. Sgt. W. A. Stewart (pilot), F/Sgt. J. Stewart (wireless operator), Sgt. R. E. Hibbert (wireless operator), Sgt. R. A. MacAllister (wireless operator), Sgt. F. S. Houston (pilot), Sgt. T. Manning (gunner), Sgt. B. C. Thompson (pilot) and Sgt. C. M. S. Lewis (observer) killed.

28/7/41 Oxford II V3685 of No. 2 FTS.
Shot down 2 miles north-east of Akeman Street Landing Ground, Oxfordshire. LAC. R. S. Smith killed.

30/7/41 00.50 hrs. Oxford II T1064 of No. 54 OTU.
Shot down at Starston Grange, Yorkshire. Sgt. C. C. Woodward killed.

31/7/41 04.05 hrs. Whitley V Z6584 of No. 10 Sqn.
Shot down one mile north of Thetford, Norfolk. Sgt. A. R. Beveridge (pilot) and Sgt. G. A. Alcock (rear gunner) killed. Sgt. Bassett (observer) and Sgt. Lawson (wireless operator) baled out safely.

13/8/41 02.20 hrs. Wellington IC T2563 'D' of No. 115 Sqn.
Set on fire in the air and crash landed at Smith's Farm, Ashmanhaugh, Norfolk. P/O. Woods (captain), Sgt. R. A. Hodges (pilot), P/O. A. J. A. Day (navigator), Sgt. C. D. Tavener (wireless operator) and Sgt. S. W. Morton (front gunner) injured. Sgt. B. G. Evans (rear gunner) killed.

12–13/8/41 Blenheim I L1245 of No. 17 OTU.
Crashed at Crow Farm, Wilburton, Cambridgeshire. P/O. W. E. A. Wand (pilot), P/O. R. P. Bell (pilot) and Sgt. E. A. Davies (wireless operator) killed.

13/8/41 00.27 hrs. Oxford II R6156 of No. 15 SFTS.
Crashed one mile north of Tackley, Oxfordshire. F/Sgt. E. Julin-Olsen killed.

13/8/41 00.27 hrs. Oxford W6229 (sic) of No. 15 SFTS.
Crashed near Sturdy's Castle Inn, near Weston-on-the-Green, Oxfordshire. LAC. C. P. Blair killed.

14/8/41 02.39 hrs. Wellington II W5536 'M' of No. 12 Sqn.
Attacked and forced to crash land at Little Coates, Lincolnshire. Sgt. Cameran (captain), Sgt. Cook (pilot) and Sgt. Thorpe (rear gunner) safe.

Sgt. Price (navigator) and Sgt. Wakeford (front gunner) injured. Sgt. Harrison (wireless operator) killed.

17/8/41 00.01 hrs. Wellington W5532 'M' of No. 104 Sqn.
Shot down at South Leverton near Scunthorpe, Humberside. Sgt. W. T. R. Stephenson (captain), Sgt. J. W. Nowlan (pilot), Sgt. S. C. Stewart (observer), Sgt. K. Hutchinson (wireless operator), Sgt. I. H. A. Henderson (wireless operator) and P/O. P. J. Murphy (gunner) killed.

20/8/41 01.05 hrs. Wellington IA N3005 of No. 11 OTU.
Shot down north east of Barrington, Cambridgeshire. F/Sgt. C. G. Andrews (pilot), Sgt. R. F. Gutteridge (pilot) and Sgt. R. H. Hazell (pilot) killed. Sgt. R. G. P. Capham (gunner) killed.

30/8/41 02.12 hrs. Wellington IC X9826 'D' of No. 115 Sqn.
Shot down over Martlesham Heath and crashed at Kesgrave, Suffolk. Sgt. J. K. Murdoch (pilot), Sgt. F. J. McGaw (pilot), Sgt. W. H. Blades (wireless operator), Sgt. W. J. Cowell (gunner), F/Sgt. A. Forse (observer) and F/Sgt. J. W. Boyce (wireless operator) killed.

31/8/41 23.00 hrs. Anson I N5074 of No. 16 OTU.
Damaged but succeeded in landing at Croughton Airfield, Northamptonshire. F/Sgt. P. C. Maries (pilot) safe. P/O. J. C. Bosch (pupil) killed. Three passengers injured.

1/9/41 02.48 hrs. Wellington 1C R1411 of No. 99 Sqn.
Shot down from 150 feet and crashed at Beck Row near Mildenhall, Suffolk. P/O. G. S. Eccles (pilot), Sgt. D. H. Hodge (pilot), Sgt. A. F. B. Broadribb (observer), Sgt. D. R. Mallett (wireless operator) and Sgt. G. E. Botall (gunner) killed. Sgt. Stevens (gunner) injured.

1/9/41 Wellington IC X9611 of No. 27 OTU.
Damaged and force landed near North Luffenham, Leicestershire. Three crew injured.

7/9/41 Whitley V Z6864 of No. 78 Sqn.
Damaged and forced to crash land near Ripon, Yorkshire. No crew casualties.

20/9/41 23.10 hrs. Hampden P5314 of No. 16 OTU.
Crashed in flames at Guist, near Croughton Airfield, Northamptonshire. Sgt. N. Van der Merwe (pilot), Sgt. D. A. Paine (navigator), Sgt. J. H. Ixer (wireless operator) and Sgt. R. Leagas (gunner) killed.

3/10/41 22.30 hrs. Stirling I N6085 of No. 7 Sqn.
Shot down and crashed at Caxton Gibbet, Cambridgeshire. Sqn/Ldr. D. I. McLeod (captain), F/Lt. S. G. Stock DFC (rear gunner), F/Sgt. H. Watson (wireless operator), Sgt. J. A. Marshall (front gunner) and F/Sgt. J. R. Walker (flight engineer) killed. P/O. J. R. Alverson (observer) and Sgt. I. Hunter (pilot) baled out safely from 700 feet.

11/10/41 21.10 hrs. Oxford II AB767 of No. 12 FTS. Collided with Lt. H. Hahn's Ju 88 and crashed at Grantham, Lincolnshire. Sgt. T. D. Graham (instructor) and Cpl. S. J. Edwards (pupil) killed.

12/10/41 21.17 hrs. Blenheim IV R3617 of No. 51 OTU.
Shot down at Sherrington, Buckinghamshire. Sgt. F. Filmer and one other killed.

I/NJG2 Losses 1940–1941

The details below record the known losses to men and machines attached to I/NJG2, from its formation to its departure to North Africa. In order to provide a complete record of the unit, accidents during non-operational flights are included. This is an important feature as the number of aircraft available for operations was reduced as a result. The system for recording the extent of damage to airframes in the Luftwaffe expresses damage in percentage terms. Thus 10% would reflect slight damage, whilst 100% would be a total loss.

Abbreviations:

Ranks:		Functions:		
Hptm.	Hauptmann	(F)	Flieger	Pilot
Oblt.	Oberleutnant	(Bo)	Beobachter	Observer
Lt.	Leutnant	(Bm)	Bordmechaniker	Flight Engineer
Ofw.	Oberfeldwebel	(Bf)	Bordfunker	Wireless Operator
Fw.	Feldwebel	(Bs)	Bordschütze	Air Gunner
Uffz.	Unteroffizier			
Ogefr.	Obergefreiter	(StKp)	Staffelkapitän	
		(GrKdr)	Gruppen-kommandeur	

29/6/40 Me 110 of 2/NJG1.
Crashed in unknown circumstances. Fw. Schwarz and Fw. Born killed.

27/7/40 Do 17Z of 5/NJG1.
Crashed near Krefeld during a non-operational flight. Fw. Gustav Buck and Fw. Herrmann Schmidt of 2/NJG2 killed.

18/8/40 03.00 hrs. Ju 88C-2 of 4/NJG1.
Shot down by P/O. R. A. Rhodes and Sgt. W. J. Gregory in Blenheim L6741 of No. 29 Sqn. Crashed into the sea off Spurn Head, Yorkshire. Ofw. Fritz Zenkel (F), Fw. Gustav Schramm (Bf) and Gefr. Hans Roth (Bm) missing.

29/8/40 Ju 88C-2 W.Nr.0256 of II/NJG1.
Crashed at Elsdorf during a training flight. Lt. Alfred Bregant (F) Gefr. Heinz Schmidt (Bf) Gefr. Karl Löneke (Bm) killed.

2/9/40 Ju 88C-2 W.Nr.0266 R4+JL of 3/NJG2.
Became lost and landed near St. Trond sustaining 80% damage.

16/9/40 Ju 88C-2 W.Nr. 0190 R4+AH of 3/NJG2.
Failed to return from a sortie to England and presumed to have crashed into the North Sea. Fw. Werner Palm (F) killed. Gefr. Hans Reinisch (Bf) and Gefr. Rudolf Haberland (Bm) missing.

14/10/40 Do 17Z-10 W.Nr.2851 R4+DK of 2/NJG2.

Crashed on return to Gilze-Rijen after combat and received 80% damage.
Uffz. Götz (F) and three others injured.

15/10/40 Me 110D W.Nr.3812 2A + BL of 4/NJG2.
Crew baled out safely in unknown circumstances.

17/10/40 Ju 88C-2 W.Nr.0251 R4 + EL of 3/NJG2.
Received 20% damage when landing at Gilze-Rijen on return from
operations.

17/10/40 Me 110D W.Nr.3385 3M + AH attached to 4/NJG2.
Crashed at Capelle during operations. Oblt. Paul Zimmermann (F) and
Gefr. Walter Makowsky (Bf) killed.

20/10/40 Ju 88C-2 W.Nr.0278 of 3/NJG2.
Sustained 60% damage when landing at Eindhoven after operations.
Fw. Kurt Schlicht (F) injured.

27/10/40 Ju 88A-1 W.Nr.6144 of 3/NJG2.
Sustained 60% damage on take off from Gilze-Rijen.

1/11/40 Ju 88C-4 W.Nr.0349 R4 + OL of 3/NJG2.
Failed to return from a sortie to England and presumed to have crashed into
the North Sea. Uffz. Mathias Lang (F), Gefr. Heinz Linke (Bf) and Gefr.
Wilhelm Geradli (Bm) missing.

9/11/40 Do 17Z-10 W.Nr.2817 R4 + HK of 2/NJG2.
Damaged by a night fighter over Lincolnshire and returned to Gilze-Rijen on
one engine. Ofw. Paul Rosenberger (Bf) and Uffz. Karl Lang (Bm) injured.
Ofw. Herbert Schmidt (F) safe.

23/11/40 Ju 88C-4 W.Nr.0347 R4 + BB of Stab I/NJG2.
Failed to return from a sortie to England and presumed to have crashed into
the North Sea. Major Karl Heinrich Heyse (F) (GrKdr), Uffz. Richard
Fiedler (Bf) and Uffz. Herbert Bauda (Bm) missing.

23/11/40 Ju 88C-4 W.Nr. 0373 R4 + BK of 3/NJG2.
Failed to return from a sortie to England and presumed to have crashed into
the North Sea. Fw. Kurt Schlicht (F), Gefr. Hans Nitz (Bf) and Uffz.
Wilhelm Marschall (Bm) killed.

23/11/40 Ju 88C of I/NJG2.
Exploded when being prepared for operations at Gilze-Rijen. Gefr. Richard
Hirschmann and Ofw. Paul Schach killed.

28/11/40 Ju 88C-4 W.Nr.0341 of I/NJG2.
Received 50% damage when landing at Gilze-Rijen.

9/12/40 Ju 88C-4 W.Nr.0369 of I/NJG2.
Forced to land at Trevent due to mechanical failure.

21/12/40 08.15 hrs. Ju 88C-2 W.Nr.0272 R4 + KL of 3/NJG2.
Shot down by the ground defences of Manby airfield, Lincolnshire and
crashed at Mill Hill, South Cockerington, Lincolnshire. Oblt. Ulrich Meyer
(F) (Stkp.), Fw. Fritz Schöttke (Bf) and Ogefr. Wilhelm Schneider (Bm)
killed.

21/12/40 Ju 88C-2 W.Nr.0182 of I/NJG2.

Intruders over Britain

Crashed on return to Gilze-Rijen. Gefr. Kurt Ludescher (F), Gefr Heinrich Dempewolf (Bs) and Gefr. Friedrich Rhode (Bf) killed.

1941

1/1/41 Ju 88C-2 W.Nr.0254 of I/NJG2.
Crash landed at Gilze-Rijen after combat with 30% damage.

9/1/41 Ju 88C-2 W.Nr.0227 R4 + CL of 3/NJG2.
Failed to return from a sortie to England and presumed to have crashed into the North Sea. Uffz. Otto Kräher (F), Uffz. Josef Diwok (Bm) and Uffz. Martin Stachowski (Bf) missing.

4–5/2/41 Do 17Z-10 W.Nr.2859 R4 + BK of 2/NJG2.
Failed to return from a sortie to England and presumed to have crashed into the North Sea. Oblt. Otto Häuser (F), Fw. Gerhard Palm (Bf) and Fw. Johannes Quade (Bs) missing.

15/2/41 Ju 88C-2 W.Nr.0239 of I/NJG2.
Force landed at Gilze-Rijen with 20% damage.

16/2/41 Ju 88C-4 W.Nr.0538 of I/NJG2.
Received 8% damage on landing at Gilze-Rijen during a non-operational flight.

17/2/41 Ju 88C-4 W.Nr.0361 of I/NJG2.
Received 40% damage on landing at Gilze-Rijen on return from operations.

17/2/41 Ju 88C-2 W.Nr.0230 of 4/NJG2.
Hit tree after take off from Gilze-Rijen and crashed during a non-operational flight. Ofhr. Hans Klarhöfer (F), Gefr. Franz Baumgärtner (Bf) and Gefr. Karl Osterloh (Bm) killed.

24/2/41 Ju 88C-4 W.Nr.0544 of 3/NJG2.
Crashed during operations at Gilze-Rijen. Fw. Johann Schuster (F), Uffz. Franz Fuchs (Bf) and Gefr. Kurt Masepohl (Bs) killed.

27/2/41 Ju 88C-4 W.Nr.0371 of 3/NJG2.
Received 15% damage on landing at Gilze-Rijen after combat.

28/2/41 Ju 88C-4 W.Nr.0660 of I/NJG2.
Received 35% damage during a non-operational flight on a take off from Gilze-Rijen.

2/3/41 Ju 88C-4 W.Nr.0377 of I/NJG2.
Received 15% damage on landing at Gilze-Rijen after combat.

2/3/41 Ju 88C-4 W.Nr.0375 of I/NJG2.
Received 15% damage on landing at Gilze-Rijen after combat.

10/3/41 23.30 hrs. Ju 88C-2 W.Nr.0343 R4 + CH of I/NJG2.
Forced to land after engine failure, at Hay Green, Terrington St. Clement, Norfolk. Oblt. Kurt Herrmann (F), Uffz. Engelbert Böttner (Bf) and Fw. Wilhelm Rüppel (Bm) captured.

14/3/41 03.30 hrs. Ju 88C-4 W.Nr.0604 R4 + GM of 4/NJG2.
Shot down by W/Cdr. S. C. Widdows and Sgt. B. Ryall in a Beaufighter of No. 29 Sqn. Crashed at Smith's Farm, Dovendale, 3 miles south-west of

Louth, Lincolnshire. Gefr. Hans Körner (F), Gefr. Karlheinz Spangenberg (Bf) and Uffz. Willi Otto Gebhardt (Bm) killed.

15/3/41 Ju 88C-4 W.Nr.0630 of I/NJG2.
Received 30% damage on landing from a non-operational flight at Gütersloh.

24/3/41 Ju 88A-1 W.Nr.6119 of I/NJG2.
Received 10% damage on landing at Alphen during a non-operational flight.

26/3/41 Ju 88C-2 W.Nr.0773 of 3/NJG2.
Received 35% damage on landing at Gilze-Rijen after a non-operational flight.

27/3/41 Ju 88C-4 W.Nr.0363 of I/NJG2.
Crash landed near Reims after engine failure during a non-operational flight and received 90% damage.

31/3/41 Ju 88C-4 W.Nr.0618 R4 + HM of 4/NJG2.
Failed to return from a sortie to England and presumed to have crashed into the North Sea after engine failure. Last reported position QU1587. Gefr. Otto Krüger (F), Gefr. August Kronewitter (Bf) and Gefr. Heinrich Kellner (Bm) missing.

9/4/41 22.10 hrs. Ju 88C-2 W.Nr.0776 R4 + CM of 4/NJG2.
Shot down by Sgt. S. Bennett and Sgt. Curtiss in Beaufighter R2122 of No. 25 Sqn. Crashed near to the Burley to Langham road, north of Oakham, Rutland. Gefr. Franz Brotz (F) killed. Uffz. Willi Lindler (Bf) and Gefr. Ewald Gorlt (Bs) captured.

17/4/41 21.23 hrs. Ju 88C-4 W.Nr.0345 R4 + BM of 4/NJG2.
Crashed at Gothic House Farm, Thorney, Cambridgeshire, in uncertain circumstances but believed to have been brought down by another I/NJG2 aircraft. Ogefr. Wilhelm Beetz (F), Gefr. Rudolf Kronika (Bm) and Gefr. Johann Mittag (Bf) killed.

18/4/41 Ju 88C-2 W.Nr.0732 of 3/NJG2.
Crashed and exploded during operations near Gilze-Rijen. Uffz. Willi Kedler (F), Gefr. Gerhard Wawra (Bf) and Uffz. Helmut Heese (Bm) killed.

18/4/41 Ju 88C-2 W.Nr.0767 of I/NJG2.
Received 20% damage on operations at Gilze-Rijen due to mechanical failure.

24/4/41 Fw. Heinrich Schwöbel of I/NJG2.
Wounded in combat.

3/5/41 I/NJG2.
Uffz. Eduard Funke (Bm) wounded during combat.

6/5/41 Ju 88C-2 W.Nr.0740 of I/NJG2.
Received 15% on landing at Gilze-Rijen after combat.

8/5/41 00.30 hrs. Do 17Z-10 W.Nr.2843 R4 + GK of 2/NJG2.
Shot down by P/O. D. W. Thompson and P/O. L. D. Britain in Beaufighter R2181 of No. 25 Sqn. Crashed at Carrington near Boston, Lincolnshire. Fw. Wilhelm Lettenmeier (F) killed. Uffz. Georg Herden (Bf) and Uffz. Herbert Thomas (Bm) captured.

8/5/41 Ju 88C W.Nr.0642 of I/NJG2.
Received 25% damage Gilze-Rijen during a non-operational flight.

27/5/41 Ju 88C-4 W.Nr.0359 of I/NJG2.
Attacked by an Me 109 during a ferry flight from Brest and landed at Lannion with 50% damage. Ofw. Herrmann Sommer (F) and Ofw. Hans Reinnagel (Bm) injured.

4/6/41 00.30 hrs. Ju 88C-2 W.Nr.0570 R4 + LK of 2/NJG2.
Flew into Skelder Moor, near Whitby, Yorkshire, in bad visibility. Lt. Johannes Feuerbaum (F), Gefr. Gerhard Denzin (Bf) and Gefr. Rudolf Peters (Bm) killed.

14/6/41 01.00 hrs. Ju 88C-4 W.Nr.0335 R4 + AM of 4/NJG2.
Shot down by P/O. D. W. Thompson and P/O. L. D. Britain in Beaufighter R2157 of No. 25 Sqn. Crashed of Wingland Marsh, near King's Lynn, Norfolk. Uffz. Helmut Bähner (F), Uffz. Jakob Ried (Bf) and Uffz. Heinz Schulz (Bm) killed.

14/6/41 00.30 hrs. Ju 88C-4 W.Nr.0550 R4 + DM of 4/NJG2.
Shot down by Sqn/Ldr. H. P. Pleasance DFC and Sgt. B. Bent in Beaufighter T4634 of No. 25 Sqn. Crashed at Narford, near Swaffham, Norfolk. Uffz. Richard Hoffmann (F) and Fw. Peter Mayer (Bm) captured, Gefr. Johann Reisinger (Bf) killed.

14/6/41 Ju 88C-2 W.Nr.0785 R4 + IM of 4/NJG2.
Flew into the North Sea when circling a dinghy containing the crew of He 111H-5 W.Nr.3883 5J + KS of 8/KG4 who had been forced to ditch after an engine failed. Uffz. Vitus Alt (F), Uffz. Hans-Georg Suckow (Bf) and Uffz. Erwin Korn (Bm) killed.

21/6/41 Ju 88C-2 W.Nr.0756 of I/NJG2.
Received 20% damage during combat and landed at Bergen.

22/6/41 01.20 hrs. Ju 88C-2 W.Nr.0827 R4 + JH of 1/NJG2.
Shot down by F/O. M. J. Herrick DFC and P/O. Yeomans in Beaufighter R2277 of No. 25 Sqn. Crashed at Deeping St. James, near Peterborough, Huntingdonshire. Ofw. Otto Wiese (F) and Gefr. Herrmann Mandel (Bm) killed. Uffz. Heinrich Beul (Bf) captured.

26/6/41 Ju 88C-2 W.Nr.0794 R4 + GM of 4/NJG2.
Damaged by return fire over the North Sea at 00.15 hrs. and abandoned over Charleville, France. Aircraft flew on to crash at Mailen, Italy. Oblt. Paul Bohn (F) (Stkp) killed. Uffz. Walter Lindner (Bm) and Fw. Hans Engemann (Bf) baled out safely.

9/7/41 Ju 88C-4 W.Nr.0848 R4 + MH of 1/NJG2.
Last radio message timed at 03.18 hrs. Crashed into the sea off the Dutch Coast at position PQ3352. Lt. Rudolf Stradner (F) missing. Uffz. Wilhelm Krieg (Bf) and Uffz. Max Oswald (Bm) killed.

14/7/41 I/NJG2.
Gefr. Hantusch (Bf) and Ogefr. Faulhaber (Bm) injured in combat.

22/7/41 01.30 hrs. Ju 88C-4 W.Nr.0842 R4 + BL of 3/NJG2.
Collided with Wellington R1334 of No. 11 OTU. over Ashwell, Hertfordshire. Lt. Heinz Völker (F), Uffz. Herbert Indenbirken (Bf) and

Fw. Andreas Würstl (Bm) killed.

24/7/41 01.10 hrs. Ju 88C-2 W.Nr.0854 R4 + LM of 4/NJG2.
Believed to have been brought down by another aircraft of I/NJG2 and crashed near Bonby Village, Lincolnshire. Ogefr. Heinrich Ladiges (F), Ogefr. Friedrich Heinemann (Bf) and Fw. Josef Beblo (Bm) killed.

20/7/41 04.20 lus. Ju 00C-4 W.Nı.0721 R1 + KK of 2/NJG2.
Crashed in unknown circumstances at Vine Farm, Wivenhoe, Essex. Lt. Dr. Lothar Bisang (F), Gefr. Werner Ulbricht (Bf) and Gefr. Fritz Rosenstock (Bm) missing.

31/7/41 Ju 88C-2 W.Nr. 0764 of 3/NJG2.
Received 25% damage on take off for operations from Gilze-Rijen. Lt. Hans Hahn (F) and Uffz. Helmut Scheidt (Bm) injured.

31/7/41 Ju 88C-2 W.Nr.0748 of I/NJG2.
Received 35% damage in forced landing at Moerdijk.

6/8/41 Ju 88C-2 W.Nr.0782 of I/NJG2.
Sustained 30% damage after making a forced landing following engine failure.

12/8/41 Ju 88C-2 W.Nr.0845 of I/NJG2.
Damaged by fighter and forced to land at Steenbergen with 60% damage. Hptm. Karl Hülshoff (F) safe. Ofw. Willi Mayer (Bf) and Ofw. Paul Licht (Bs) injured.

13/8/41 Ju 88C-4 W.Nr.0375 of I/NJG2.
Sustained 40% damage on landing at Gilze-Rijen.

17/8/41 Ju 88C-2 W.Nr.0851 R4 + HM of 4/NJG2.
Failed to return from a sortie to England and crashed into the North Sea. Lt. Rudolf Pfeiffer (F) and Uffz. Alfred Ranke (Bm) missing. Gefr. Otto Schierling (Bf) killed.

2/9/41 Ju 88C-4 W.Nr.0592 R4 + CM of 4/NJG2.
Failed to return from a sortie to English East Coast and crashed in the North Sea. Fw. Walter Kleine (F) and Fw. Helmuth Fiedler (Bm) missing. Fw. Hans Engmann (Bf) killed.

5/9/41 Ju 88C-4 W.Nr.0377 of I/NJG2.
Received 20% damage when undercarriage collapsed at Gilze-Rijen.

15/9/41 Ju 88C-4 W.Nr.0584 (100%) and Ju 88C-2 W.Nr.0779 (10%).
Both damaged at Gilze-Rijen.

16/9/41 21.25 hrs. Ju 88C-4 W.Nr.0839 R4 + NH of I/NJG2.
Shot down by Sqn/Ldr. G. L. Raphael DFC and Bar and ACI Addison DFM in a Havoc II of No. 85 Sqn. Crashed into the sea off Clacton-on-Sea, Essex. Ofw. Erwin Veil (F), Uffz. Angelbert Wegener (Bf) and Ofw. Heinrich Welker (Bm) captured.

19/9/41 Do 17 L-Z W.Nr.2867 of I/NJG2.
Received 10% damage when undercarriage collapsed at Gilze-Rijen.

21/9/41 Ju 88C-2 W.Nr.0720 of I/NJG2.
Crashed at Gilze-Rijen during a non operational flight. Oblt. Bernhard Pajung (F) and Gefr. Willi Gutt (Bs) injured. Uffz. Franz Lindner (Bf) killed.

3/10/41 Ju 88C-2 W.Nr.0791 of I/NJG2.
Forced to land at Cadzand after fuel shortage. Fw. Hans Berschwinger (F) injured.

11/10/41 21.20 hrs. Ju 88C-4 W.Nr.0351 R4 + NL of 3/NJG2.
Collided with Oxford AB767 of No. 12 FTS. over Grantham and fell at Barrowby Village, Lincolnshire. Lt. Hans Hahn (F), Uffz. Ernst-Wilhelm Meissler (Bf) and Uffz. Helmut Scheidt (Bm) killed.

12/10/41 Ju 88C-2 W.Nr.0756 of I/NJG2.
Damaged on return to Gilze-Rijen on one engine. Ofw. Jung and crew safe.

16/10/41 Ju 88C-2 W.Nr. 0788 of I/NJG2.
Sustained 50% damage in a forced landing at Parow during a non-operational flight.

24/10/41 Ju 88C-2 W.Nr.0236 of I/NJG2.
Crash landed during a non-operational flight at Brussels and received 65% damage. Gefr. Ernst Witt (Bs) injured.

Losses of Allied aircraft attributable to intruder action

1943

24/8/43 03.00 hrs. Lancaster B.I. EE105 'Q' of No. 97 Sqn. Shot down over Marham and crashed at Shouldham, Norfolk. Sgt. C. S. Chatten (pilot) wounded. Sgt. C. Baumber (flight engineer), P/O. L. R. Armitage (navigator), Sgt. Standen (bomb aimer), Sgt. Reffin (gunner) and Sgt. L. V. Smith baled out safely. F/Sgt. J. R. Kraemer (mid-upper gunner) killed.

7/9/43 Stirling I W7455 of No. 1657 CU.
Forced to crash land at Great Thurlow, Suffolk. P/O. L. F. Smith (instructor) killed. Sgt. C. J. Gilkes (pilot), P/O. N. E. Miles (navigator), F/Sgt. G. R. Greaves (wireless operator), Sgt. D. E. Reddy (bomb aimer) seriously injured. Sgt. Oulton (flight engineer), Sgt. J. M. Hardman (bomb aimer) and Sgt. E. V. Cramp (gunner) slightly injured.

23/9/43 00.43 hrs. Lancaster B.I. W4948 'S' of No. 57 Sqn.
Shot down in the circuit of East Kirby and crashed near Spilsby, Lincolnshire. P/O. S. Duff (pilot), P/O. P. N. Rolfe (navigator), Sgt. H. R. Ellmer (wireless operator), Sgt. R. Smith (mid-upper gunner) and F/Sgt. W. Pryde (rear gunner) killed. Sgt. Cherrington (flight engineer) and Sgt. R. C. Brown (bomb aimer) baled out safely.

28/9/43 01.20 hrs. Lancaster III ED410 'X2' of No. 101 Sqn.
Crashed near Wickenby, Lincolnshire. P/O. D.W. Skipper, Sgt. P. Hands, Sgt. T. C. Kerr, Sgt. P. Meredith, Sgt. J. D. Gulliver, Sgt. W. J. Phillips, Sgt. S. Harris and Sgt. R. V. Liersch killed.

1944

31/3/44 Mosquito XVII of No. 25 Sqn.
Shot up whilst taxiing at Coltishall, Norfolk. Sub/Lt. Adams and Sub/Lt. Smith safe.

31/3/44 04.25 hrs. Lancaster III LM509 'C' of No. 12 Sqn.
Damaged over Norwich, but landed at Wickenby with starboard outer engine and all hydraulics hit. F/Sgt. A. F. T. L'Estrangem and crew safe. Sgt. A. Davenport (rear gunner) injured.

12/4/44 Stirling III LJ450 'F' of No. 1654 CU.
Shot down in flames over Bassingham Bombing Range, Lincolnshire. F/Sgt. J. J. G. Nicholson (pilot), Sgt. J. E. Lowe (navigator), Sgt. G. J. Lewis (bomb aimer) and Sgt. K. L. McFarlane (rear gunner) killed. Four others baled out safely.

12/4/44 00.50 hrs. B17-G 42-97556 of the 96th BG.
Crashed and exploded at Great Glemham Park, Suffolk. Lt. D. M. MacGregor and eight others injured. Three killed.

12/4/44 00.30 hrs. Spitfire of No. 64 Sqn.
Shot down at Skeyton near Coltishall, Norfolk. F/Sgt. Maunders baled out safely.

12/4/44 Mosquito of No. 60 OTU.
Shot down near Grantham, Lincolnshire. F/O. Byrne and Sgt. Payne baled out safely.

19/4/44 02.09 hrs. Lancaster II ED631 'B' of No. 115 Sqn.
Undercarriage collapsed on runway of Witchford Airfield, Cambridgeshire. Sgt. Lemoine and crew safe.

19/4/44 02.10 hrs. Lancaster II LL667 'KO-R' of No. 115 Sqn.
Shot down on landing at Witchford Airfield, Cambridgeshire. P/O. J. Birnie (pilot), F/Sgt. D. Jones (navigator), F/Sgt. A. Feldman (bomb aimer), Sgt. E. Kerwin (wireless operator), Sgt. G. Bailey (rear gunner), Sgt. W. McMillan (mid-upper gunner) and Sgt. J. Ferguson (flight engineer) killed.

19/4/44 03.48 hrs. Lancaster I LL867 'A4-J' of No. 115 Sqn.
Shot down on landing at Witchford Airfield, Cambridgeshire. F/Lt. C. Eddy (pilot), F/O. A. Smith (navigator), F/Sgt. H. Pugh (bomb aimer), F/Sgt. J. Maddox (wireless operator), W/O. H. Benndis (rear gunner), Sgt. A. Langridge (mid-upper gunner) and Sgt. W. Murphy (flight engineer) killed.

19/4/44 02.30 hrs. Lancaster I ME743 'Y' of No. 625 Sqn.
Shot down in flames and crashed near Kelstern Airfield, Lincolnshire. P/O. J. P. Cosgrove (pilot), Sgt. A. Bennett (flight engineer), Sgt. G. Jeeves (bomb aimer), F/Sgt. R. A. Mercer (navigator), Sgt. C. Williams (wireless operator), Sgt. C. J. Page (mid-upper gunner) and Sgt. D. H. Beechey (rear gunner) killed.

21/4/44 05.15 hrs. Master II of No. 7 (P)AFU.
Shot down one-and-a-half miles north of Peterborough Airfield, Lincolnshire. F/O. J. Banister (pilot) killed.

22/4/44 B24-J 44-40085 of the 565th Sqn. 389th BG.
Crashed on landing at Hethel Airfield, Norfolk and demolished a signals hut killing the two men inside. Lt. Foley and crew safe.

22/4/44 22.17 hrs. B24-J 42-109915 of the 567th Sqn. 389th BG.
Shot down and crashed at Cantley, Norfolk. Lt. Wilkerson (pilot) and one waist gunner baled out safely. Eight others killed.

22/4/44 22.25 hrs. B24-H 42-94744 of the 714th Sqn. 448th BG.
Crashed on to a railway embankment near Worlingham, Suffolk. 1st/Lt. M. L. Alspaugh (pilot), Lt. D. Watters (pilot), 2nd/Lt. W. A. Carison (navigator), 2nd/Lt. W. E. Edwards (bomb aimer), Sgt. D. L. Halter (wireless operator), Sgt. C. Adams (flight engineer), Sgt. O. W. Worsman (gunner), S/Sgt. R. G. Chartiers (rear gunner), Sgt. H. A. Barney (gunner) T/Sgt. J. E. Adamson (gunner) baled out safely.

22/4/44 B24-H 42-73497 'Vadie Raye' of the 715th Sqn. 448th BG.
Landed in flames on Seething Airfield, Norfolk. Cpt. A. D. Skaggs (pilot), Cpt. W. G. Blum (pilot) and Sgt. G. Glevanik (flight engineer) landed safely with aircraft. T/Sgt. S. C. Filipowicz jumped out injured. S/Sgt. F. T.

Sheehan (gunner), Sgt. E. Gaskins (gunner) and Sgt. W. Jackson (gunner) baled out safely.

22/4/44 B24 41-28595 'Ice Kold Katie' of the 713th Sqn. 448th BG.
Overshot the runway at Seething and later hit by B24 41-28240 which sliced off the upper tail fins and broke the fuselage in half. Crew safe.

22/4/44 B24 41-28240 of the 713th Sqn. 448 BG.
Overshot the runway at Seething and collided with B24 41-28595. Crew safe.

22/4/44 22.07 hrs. B24-H 42-52608 of the 715th Sqn. 448th BG.
Shot down into the sea 1 mile off Hopton, Suffolk. 1st/Lt. C. C. Pitts and nine others killed.

22/4/44 22.20 hrs. B24-H 41-28843 'N' of the 715th Sqn. 448th BG.
Shot down and crashed near Benacre Church, Kessingland, Suffolk. 2nd/Lt. E. V. Pulcipher and nine others killed.

22/4/44 22.20 hrs. B24-H 42-64490 'Cee Gee II' of the 735th Sqn. 453rd BG.
Hit 15 miles off the Suffolk coast and crashed at Girling's Farm, Reydon Marsh, Suffolk. Lt. J. S. Munsey (pilot), Lt. R. O. Crale (pilot), T/Sgt. J. F. McKinney (waist gunner) and T/Sgt. W. C. Grady (wireless operator) killed in aircraft. T/Sgt. G. G. Conway (top gunner) baled out but drowned. S/Sgt. R. W. McClure (rear gunner) 2nd/Lt. L. Helfand (navigator), Lt. A. Orlowski (waist gunner), Sgt. K. G. Laux (front gunner) and Sgt. N. W. Brown (ball gunner) baled out safely.

22/4/44 B24-H 41-28644 of the 453rd BG.
Undercarriage collapsed on landing at Tibenham airfield, Norfolk. No crew casualties.

22/4/44 22.34 hrs. B24-J 42-100357 of the 458th BG.
Made a crash landing with right wing in flames near 'The Bull', 1 mile from Horsham St. Faith, Norfolk. Lt. Stilson and crew safe.

22/4/44 22.10 hrs. B24-H 42-52353 of the 754th Sqn. 458th BG.
Crashed near Daniel's Road, Lakenham, Norfolk. Lt. T. G. Harris and one other safe. S/Sgt. H. E. Found, 2nd/Lt. M. C. Marshall, T/Sgt. F. X. McKenna, S/Sgt. F. G. Morin, 2nd/Lt. R. L. Moses, Sgt. C. L. Oder, T/Sgt. W. M. R. Pearce and S/Sgt. A. Silverman killed.

22/4/44 22.30 hrs. B24-H 42-52536 of the 788th Sqn. 467th BG.
Shot down from 500 feet and crashed at Withersdale St. Mendham, Suffolk. 2nd/Lt. J. H. Maxey (captain), 2nd/Lt. J. A. Roden (pilot), 2nd/Lt. W. E. Landis (navigator) 2nd/Lt. R. E. Wilson (bomb aimer), S/Sgt. L. J. Violette (flight engineer), S/Sgt. G. E. Carter (wireless operator), S/Sgt. R. E. Orr (gunner), Sgt. J. R. Howe (gunner), S/Sgt. C. D. McGonigle (bottom gunner) and S/Sgt. R. E. Horak (tail gunner) killed.

22/4/44 22.22 hrs. B24-J 42-52445 of the 791st Sqn. 467th BG.
Crashed near Barsham, Suffolk. 1st/Lt. S. C. Reid jr. 2/Lt. W. W. Mason (captain), 2/Lt. J. G. Ferguson (navigator), Lt. L. A. Alier (bomb aimer), Sgt. S. L. Dory (flight engineer) and T/Sgt. W. W. Kovalenko (wireless operator) killed. Sgt. E. W. Hoke killed due to parachute failure. Sgt. M. M. Shanks (gunner), Sgt. G. Hamilton (gunner) and Sgt. J. H. Biggs (tail gunner) baled out safely.

22/4/44 Albermarle V1610 of No. 42 OTU.
Shot down whilst on a training flight near Lowestoft, Suffolk. Sgt. J. E. Hutchinson, Sgt. A. A. Whittome and Sgt. K. Rushby killed. Sgt. J. Davis and Sgt. R. W. Thorogood baled out safely.

25/4/44 04.10 hrs. Lancaster III DV177 'K2' of No. 626 Sqn.
Shot down in flames and crashed at USAAF Station Boxted, Essex. W/O. M. L. McPherson (pilot), W/O. F. W. Gunn (navigator), Sgt. D. Randle (wireless operator), F/Sgt. J. L. Shell (bomb aimer), Sgt. J. D. Mayger (flight engineer), W/O. R. E. H. Cameron (mid-upper gunner) and Sgt. E. J. Fancy (rear gunner) killed.

25/4/44 04.20 hrs. Halifax III LK789 'L' of No. 76 Sqn.
Shot down near Welney, Norfolk. P/O. D. R. Dibbins (pilot), F/Sgt. J. R. Bathe (bomb aimer), Sgt. K. C. Oswald (navigator), Sgt. J. G. Davenport (flight engineer), Sgt. N. M. Harrison (wireless operator) and Sgt. G. N. Head (gunner) killed. F/Sgt. J. Anderson (gunner) injured.

27/4/44 04.30 hrs. Oxford I LX196 of No. 18 (P)AFU.
Collided with an Me 410 of KG51 when in the circuit of Church Lawford and crashed at Frankton near Rugby. P/O. C. G. W. Moore killed.

23/5/44 02.55 hrs. Lancaster I NN695 'X' of No. 619 Sqn.
Crashed at East Wretham, Norfolk. F/O. R. H. Redshaw (pilot), Sgt. L. G. Richardson (flight engineer), F/Sgt. S. B. Bandur (navigator), Sgt. K. W. Harmer (wireless operator), Sgt. R. A. McKay (mid-upper gunner) and P/O. F. J. Baker (rear gunner) killed. Sgt. Leeson (bomb aimer) baled out safely.

23/5/44 03.34 hrs. Lancaster III JB417 'R' of No. 582 Sqn.
Damaged over Little Staughton, Bedfordshire, but landed safely. Sqn/Ldr. H. W. B. Heney (captain) and crew safe.

22–23/5/44 Anson I LT476 of No. 13 OTU.
Damaged over Little Staughton, Bedfordshire, but landed safely. F/O. P. B. Davidson (pilot) killed. F/Sgt. R. N. Blyth (navigator) injured. W/O. G. Lister (navigator) and Sgt. McConchie safe.

29/5/44 02.39 hrs. Stirling I R9298 of No. 1657 CU.
Crashed on Stradishall Airfield, Suffolk and collided with Stirlings LK506 and R9283. F/O. W. A. C. Yates (pilot), Sgt. N. Nicholson (navigator), Sgt. G. Wood (wireless operator), Sgt. J. Carter (bomb aimer), Sgt. T. Farley (gunner), Sgt. J. W. Grainger (gunner) and Sgt. S. Sterry (flight engineer) killed.

7/6/44 23.25 hrs. B24-H 42-94911 of the 4th Sqn. 34th BG.
Crashed at Joe's Road, Blacksmith's Green, Wetheringsett, Suffolk. Lt. Rowley (pilot), Sgt. Humphreys (bomb aimer), T/Sgt. J Blackham (top gunner), T/Sgt. W. Reschke (waist gunner), T/Sgt. C. Forrister (wireless operator) and one other baled out. 2nd/Lt. A. Grabowski (navigator), Sgt. R. Erisch (rear gunner) and Sgt. W. Johnson (ball gunner) killed.

7/6/44 23.25 hrs. B24-H 42-52738 of the 34th BG.
Crashed on Mendlesham Airfield, Suffolk. 2nd/Lt. H. D. Eastman (pilot) and eight others baled out safely. Top gunner killed.

7/6/44 23.50 hrs B24-H 41-29572 of the 34th BG.
Crashed at Nedging, Suffolk. Nine of crew baled out safely but one killed due to parachute failure.

8/6/44 B24-H 42-52695 of the 34th BG.
Made a crash landing at Eye Airfield, Suffolk. No casualties reported.

28/6/44 02.26 hrs. Lancaster III NE145 'D' of No. 90 Sqn.
Crashed at Canada Farm, Icklingham, Suffolk. P/O. C. J. Todd (pilot), Sgt. R. J. Ferrans (navigator), Sgt. J. K. Horn (flight engineer), F/Sgt. R. J. T. Hawkes (bomb aimer), Sgt. W. A. Burnett (wireless operator), Sgt. D. J. Smith (mid-upper gunner) and Sgt. C. T. Sayer (rear gunner) killed.

28/6/44 Lancaster I LM164 'V' of No. 90 Sqn.
Damaged when attempting to land at Tuddenham. F/Lt. A. H. Burton DFC and four others safe. F/Sgt. W. P. Smith (rear gunner) killed.

28/6/44 B24-H 42-95321 of the 801st. BG.
Crashed at Eaton Socon, Bedfordshire. Three killed, one seriously injured, remainder safe.

Me 410 losses during intruder operations 1943–1944

Unlike the operations of I/NJG2, the intruder operations flown by Me 410s in late 1943 and 1944 were only part of the unit's task. As the main function of V/KG2 and II/KG51 was bombing, only losses that can be confirmed as having occurred during intruder operations are detailed. Unfortunately it has not been possible to identify the designation of the second crew man in each of the following Me 410s. It can be taken that the first named in each entry was the pilot (flieger) and that the second, by nature of his duel role, was either a Bordfunker or Bordschütze.

24/8/43 03.15 hrs. Me 410 A-1 W.Nr.420214 U5 + CF of 15/KG2.
Shot down by a British night fighter 8km off Zeebrugge, Belgium. Oblt. Wilhelm Schmitter (Stkp) and Ofw. Heinz Gräber baled out and rescued.

22/4/44 Me 410A-1 W.Nr.420458 9K + HP of 6/KG51.
Shot down by return fire from a B-24 it was attacking and crashed at Ashby St. Mary, Suffolk. Oblt. Klaus Krüger and Fw. Michael Reichardt killed.

22/4/44 Me 410A-1 W.Nr.420314 9K + MN of 5/KG51.
Failed to return from a sortie to England. Believed to have been damaged by return fire from B-24s and crashed into the North Sea. Hptm. Dietrich Puttfarken (GrKdr) and Ofw. Willi Lux missing.

27/4/44 04.30 hrs. Me 410A-1 W.Nr.420445 9K + ZP of StabII/KG51.
Collided with Oxford LX196 of No. 18 (P)AFU near Church Lawford airfield and crashed at Frankton, near Rugby. Lt. Wolfgang Wenning and Fw. Gustav Delp killed.

12/5/44 Me 410A-1 W.Nr.420201 9K + DN of 5/KG51.
Shot down by a British night fighter north east of Beauvais, France. Oblt. Claus Bieber and Fw. Heinz Closken killed.

29/5/44 Me 410A-1 W.Nr.420006 9K + KP of 6/KG51.
Failed to return from a sortie to England. Believed to have crashed into the North Sea. Fw. Ernst Dietrich and Uffz. Walter Schaknies missing.

2/6/44 Me 410A-1 W.Nr.420448 9K + MM of 4/KG51.
Shot down by a British night fighter near Nouilly, France. Lt. Martin Kneis injured.

6/6/44 Me 410A-1 W.Nr.420428 9K + AM of 4/KG51.
Shot down by a British night fighter when landing and crashed at St. Andre sur l'Eure. Ofw. Herrmann Bolten injured. Fw. Wilhelm Lohe killed.

7/6/44 Me 410A-1 W.Nr.420654 9K + HM of 4/KG51.
Failed to return from a sortie to England. Believed to have crashed into the North Sea. Hptm. Werner Dürr and Fw. Walter Heinemann missing.

7/6/44 Me 410A-1 W.Nr.420200 9K + IM of 4/KG51.
Failed to return from a sortie to England. Believed to have crashed into the North Sea. Uffz. Karl-Heinz Mond and Uffz. Hugo Hagel missing.

7/6/44 Me 410A-1 W.Nr.120018 9K + DP of 6/KG51.
Failed to return from a sortie to England. Believed to have crashed into the North Sea. Fw. Hans Seemann and Uffz. Karl-Heinz Steffen missing.

15/6/44 Me 410A-1 W.Nr.420417 9K + GN of 5/KG51.
Failed to return from a sortie to England. Believed to have crashed into the North Sea. Uffz. Heinrich Ramm and Uffz. Karl Seeland missing.

25/7/44 Me 410B-2 W.Nr.470136 9K + GM of 4/KG51.
Failed to return from a sortie to England. Believed to have crashed into the North Sea. Uffz. Walter Brügel and Uffz. Rudolf Sperlich missing.

Losses of RAF aircraft on the night of March 3rd – 4th, 1945

As the losses detailed below occurred in a relatively short period of time, the accuracy of some times are open to question. The times given are those quoted in contemporary records, but even these have been found to differ. Losses are therefore listed in the sequence in which they appear in the text.

00.08 hrs. Fortress II KH114 'B' of No. 214 Sqn.
Damaged on return from a 'Window' operation and landed at Woodbridge, Suffolk. F/Sgt. R. V. Kingdon and crew safe.

00.10 hrs. Mosquito XIX MM640 'H' of No. 169 Sqn.
Shot down near Coltishall on return from a bomber support sortie to Kamen and crashed at The Avenue, Buxton, Norfolk. Sqn/Ldr. V. J. Fenwick and F/O. J. W. Pierce killed.

00.16 hrs. Fortress III HB815 'J' of No. 214 Sqn.
Crashed at Lodge Farm, Oulton, Suffolk. F/O. Bennett, F/Sgt. H. Barnfield, Sgt. F. Hares, F/Sgt. L. A. Hadder, Sgt. P. J. Healy and Sgt. L. E. Billington killed. F/Sgt. W. Briddon, Sgt. A. McDermid, W/O. R. W. Church and W/O. L. J. Odgers safe.

00.39 hrs. Fortress HB802 'O' of No. 214 Sqn.
Attacked over Peterborough and landed at Brawdy.

00.20 hrs. Halifax NP913 'J' of No. 640 Sqn.
Attempted to land on three engines but lost height and crashed into Thicks Wood, short of Woodbridge Airfield. P/O. P. B. Manton (pilot), Sgt. E. R. Knowles (air bomber), Sgt. K. R. Stocker (navigator), Sgt. J. H. Law (wireless operator), Sgt. J. P. Pridding (mid-upper gunner), F/Sgt. C. E. Cox (flight engineer) killed. Sgt. E. J. V. Thompson (rear gunner) injured.

00.25 hrs. Halifax III NA107 'T' of No. 171 Sqn.
Shot down on return from a 'Mandrel' operation and crashed at Walnut Tree Farm, South Lopham, Norfolk. Sqn/Ldr. P. C. Procter (pilot), W/O. A. P. Richards (mid-upper gunner) and F/O. E. V. Stephenson (rear gunner) injured. F/O. B. T. Twinn (navigator), F/O. W. Braithwaite (air bomber), F/Lt. N. G. Errington (wireless operator), F/Sgt. H. Laking (flight engineer), F/O. W. G. Hayden (special wireless operator), baled out safely.

00.29 hrs. Lancaster III PB476 'Y' of No. 12 Sqn.
Dived into the ground at Weekly Cross, Alford, Lincolnshire. P/O. Ansdell (pilot), F/O. Hunter (navigator), F/O. Heath (air bomber), Sgt. Shaffer (flight engineer), Sgt. Parry (wireless operator), Sgt. Walker (mid-upper gunner) and Sgt. Mellor (rear gunner) killed.

00.30 hrs. Halifax III PM437 'X' of No. 158 Sqn.
Dived into hillside at Sledmere Grange, north of Driffield, Yorkshire. F/Lt. C. A. Rodgers (pilot), F/O D. J. Harris (navigator), F/Sgt. R. H. Houldey

(air bomber), F/Sgt. J. W. Middleton (wireless operator), Sgt. J. J. E. Dent (mid-upper gunner), Sgt. E. A. J. Fanrow (rear gunner) and P/O. C. J. W. Muir killed.

00.40 hrs. Halifax III NR250 'N' of No. 466 Sqn.
Crew baled out over Waddington and aircraft flew on to crash at Friskney, near Skegness, Lincolnshire and demolished a cottage. P/O A. F. Schrank (pilot), F/Sgt. J. A. Todd (air bomber), F/Sgt. J. W. Tobin (navigator), F/Sgt. J. A. Hadlington (wireless operator), F/Sgt. J. H. Kernaghan (rear gunner), Sgt. P. Stewart (mid-upper gunner) and Sgt. J. W. Hodgson (flight engineer) baled out safely.

00.40 hrs. Halifax III 'E' NA584 of No. 76 Sqn.
Damaged when landing at Holm. F/O. R. C. MacDougal (mid-upper gunner) killed. P/O. Oleynik (pilot) and crew safe.

00.51 Halifax III MZ917 'R' of No. 158 Sqn.
Damaged but landed at Lissett. Sgt. A. Tait (rear gunner) injured. Remainder of crew safe.

00.57 hrs. Lancaster III PB118 'Q' of No. 1654 CU.
Crashed at Church Warsop, Nottinghamshire. F/Sgt. R. W. Pinkstone (pilot), F/Sgt. H. Evans (flight engineer), Sgt. J. Pringle (air bomber) and Sgt. J. S. Morgan (rear gunner) baled out injured. Sgt. C. G. Rouse (navigator) and Sgt. J. F. Morgan (rear gunner) baled out safely. Sgt. R. Campbell (mid-upper gunner) killed.

00.59 hrs. Halifax III LV255 'G' of No. 192 sqn.
Crash landed at Ainlies Farm, Fulmodeston, Norfolk. F/O. E. D. Roberts (pilot) and Sgt. K. A. Sutcliffe (mid-upper gunner) seriously injured. F/O. R. G. Todd (special operator) baled out injured. F/O. W. Darlington (navigator), W/O. W. S. Clementson (wireless operator), Sgt. J. C. Anderson (flight engineer), F/Sgt. R. G. Holmes (air bomber) and Sgt. R. T. Grapes (rear gunner) killed.

01.00 hrs. Lancaster I NG502 'J' of No. 460 Sqn.
Crash landed at Barfield House, Langworth, Lincolnshire. F/O. W. B. Warren (pilot) and F/Sgt. F. D. Kelly (air bomber) safe. F/O. S. R. Gannon (navigator), F/Lt. G. R. Grinter (mid-upper gunner) and F/O. R. J. Jackson (rear gunner) injured. F/Sgt. R. E. Davey (wireless operator) and Sgt. A. Streatfield (flight engineer) killed.

01.02 hrs. Lancaster I PB708 'M' of No. 1654 CU.
Attacked over Wigsley Airfield. W/O. Kann (rear gunner) baled out. F/O. Mosby (pilot) landed safely at High Ercall.

01.05 hrs. Lancaster I PD444 'F' of No. 1662 CU.
Attacked over Doncaster, but landed safely.

01.05 hrs. Lancaster III LM748 'H' of No. 1654 CU.
Dived into the ground at Stapleford, near Newark, Nottinghamshire. F/Sgt. A. E. Lutz (pilot), Sgt. F. Shaw (air bomber), F/Sgt. H. F. Cox (flight engineer), Sgt. A. G. Davy (rear gunner), F/O. J. A. C. Chapman (navigator), Sgt. A. F. Wawby (wireless operator) and Sgt. H. Frost (mid-upper gunner) killed.

01.10 hrs. Halifax III MZ654 'R' of No. 1664 CU.
Attacked and damaged over Dishforth, Yorkshire. Sgt. E. P. Mangin
(wireless operator), Sgt. A. K. Ballantyne (air bomber) and Sgt. J. Wilson
(flight engineer) baled out injured. F/O. J. L. Maunders (pilot), F/O. J. D.
Cruikshank (navigator), F/O. W. E. McQuestion (mid-upper gunner) and
F/O. R. P. Maitland (rear gunner) stayed with aircraft and landed safely.

01.12 hrs. Halifax III NA612 'S' of No. 1664 CU.
Crashed in flames at Brafferton, Yorkshire. P/O. K. W. Griffey (pilot), Sgt.
J. W. Buttrey (navigator), F/O. G. Lloyd (air bomber) W/O2. L. T. Chevier
(wireless operator), Sgt. S. Forster (flight engineer), Sgt. L. Boardman (mid-
upper gunner) and Sgt. J. E. Fielder (rear gunner) killed.

01.10 hrs. Halifax III NR179 'C' of No. 466 Sqn.
Dived into the ground near Elvington, Yorkshire. F/O. A. P. Shelton (pilot),
F/Sgt. R. P. Johnson (air bomber), F/Sgt. G. N. Dixon and Sgt. W. E.
Welsh (flight engineer) killed. F/Sgt. P. Hogan (navigator), F/Sgt. V. Bullen
(rear gunner) and F/Sgt. G. Lain (mid-upper gunner) baled out safely.

01.15 hrs. Halifax III NR235 'Q' of No. 347 Sqn.
Crashed in flames at Sutton on Derwent, Yorkshire. Sqn/Ldr. J. Terrien
(pilot) killed. Lt. R. Mosnier (navigator), 2nd/Lt. R. Michelon, F/Sgt. C.
Dugardin (wireless operator), Ajt. G. Puthier (flight engineer), Sgt. A.
Dunand (rear gunner) and Sgt. R. Delaroche (mid-upper gunner) baled out
safely.

01.05 hrs. Halifax NA680 'H' of No. 347 Sqn.
Shot down in flames and crashed near Sleeford, Lincolnshire. Capt. Laucou
(pilot) and Sgt. Le Masson (flight engineer) killed. 2nd/Lt. Giroud (air
bomber), Asp. L. Viel (navigator), Sgt. C. Pochont (wireless operator), Sgt.
P. Charriere (mid-upper gunner) and Sgt. Hemery (rear gunner) baled out
safely.

01.10 hrs. Lancaster III ME323 'P' of No. 12 Sqn.
Crashed at East Stockwith, near Blyton, Lincolnshire. F/O. Thomas (pilot),
F/Sgt. Horstman (navigator), F/Sgt. Davis (wireless operator), F/Sgt.
McCaffery (flight engineer), F/Sgt. Pridmore (air bomber), F/Sgt. Cryer
(mid-upper gunner) and F/Sgt. Weston (rear gunner) killed.

01.15 hrs. Lancaster III ND387 'K' of No. 1651 CU.
Crashed near Cottesmore, Leicestershire. F/Sgt. Howard (pilot), Sgt.
Darling (flight engineer). Sgt. Pullan (navigator), F/O. Millar (air bomber),
F/Sgt. Wilson (wireless operator), Sgt. Taylor (mid-upper gunner) killed.
Sgt. Thompson (rear gunner) injured.

01.15 hrs. Lancaster III ME442 'V' of No. 44 Sqn.
Crashed in flames at Brocklesby Park, Grannington, Lincolnshire. F/O. J. J.
Ryan (pilot), Sgt. T. H. Jarman (flight engineer), Sgt. R. R. Russell
(navigator), Sgt. A. J. Terry (air bomber), Sgt. H. Birch (wireless operator),
Sgt. H. Payne (mid-upper gunner) and Sgt. W. H. Rogan (rear gunner)
killed.

01.18 hrs. Lancaster I NG325 'H' of No. 189 Sqn.
Dived into the ground near East Rudham Railway Station, Norfolk.

F/O. S. J. Reid (pilot), Sgt. F. N. Benson, Sgt. R. W. McCormack, F/O. J. T. Nelson, Sgt. M. R. Bullock, F/O. H. G. Harrison and F/Sgt. G. F. Caley killed.

01.35 hrs. Lancaster III JB699 'F' of No. 1651 CU.
Dived vertically into the ground at Cottesmore Airfield, Leicestershire. F/Lt. Baum (pilot), F/O. Davies (navigator), Sgt. Smith (flight engineer), Sgt. Warne (air bomber), Sgt. Gardener (wireless operator), F/O Brook (mid-upper gunner) and Sgt. Platt (rear gunner) killed.

01.36 hrs. Halifax III MZ680 'R' of No. 76 Sqn.
Crashed in flames at Cadney Brigg, Lincolnshire. P/O. H. Bertenshaw (pilot), F/Sgt. G. A. Austin (navigator), Sgt. H. Wood (flight engineer), F/Sgt. D. Skilton (wireless operator), F/Sgt. G. F. French (air bomber), Sgt. Shearman (mid-upper gunner) and Sgt. H. Sporne (rear gunner) baled out safely.

01.45 hrs. Halifax III HX322 'V' of No. 10 Sqn.
Dived into the ground at Spellow Hill, near Knaresborough, Yorkshire. F/Lt. Laffoley (pilot), P/O. Thorneycroft (air bomber), F/Sgt. P. Field (wireless operator), F/Sgt. Bradshaw (rear gunner) and Sgt. C. H. Finch (flight engineer) killed. P/O. W. Kay (mid-upper gunner) injured. P/O. K. H. V. Palmer (second pilot) and F/Sgt. S. Hamilton (navigator) safe.

02.09 hrs. Halifax III NR229 'D' of No. 346 Sqn.
Crash landed at Hurworth, near Croft, Yorkshire. Capt. Notelle (pilot), 2nd/Lt. Boissey (flight engineer), Lt. Flous (air bomber) and Sgt. Malia (rear gunner) injured. Lt. Martin (navigator), Sgt. Santoni (wireless operator) and Sgt. Neri (mid-upper gunner) safe.

Hudson 'M' of No. 161 Sqn.
Damaged near Feltwell. F/O. Regan (pilot) and crew landed safely.

Lancaster NR210 'Z' of No. 77 Sqn.
Damaged but landed safely. F/Sgt. H. Mustoe (rear gunner) injured. F/O. J. M. Geddes (pilot) landed aircraft safely.

Halifax III NR240 'N' of No. 158 Sqn.
Damaged but landed safely at Middleton St. George. F/Sgt. K. M. Anderson (pilot) and crew safe.

03.59 hrs. Mosquito XX NT357 of No. 68 Sqn.
Crashed at Horstead Hall, Norfolk on return to Coltishall due to engine failure. F/O. Aust (pilot) and F/O. Halestrap (wireless operator) killed.

Other losses due to intruders. February–March 1945

21/2/45 22.30 hrs. Stirling IV LK126 of No. 195 Sqn.
Landed in flames on Shepherd's Grove Airfield. F/Lt. D. R. Campbell (pilot), F/O. P. Boddington (navigator), F/Lt. C. E. Bassett (air bomber), F/Sgt. S. McQuillan (wireless operator), F/Sgt. D. L. Vince (flight engineer) and Cpt. G. Slater, safe. W/O. J. B. McGovern (rear gunner) killed.

17/3/45 18.00 hrs. Lancaster NG132 'E2' of No. 550 Sqn.
Crashed into the Humber Estuary, north of Immingham. F/Sgt. Lockyer (pilot), Sgt. Lucey (rear gunner), Sgt. Berry (navigator), Sgt. Elliot (wireless

operator) and Sgt. Matthews (mid-upper gunner) killed. W/O. Farmer (air bomber) missing. Sgt. Drawbridge (flight engineer) safe.

20/3/45 21.45 hrs. Stirling IV LK116 of No. 620 Sqn.
Shot down near Great Dunmow, Essex. Sqn/Ldr. G. O. S. Whitty DFC (pilot), P/O. G. E. Ames (pilot), W/O. J. G. J. Williams (navigator), F/Sgt. G. R. Douglas (air bomber), W/O. A. P. Bell (gunner) and one passenger killed. Flight engineer baled out safely.

20/3/45 21.45 hrs. Halifax 'OG-U' of No. 1665 CU.
Shot down near Wittering, Cambridgeshire. six of crew baled out safely. P/O. P. E. Nettlefield and two others killed.

Luftwaffe losses in 'Operation Gisela', March 3rd – 4th, 1945

Ju 88G-6 W.Nr.620588 4R + JL of 3/NJG2.
Failed to return from operations and presumed to have crashed into the North Sea. Fhr. K. Vogel (F), Fw. J. Fritsch (Bf), Uffz. H. Hellmich (Bf) and Uffz. A. Engelhardt (Bs) missing.

Ju 88G-6 W.Nr.620644 4R + CL of 3/NJG2.
Crashed due to fuel shortage on return. Uffz. A. Schlichter (F) and Ogefr. R. Kautz (Bs) killed. Fw. Kolbe and Ogefr. R. Theimer (bf) baled out.

Ju 88G-6 W.Nr. 620192 of I/NJG2.
Crashed near Lübbecke, Germany. Fj.Fw. J. Wyleciol (F), Fw. K. Thomann (Bf), Uffz. G. Pfauter (Bf) and Uffz. E. Schnitzer (Bs) killed.

Ju 88G-6 W.Nr.710580 of I/NJG2.
Received 25% damage when landing at Vechta, Germany.

Ju 88G-6 W.Nr.622474 of I/NJG2.
Received 25% damage at Diepholz, Germany.

Ju 88G-6 W.Nr.622154 of I/NJG2.
Crashed north-west of Würzburg. Crew safe.

Ju 88G-6 W.Nr.622140 4R + LT of 9/NJG2.
Shot down north-east of Campen Lighthouse, near Emden, Germany. Fw. H. Schenk (F), Uffz. H. Kunst (Bf), Ogefr. F. Habermalz (Bs) and Uffz. F. Däuber (Bm) killed.

Ju 88G-6 W.Nr.622822 of III/NJG3.
Received 25% damage in a forced landing near Oldenberg, Germany after engine failure. Ogefr. Kurt Röder (Bs) injured. Rest of crew safe.

Ju 88G-6 W.Nr.6222(sic) of II/NJG3.
Sustained 35% damage in a forced landing near Wartenberg, Germany after fuel shortage. Crew safe.

Ju 88G-6 W.Nr.621821 of III/NJG3.
Crashed at Beilen, Holland after being hit by flak. Lt. Hans Flach (F), Uffz. Gottfried Nass (Bf), Fw. Karl Huber (Bf) and Fw. Franz Fleischer (Bw) injured.

Ju 88G-6 W.Nr.620785 of IV/NJG3.
Crashed during a meteorological flight at Dickhausen 04.40 hrs. Uffz. L. Kowalski (F) and Ogefr. M. Komatz (Bf) killed. Uffz. Burger (Bw) safe.

Ju 88G-7 W.Nr.0018 of IV/NJG3.
Failed to return from operations and presumed to have crashed into the North Sea. Ofw. W. John (F), Fw. L. Dunst (Bf), Ogefr. A. Gerhard (Bf) and Ogefr. W. Krause (Bw) missing.

Ju 88G-6 W.Nr.621293 of IV/NJG3.

Failed to return from operations and presumed to have crashed into the North Sea. Uffz. W. Lohse (F), Uffz. H. Horsch (Bf) and Ogefr. F. Neumann (Bf) missing.

Ju 88G-6 W.Nr.620745 D5 + AE of IV/NJG3.
Abandoned by crew near Knesebeck, Germany after fuel shortage. Major B. Ney (F) Grkdr. and Fw. W. Bolenz (Bf) injured. Ofw. Schlick safe.

Ju 88G-6 W.Nr.620028 D5 + AX of 13/NJG3.
Flew into the ground at Sutton on Derwent, near Elvington, Yorkshire 02.00 hrs. Hptm. Johann Dreher (F) Stkp., Fw. Gustav Schmitz (Bf), Ofw. Hugo Böker (Bf) and Fw. Martin Bechter (Bw) killed.

Ju 88G-6 W.Nr.622829 3C + EK of 2/NJG4.
Crashed due to fuel shortage at Ellenstädt, Germany after three crew had baled out. Lt. W. Rinker (F) injured.

Ju 88G-6 W.Nr.621305 3C + FL of 3/NJG4.
Crashed after two crew baled out near Hardenberg. Lt. H. Emsinger (F) killed.

Ju 88G-6 W.Nr.622056 3C + BC of I/NJG4.
Received 30% damage in combat. Ofw. F. Specht (Bw) wounded.

Ju 88G-6 W.Nr.622959 of I/NJG4.
Abandoned by crew due to fuel shortage at Wunstorf, Germany. Crew safe.

Ju 88G-6 W.Nr.622132 of I/NJG4.
Abandoned by crew due to fuel shortage near Osnabrück, Germany. Ofw. K. Gabler (F) injured. Rest of crew safe.

Ju 88G-6 W.Nr.620976 of II/NJG4.
Sustained 25% damage in collision with Ju 88G-6 W.Nr.621072 at Leeuwarden, Holland. Crew safe.

Ju 88G-6 W.Nr.621072 of II/NJG4.
Sustained 15% damage in collision with Ju 88G-6 W.Nr.620976 at Leeuwarden, Holland. Crew safe.

Ju 88G-6 W.Nr.621805 3C + KN of 5/NJG4.
Flew into the ground near Metfield, Suffolk whilst attempting to attack a B-24 at 02.00 hrs. Ofw. Leo Zimmermann (F), Ofw. Paul Vey (Bf), Uffz. Heinz Pitan (Bf) and Uffz. Hans Wende (Bw) killed.

Ju 88G-6 W.Nr.710839 of II/NJG4.
Received 25% damage when landing at Steenwijk, Holland during a non-operational flight. Crew safe.

Ju 88G-6 W.Nr.621792 3C + DS of 8/NJG4.
Failed to return from operations and crashed into the Ijsselmeer. Oblt. W. Paulus (F), Ogefr. E. Hafels (Bf) and Ogefr. H. Müller (Bm) missing. Body of Ogefr. A. Hörger (Bw) washed ashore in the Ijsselmeer.

Ju 88G-1 W.Nr.712203 of III/NJG4.
Crashed near Giessen, Germany. Cause unknown. Ogefr. Herrmann Hangs (Bf) missing. Rest of crew not known.

Ju 88G-7 W.Nr.710438 of III/NJG4.

Sustained 75% damage in a forced landing near Steenwijk, Holland, after mechanical failure. Crew safe.

Ju 88G-1 W.Nr.712405 of III/NJG4.
Received 10% damage at Vechta, Germany. Crew safe.

Ju 88G-6 W.Nr.620397 C9 + RR of 7/NJG5.
Flew into the ground at Welton, Lincolnshire 01.45 hrs. Fw. Heinrich Conze (F), Uffz. Rudolf Scherer (Bf), Ogefr. Werner Nollau (Bf) and Uffz. Alfred Altenkirch (Bs) killed.

Ju 88G-6 W.Nr.620651 C9 + CS of 9/NJG5.
Failed to return from operations and crashed into the North Sea. Hptm. H. Bobsien (F), Fw. F. Dessemeier (Bf) and Ogefr. F. Purth (Bs) missing. Ofw. H. Steinadler (Bf) killed.

Ju 88G-6 W.Nr.620512 of III/NJG5.
Received 20% damage in a mid-air collision at Wittmundhafen, Germany. Crew safe.

Ju 88G-6 W.Nr.621611 of III/NJG5.
Received 50% damage in a forced landing east of Leer, Germany. Uffz. E. Berger (Bs) injured. Rest of crew safe.

Ju 88G-6 W.Nr.622832 of III/NJG5.
Abandoned due to fuel shortage near Buxtehude, Germany. Crew safe.

Ju 88G-6 W.Nr.620816 of III/NJG5.
Abandoned due to fuel shortage near Vechta, Germany. Crew safe.

Index

202